The Functional-Notional Approach
From Theory to Practice

The Functional–Notional Approach

From Theory to Practice

Mary Finocchiaro
Christopher Brumfit

90-1922

OXFORD UNIVERSITY PRESS • 1983

Oxford University Press

200 Madison Avenue
New York, N.Y. 10016 USA

Walton Street
Oxford OX2 6DP England

OXFORD is a trademark of Oxford University Press.

Library of Congress Cataloging in Publication Data

Finocchiaro, Mary Bonomo.
The functional-notional approach.

Bibliography: p.
Includes index.
1. English language—Study and teaching—Foreign students.
I. Brumfit, Christopher. II. Title.
PE1128. A2F515 1983 428.007 82–22307
ISBN 0-19-434106-2 (pbk.)

Copyright © 1983 by Oxford University Press, Inc.

First published 1983
Third impression 1985

Printed in the United States of America

To the many teachers and colleagues
throughout the world
with whom we have worked
and who have shared their knowledge
with us.

Contents

Acknowledgments

It is a privilege to be able to affirm that it was Joseph Bertot, then Cultural Attaché at the American Embassy in Holland, who encouraged me to study the work of the Council of Europe and particularly the materials prepared by Professor van Ek. Several times over a period of two years, he invited me to go to Holland to speak on the Functional-Notional Syllabus and to discuss problems and issues with Dr. van Ek and others. Those visits and discussions revealed a whole new world of exciting language teaching possibilities to me. To say that I became an enthusiatic convert would be an understatement.

Ms. Anne Newton, editor of the *English Teaching Forum,* motivated me further by publishing an article of mine on the Functional-Notional syllabus in a recent issue of the *Forum.* Her questions and comments contributed to a more definitive resolution of some ideas which were still in the "well, maybe" stage. I am extremely grateful to Ms. Newton for her encouragement and the benefit of her thoughts.

I extend heartfelt thanks to the International Communication Agency of the American Embassy in Rome which permitted me to leave Rome whenever necessary to attend and give lectures and demonstrations as well as to the British Council in Rome whose directors lent me materials and invited me to attend lectures and discussions by van Ek, Wilkins, Alexander, Morrow, Brumfit, and many others.

I am particularly grateful to the teachers and educators in such far-flung places as Spain, Portugal, Tunis, Yugoslavia, Greece, Italy, Mexico, Thailand, and the United States. Their questions and requests gave me the certainty that the enthusiasm I had gained in Holland was not a casual, temporary feeling and that—perhaps a book such as this one—would find readers eager to try this innovative approach to learning and teaching in their classes.

My esteemed colleague and friend Christopher Brumfit was kind enough to review the first four chapters and to make valuable suggestions which I attempted to incorporate in spirit and in words. His recommendations, his vast knowledge, and the relationship he established with teachers in the many places where I heard him lecture made me urge him to coauthor this book. I am deeply honored that he was willing to do so. I was not aware at the time that I would gain an unexpected reward. His wife, Ann Brumfit, an experienced master teacher, has reviewed the entire manuscript—adding or deleting where necessary—making it altogether more appropriate for teacher and curriculum writers anywhere.

I owe many thanks to the members of the New York branch of Oxford University Press and particularly to William Halpin, Marilyn Rosenthal, Debra Sistino, and Susan Kulick.

To all of you, my unlimited gratitude.

Rome   M.F.
1981

Preface

It is many years since I have felt a quickening of interest about any theoretical or methodological aspect of foreign language learning or teaching. With nearly everything written or spoken about in the field, I either had a feeling of *déjà vu* or thought, "Yes, this could be exciting, but is it feasible everywhere?" Having taught for decades and given teacher-training seminars in many parts of the world, I realized how unrealistic some doctrines or methods were. I could not help but remember countries where the language "classroom" was a corner of a garden next to a noisy playground, others where the minimum class size was eighty, still others where the chalkboard—if we were fortunate—was a warped piece of plywood to be written on with yellow crayon, others where there was no electric current.

Worse still, for too long a time, the very people who espoused new theories and strategies hesitated to work with classroom teachers. For many years I raised my voice hopelessly requesting that persons in teacher training institutions be trained to mediate between the theoretician and the classroom teacher. Most frustrating to me was the fact that often school supervisors or directors became over-enthusiatic about the obscure but elegantly worded theories which had gained currency and insisted that their teachers adopt the new theory or the new methodology. I need not remind us of the results: Many teachers were frustrated and unhappy; most learners did not really know what to do with the bits and pieces of grammar and vocabulary they had acquired. But two exciting movements have taken place to restore my faith in the profession:

A. Organizations such as International TESOL (Teaching English to Speakers of Other Languages) and IATEFL (International Association of Teachers of English as a Foreign Language) hold one or two annual conventions where theoreticians and teachers meet and discuss problems of mutual concern. The meetings are held in many cities of the United States (as well as in Mexico, Puerto Rico, Hawaii, etc.) and in many cities in Great Britain, in Hungary, Poland, and countries too numerous to mention.

B. The Council of Europe has carried out research since 1969 with two major aims:

To change the content and sequence of the language to be taught (after making a thorough analysis of the needs of learners and the use to which most human beings wish to put the language they acquire).

To arrange for credit-transfer to other countries or regions to which learners may wish to migrate. Credit-transfer would depend on the proficiency attained by the langauge learners in consonance with their needs as they complete the sociocultural and sociovocational units and modules in the curricula and syllabi now in preparation.

It is only natural that these major efforts should have given rise to the establishment of numerous teacher-training programs in universities and other institutions all over the world dedicated to the preparation of skilled teachers and thus to the formation of successful, well-integrated language learners.

While the Coucil of Europe Project was originally designed for adults in a European community situation who needed to learn a language after their formal period of education had been completed, my many years of experience of teaching and supervising language studies in the United States and in countries in many parts of the world made me aware of the broader implications of the Council of Europe's work not only in countries beyond Europe, but also at *all* levels of school systems and with *any* language one would wish to learn.

I was aware also that more needed to be said about integrating the Functional-Notional Syllabus with traditional approaches, and about the role of reading and writing. Moreover, much of the Council material consisted of monographs which were not easy to procure. I thought therefore, that it might be useful to teachers, educators, and lay people who have begun to hear about the Syllabus and the research being done to make available a short book on the subject. This book is the result of our reading of all the Council of Europe materials and of our listening and talking to people like Professors Trim, van Ek, Wilkins, Alexander, Morrow, Johnson, and others whose names you will find in it. It results too from the lectures and demonstrations we have given in the past four years as well as from the questions we have asked ourselves continually. Would this approach have worked with us and all the other teachers we have observed over the years? Our answer was an unqualified affirmative.

The work of the Council has been given several labels: A Notional Syllabus, A Functional Syllabus, and more recently, A Functional-Notional Syllabus. It has been referred to as "The Common Core in a Unit-Credit System." In this book, we shall refer to it as the functional-notional curriculum since the functional (communcative) purpose of the people who use language is central to the project.

While the monographs prepared to date by the Council team have been primarily concerned with a syllabus—that is, with detailed listing of the linguistic and cultural content of a course of study—we have thought it desirable to extend the material by making suggestions for the preparation of multi-lingual curricula for learners of all ages, anywhere!

A curriculum, as we all know, includes not only the linguistic-cultural content of a language program at various levels of learning but also the skills and abilities we help our learners develop through a variety of in-class and out-of-class tasks and activities. These are specifically designed to foster the progressive growth of internalized linguistic competence and of overt oral and written performance but primarily of communicative competence.

Since 1977, the Council has set into motion research studies for all languages (not English and French alone) and for secondary schools and universities as well as for continuing education programs.

This book will include, therefore, notes on general methodology, on the strategies which have been found most effective in helping learners use the language *appropriately* in a *variety* of *real-world situations,* and on the teaching of reading and writing. It will also deal at some length with the teaching of grammar, since a misunderstanding appears to have arisen in the minds of some educators that with a functional-notional approach, "grammar is out."

The suggestions for discussion you will find in this book will be applicable both where a language is taught as a second language; that is, where it is the dominant language spoken in the community in which the newcomer plans to live temporarily or permanently, or where it is taught as a foreign language either in the native country or in the country to which he will transfer.

It is our hope that this book will be read by lay people, interested parents, administrators, teachers of foreign languages, and many others who are interested in the closer collaboration and mutual interaction of peoples of all nations. To this end, we make every effort to avoid technical terms and what has been labeled "pedaguese."

I should like to make two minor comments before closing these preforatory remarks.

1. The examples are given in English, first, because English has become the accepted lingua franca of the world, and second, because it will be one of the major languages of any readers, no matter what other languages they teach.
2. In order to avoid using his/her or s/he throughout, we and the editor

have thought it less confusing to use *his* and *he* to designate persons of both sexes.

3. Many of the ideas noted under *Developing Communcative Abilities* and a number of the exercises found under *Time-Honored Practice Activities* are just that. They have appeared in numerous texts since the 1920s. They have been given out by me in handouts at numerous seminars. Moreover, some have been incorporated in three methodology texts I have published either alone or in collaboration. We feel they belong in this manual for two reasons: a. They underscore the continuity and evolution of foreign language teaching. b. We wished to make the content of this book as inclusive as possible so that teachers would not be forced to turn to other sources when presenting or practicing elements of the sound or grammatical systems—both integral facets of a communicative approach.

Rome   M.F.
1981

The Functional-Notional Approach
From Theory to Practice

1 The Last Century in Language Learning and Teaching: A Brief Overview

CONTINUITY AND CHANGE IN LANGUAGE TEACHING

It is becoming increasingly obvious to members of language teaching organizations that there is a renascence of faith and interest in foreign language studies. Every year more and more conferences are held, and more and more teachers join professional associations. Throughout the world teachers of foreign languages continue to address themselves to the fundamental questions which underlie their work, questions like:

1. How do people of various age levels learn a second language?
2. How can students be motivated to continue their study of a second language, or to initiate the study of a third language, when it is not required either for admission to a higher level academic program or to secure employment?
3. How can educators improve teaching, so that students no longer complain that they studied Language X for several years in school and still can't say (or understand) a word?

Yet it is unfortunately true that these questions are not new—they have plagued those interested in foreign language instruction for centuries, and at different times many different answers have been given to them. The new approaches that we adopt now will evolve from earlier approaches, and will reflect ideas of the past as well as those of the present. It is usually only in times of major political crisis that there are massive revolutions in educational practice; indeed, many countries seem only to invest heavily in language teaching programs during periods of international conflict.

Language teaching does develop, however, for as teachers seek to improve they react against the excesses of immediately preceding methodologies by devising new ones which correct the weaknesses of the old. But these too, if interpreted simply, will have their own weaknesses, and the process continues. There will, indeed, be some periods when fashions change far too rapidly. The 1970s was perhaps one of these periods, when the erratic swings of the pendulum in methodology caused many good language teachers to shrug and mutter, "A plague on all your houses," and continue with the well-tried procedures with which they felt secure.

Foreign language teaching at any one time will of course include procedures drawn from many different traditions. There will, however, be a wide range of accepted basic assumptions underlying teaching which will provide answers to the questions listed above. In order to understand the need for innovation, as well as the reasons for any change being accepted only cautiously by many teachers, it is desirable to look briefly at several of the methodological approaches which have held sway during the twentieth century and the linguistic theories underlying them.

GRAMMAR-TRANSLATION METHOD

Let us start with the traditional *grammar-translation method* which is still in use in many school systems. We inherited this method from the teaching of Latin, a language which was not usually taught for active use in any language community. Since Latin is not spoken in everyday communication, the analysis of Latin, and the grammar-translation method, ignores authentic spoken communication and the social variation of language which goes with it, and concerns itself primarily with the written language of classical literature.

Traditional linguistic analysis, based on the most suitable procedure for describing Latin, recognizes different types of sentences (declarative, interrogative, etc.) and divides vocabulary into different parts of speech (noun, verb, preposition, etc.). In Latin, whether a noun is the subject or object of a verb and many relations which we show in English through prepositions ("He cut it *with a knife*") are expressed through different endings attached to the word stem. These different endings reflect different cases so that the grammar of nouns is classified in terms of nominative, accusative, genitive, and other cases in which the meaning relations in the sentence are reflected by the different case endings used. In English, where the only remaining case ending is the genitive (Shirley's book), such a classification has less value. Nonetheless, the sense relations expressed by case endings are still of interest to linguists, and some of these ideas have influenced the functional-notional curriculum (p. 32). Generally, though, the "grammar" part of "grammar-translation" was attacked, partly because the grammar used was actually inappropriate to English, and partly it was felt that too much emphasis on grammar led to learning about the language rather than learning to use the language. However, while the basic patterns of the language were often learned in a very formal way, together with lists of words, the translation procedure was supposed to help students to *use* the language successfully.

Translation was a particularly important device when much international communication was conducted through written Latin, but when used as the main procedure for teaching spoken languages, it led to too much concentration on the written, and particularly literary, forms and too little on natural speech. But translation, both oral and written, may still have a role to play, even though the reaction to the excessive use of grammar-translation led some teachers to reject both parts of the method on principle.

THE DIRECT METHOD

An alternative was provided by the *direct method*, which became popular throughout the early years of the twentieth century. This method emphasized aural-oral skills and rejected the use of the student's mother tongue at all. Reading and writing were deferred for months—and in some programs for years—in the fear that the sight of the written symbols would confuse learners in their use of the sounds.

Unfortunately, gradation and sequence of materials were not based on realistic spoken speech, and some of the materials used in direct method classes have remained as classic examples of artificially constructed sentences. Students may have learned to say such unreal sentences as "La plume de ma tante est sur le bureau de mon oncle," but they may still have loved learning French, particularly if the teacher was enthusiastic, hardworking, and caring. They may never have practiced in class how to buy a ticket for the metro, but they had been exposed to enough unrealistic French to be able to make the jump to the real thing when the occasion arose. The direct method provided the chance for intensive immersion in the second language and tried to emphasize effective language use rather than the intellectual analysis characteristic of grammar-translation.

Many techniques were developed to try to make direct method as effective as possible. One series of procedures, associated with the Frenchman Gouin, accompanied language use with appropriate actions. Statements and questions were illustrated with actions, and students repeated both the language model and the action. For example, a sequence might be, "I'm getting up. I'm going to the blackboard. I'm writing my name." The statements were followed by related questions such as, "Where are you going?" and later still by questions to class members such as, "Where is he going?/Where did he go?"

Unfortunately, however, all the statements used were related to the classroom. Teachers did not generally think of students using language beyond the classroom. Any connection with real life was expected to come later and was not the business of the school.

READING METHOD

Direct method procedures were widely used in the United States and Canada, but dissatisfaction with these led to a commission headed by Professor Coleman making a study of foreign language teaching, published in 1929, which argued against such heavy emphasis on the spoken language. The report proposed that teaching should focus on *reading* as a more attainable and appropriate goal for school students. Until the Second World War, then, intensive and extensive reading was accompanied by the teaching of grammar rules based principally on the structures found in the reading passages.

STRUCTURAL APPROACH

Then, in the 1940s, three major occurrences in America forced a change in the "reading only" objective. When the United States entered the Second World War, it found that there were few people who could speak a foreign language—an ability desperately needed at that time. So crash programs of eight or more hours a day to teach the aural-oral skills were started in many parts of the United States.

The other two occurrences were more theoretical. The ideas of the psychologist Skinner began to be used as a way of explaining what happens when we teach and learn languages, and linguists like Bloomfield and Fries started to apply the ideas of structural linguistics to language teaching. What emerged has been loosely called the *structural approach* (or even the linguistic approach).

The aspect of Skinner's work which was associated most strongly with this approach was the view of language learning as habit formation. It was held that the patterns of the language, as defined by structural linguistics, needed to be "over-learned" by students so that they would be produced correctly as a matter of unconscious habit. Consequently, meaningless repetition of correct forms was considered valuable. At the same time, it was maintained that contrasts between the structure of the native language and the target language (the second or foreign language being studied) caused conflict, because the patterns of the target language would fight against the established patterns of the native language. Teaching procedures should attack this conflict, or "interference," by intensive exposure to the correct patterns of the target language through drills and pattern practice.

AUDIO-LINGUAL METHOD

It took some time for this theoretical discussion to develop into a fully-fledged "method," and this was the first time that language teaching methods became primarily responsive to linguistic and psychological theory rather than to the intuitions and arguments of successful teachers. What emerged was the *audio-lingual method*, which flourished between about 1950 and 1965. As with the earlier methods, however, it was often interpreted too simplistically, in over-reaction to the direct and reading methods. The fashion now was for long dialogs, usually centered on one or more carefully graded structures. "Mimicry and memorization of the dialog" became the slogan for too many years, perfect pronunciation was sought often at the expense of anything else, and lexical meaning was considered unimportant. Learners parroted incomprehensible material, reading was deferred, the study of grammar ("talking about language") was banned in many school systems, and pattern practice drills were the main activities of the lesson.

And since students were being taught to parrot patterns they often became very good at doing it—without communication and without interaction. In fact learners were often prevented from saying what they wanted to say because that was against the "rules" of the theory. Audio-lingual theory, as presented to teachers, was very strong on what students ought *not* to do: they should not write down versions of what they heard, they should not attempt to use linguistic forms they had not been drilled in, they should not learn words out of context, and so on. It was often presented with complete conviction, as if there was one—relatively understandable—way in which we all learned languages and which we could apply to the classroom. It was supported by linguistic and psychological theory—and apparently also by successes in teaching military personnel during and after the war.

But soldiers are not school students, and the procedures developed by Fries, Lado, and others contained many freer elements than were accounted for in the strong form of the theory. Perhaps the effectiveness of the procedures could be attributed to causes other than those provided by the theory, and certainly the same degree of success was not observable in language classes in high school. During the time that the United States was showing a seemingly indestructible attachment to the audio-lingual method, many countries in Europe were using the *audio-visual method*. Tape recorders, film strips, flannelboards (see p. 170) and other pictorial devices were designed to teach carefully graded structures in specific linguistic contexts and social situations which would clarify their use. While it is true that the spoken language was given precedence and that the film strips and/or films gave students insight into both linguistic features and paralinguistic features of communication (distances maintained by speakers, gestures, or facial expressions), too much emphasis was often placed on mechanical repetition of the tape and the objective was generally mastery of sentence pattern rather than creative or real communicative use of language. Often, the teacher followed the tape and film strip slavishly and permitted no deviation from the structural progression of the text. Relevant interests of the learners were generally ignored.

SITUATIONAL METHOD

Concurrently, many teachers and many texts espoused what was, and still is, called the *situational method*—a development from Gouin (see p. 5, 6). Units in the text generally started with a situational title, for example, "At the Supermarket" or "At the Beauty Shop," and nearly every utterance in the dialog stemmed from that theme or that center of interest. Many good techniques came out of the situational method. Actions were simulated to illustrate the utterances; numerous pictures and other real objects were used. It was possible to practice many questions and answers with the dialog utterances and even talk about likes and dislikes, e.g. "Do you like cereal in the morning?" "Do you like your hair cut short at the sides?"

But there were and are shortcomings in the method. Once started on the path of the supermarket or the beauty shop, there was little or no deviation. Learners were generally not shown how a structure or an expression in a particular unit could be used in another. The utterances were all related to one social situation. More important, situations cannot be graded. The sequencing of situations was generally random, making it well-nigh impossible to grade the structures without falsifying the situation. Today many situationally based texts are encouraging greater leeway. There is awareness that in real-life speech we do not generally adhere to the same vocabulary area in a conversation. In any case, as we shall see, "situation" (but not a situational method) is a vital component of a functional-notional curriculum, which is the subject of this book.

LEARNING THEORIES

It was a strong tenet of audio-lingualism that grammar should be learned unconsciously, and—as we have seen—this view was defended by reference to Skinner's theory of learning. In 1959 that view of the nature of language learning was savagely attacked by Chomsky, and in the years that followed he set out to produce a linguistic theory which would supersede the structuralist model of Bloomfield and his followers. The resulting development of *transformational-generative grammar* did not have a direct impact on language teaching on any large scale, but an alternative learning theory, *cognitive-code*, was developed that placed emphasis more on the conscious understanding of the rules which lead to the production of linguistic patterns than on unconscious learning of the patterns themselves. Once again, as earlier with grammar-translation, rules would be learned and then applied to the elements of the language, and the use of the intellect again became respectable.

Without wanting to enter into a controversy which has spilled over hundreds of printed pages and which has dominated language conferences in the last decade, we would like to suggest that both cognitive-code and habit-formation theories (not one or the other) have a role to play in language acquisition and learning. Certainly, students should not be discouraged from thinking about the language and making use of generalizations—but equally the value of simple repetition, for many students, should not be ignored. In this, as in other matters, the teacher should be sensitive to the individual needs of students.

THE BASIS OF THE
FUNCTIONAL-NOTIONAL APPROACH

It is this sensitivity to individual needs which is the major characteristic of the functional-notional approach to language teaching. Many methodologies seem to ignore the fact that the ability to use real, appropriate language to communicate and interact with others is—and should be—the primary goal of most foreign language learning. The organization and design of the curriculum deriving from a functional-notional approach contributes to the goal of communication and interaction from the first day of study—at whatever age or learning level.

It would be unnecessarily restrictive to refer to functions and notions as the basis for a method, in the sense that the movements referred to above can be classified as methods. A "method" can be defined as a coordinated body of techniques and teaching procedures, related to a shared body of assumptions about the nature of language teaching and learning. Sometimes a "method" is packaged and marketed in advance, but more often that not, as with grammar-translation or direct methods, we recognize their consistencies as they develop out of our practice in classrooms. At the moment, the functional-notional approach is a body of ideas which reflect and synthesize much contemporary thought about language teaching. Implementation of these ideas has more often than not been in terms of syllabus specifications rather than teaching methodology. But we hope to show in this book that a functional-notional basis for teaching will have a major impact on both course design and teaching procedures.

Let us start, though, by explaining the origins of the approach. It arose primarily out of work commissioned by the Council of Europe, a body which was founded in 1949 and which now includes all Western European countries. The Council for Cultural Co-operation of the Council of Europe became particularly interested, in the 1960s, in both language teaching and what it called "permanent education" (i.e., continuing adult education after formal schooling has been completed). Following a seminar in Switzerland in 1971, a group of experts was set up which decided that the foreign language needs of adult Europeans should be approached through three initial investigations:

A. "to break down the global concept of language into units and sub-units based on an analysis of particular groups of adult learners, in terms of the communicative situations in which they are characteristically involved. This analysis should lead to a precise articulation of the notion of 'common core' with specialist extensions at different proficiency levels";

B. "to set up on the basis of this analysis an operational specification for learning objectives";

C. "to formulate, in consultation with the Steering Group on Educational Technology of the Council of Europe, a meta-system defining the structure of a multi-media learning system to achieve these objectives in terms of the unit/credit concepts"(Trim et al. 1973).

Language should, then, be broken down into appropriate units for acquisition, and credits should be awarded for mastery of units towards any necessary qualification in linguistic proficiency. The crucial question was what kinds of units were the most appropriate ones for describing the learning of foreign languages. Further work by the Council of Europe experts, combined with interest and discussion by outside commentators, has led to an identifiable position within the general movement towards communicative teaching of the 1970s.

At the onset the Council's studies focused upon the social and vocational or academic needs of adult learners of English and French. (Since 1977, it includes the study of all European languages and at secondary, college, and university levels of a school system.) It explored in depth the language and cultural content which would enable these adults to communicate and interact with speakers of other languages either in a foreign country or in their native land. The adult learners included future workers in foreign countries, tourists, or people engaged in academic, cultural, technical, or economic activities. The language and cultural content was designed to encompass situations and topics of immediate concern to them. More will be said of this content in the following chapters.

Of paramount interest, in our estimation, is the fact that the research team has been evolving a system for granting credits to any person who will have learned single modules, units, or entire texts of the material. This system is to be established according to criteria agreed upon by all nations wishing to take part in such an accreditation system.

In our estimation, this aspect of the project will be of tremendous benefit to learners, teachers, and administrators everywhere. We cannot help but hope that the basic idea of credit recognition and transfer will spread and flourish. It is urgently needed in those states within the United States and in regions and countries in many parts of the world which receive immigrants continually. The majority of migrant adults and their children are often forced to enter schools at levels which they had completed in their native lands. Record cards, curricula, and testing programs are not considered equivalent to those prevailing in the admitting schools. The problems arising out of this situation are too well-known to those of us who have headed administrative programs for migrants and who have participated in conferences sponsored by UNESCO, TESOL,

AILA, IATEFL, and other organizations devoted to alleviating the problems of migrants.

The functional-notional approach springs, then, from an attempt to classify exactly what aspects of a language have been mastered by a particular student. Thus the early work in this area was concerned with suitable bases for such a classification. It was suggested, particularly, that language was much more appropriately classified in terms of what people wanted to *do* with the language (functions) or in terms of what *meanings* people wanted to convey (notions) than in terms of the grammatical items as in traditional language teaching models. It was argued, particularly, that we all understand that we use language to apologize, greet, persuade, recommend, or praise, and we all understand that we use language to express certain meanings, time or spatial relations, for example, but we do not all agree that we use language to exemplify grammatical categories invented by linguists! Thus a functional-notional organization of language teaching will incorporate a classification of language which closely matches ordinary people's perception of what language is for. The ways in which insights deriving from this approach can be adapted fruitfully to school foreign and second language teaching are the contents of the rest of this book.

2 A Functional-Notional Approach to Language Learning

A PRELIMINARY DEFINITION OF FUNCTIONS AND NOTIONS

In this section we introduce a simple description of the ways in which functions and notions operate in language use. As we have seen in Chapter 1, a functional-notional approach concentrates on the purposes for which language is used. Any act of speech is functionally organized (that is, it is an attempt to *do* something) for a particular situation in relation to a particular topic. The language that we actually produce changes when these elements change, because we have learned to adjust our language use to be appropriate for the conditions in which we use it.

We shall see below how different communicative purposes, situations, and topics lead us to adapt our messages so that they will be most clearly understood. When we use language we are constantly adapting and adjusting our messages in this way, and a good language teaching curriculum must recognize this.

A functional-notional approach to language learning places major emphasis on the *communicative purpose(s)* of a speech act. It focuses on what people want to do or what they want to accomplish through speech. Do they want to introduce people to each other? Do they want to invite someone to their home? Do they want to direct someone to do or not to do something? Do they want to talk about a picture, a book, a film, or something in the room they are in? Do they want to give sway to their creative impulses and recite a poem? The above are simple examples of the *functions* of language which all human beings wish to express at one time or other; in other words, to let others know their purpose or aim in speaking in the first place.

For example, inviting (function) using words like "I invite" or "I'd like to invite" might not make the speaker's message clear. In order to do so, a speaker would have to say something like, "What are you doing this weekend?" If the response is, "Nothing much," the first speaker might say, "I'd like to invite you to my house for Friday dinner." (As we will have occasion to note later, there are numerous other ways in which the speaker could have extended the invitation without even using the verb "invite.") But the essential point to clarify at this time is that *functional* language must also incorporate specific *notions*; that is, the vocabulary items that, in the example above, might answer the questions *who, when, where,* and *why.* Other notions we may examine with other functions might answer the questions *how long, how far, how much,* etc.

Let us clarify the concept of specific notions, by saying that the words following the functional expression would generally be considered notions. Thus *notions* are meaning elements which may be expressed through nouns, pronouns, verbs, prepositions, conjunctions, adjectives, or adverbs. *Notions* may be substituted by other appropriate words, depending on the topic being discussed, the situation, and the persons involved in the speech act. For example, the invitation above might have been, "I'd like to invite (or ask) your son to come to my club for lunch on Saturday."

The basic *communicative purposes* of the speaker may be expressed in two principal ways, depending on the function: We would use either A. *formulas,* that is, *fixed expressions*; or, B. *communicative* or *functional expressions.*

A.   Note these English examples of *formulas.*
     FUNCTION: greeting
               (informal, usable at any time): "Hello"
               (time-bound, formal): "Good evening"
     FUNCTION: leavetaking
               (informal): "So long" or "Bye"
               (formal): "Good-bye"
     FUNCTION: acknowledging an introduction
               (formal): "How do you do?"
               (informal): "Pleased/Nice/Happy to meet you."
     FUNCTION: expressing and acknowledging gratitude
               (formal or informal): "Thank you." "You're welcome."
     FUNCTION: responding to a request, such as:
               "Do you mind if I smoke?" "Not at all."

In English, formulas are *fixed.* We could not, for example, say "How does she do?" or "How did you do?" in an introduction. In other languages, fixed formulas also exist but not necessarily in the same social situation. For example in Italian, we use the informal, *"Ciao,"* both for greeting and leavetaking; in Turkish, the host or hostess uses one fixed formula and the guest who is leaving uses another.

B.   On the other hand, in all languages generally *communicative* (functional) expressions can be changed for gender, number, tense, aspect, emphasis, or other communicative purposes. Note these English examples:

FUNCTION: making a suggestion: "How do you feel about going to the beach?" Here the *do* may become *does* or remain *do* with plural nouns or pronouns and *you* may be substituted by *he, she, they, the boys*, etc.

FUNCTION: expressing anger: In "I'm very angry with you," nearly every word can be changed. *I'm* can be *He's, She's, We're, They're; very* can be *pretty* or *quite; angry* can be *annoyed, furious*, etc.; *you* can be *him, her, them, the girls*. In a tag question, the utterance may be, "*You're* very angry with *me/her/us/them*, aren't *you*?"

FUNCTION: making a request or asking for an opinion: "Would (you) mind not going out today?" could become, "Would you have minded not going out last night?"

Naturally a communicative function can include *both* a formula and a communicative expression, for example, greeting/expression of concern: "Good morning. How does your mother feel today?"

While the basic *functions* to be expressed depend solely on the purpose(s) of the speaker, the specific *notions* depend on three major factors: a. the *functions* b. the elements in the *situation,* and c. the *topic* which is being discussed.

We shall have occasion to return to these factors many times, but briefly stated, a situation includes:

1.   The *persons* who are taking part in the speech act. Are they about the same age? Are they males or females? Which language are they using to speak? (their native tongue? the native language of one of them? a second language for one or both of them?) How many people are there? What are their social roles? (Is it a mother talking to her child? a student talking to a teacher? a doctor talking to a patient?) What are their attitudes toward each other? (Are they friends, enemies, strangers, or acquaintances?)

2.   The *place* where the conversation occurs. Is it in the speaker's native land or is it in a foreign country or region which he is visiting or to which he has moved? Is it in a house, an office, a place of worship, a movie, or a park? Must the speech act be brief and spoken in a whisper or can it be in a normal voice and sustained?

3. The *time* it is taking place. Is it a usual daily occurrence? Is it a frequent or infrequent happening? What is the duration—the length—of the conversation? Is it time-bound or time-free, e.g., "Good evening" or "Hello"?

4. The *topic* or *activity* which is being discussed. The psychological attitude and the reaction of the listener will differ depending on the type of invitation, for example. Is it a pleasant social invitation or might it be a teacher or a guidance counselor asking (inviting) a student with the words, "I'd like to see you in my room at three today to talk about the mistakes in your composition"? The *function* + the *situation* + the *topic* give rise to the specific *notions* (underlying the nouns, verbs, adjectives, adverbs, prepositions and other words) which complete the function (the communicative purpose) and clarify it. These, in turn, give rise to the exponents in the speech act.

Exponents are the language *utterances* or *statements* which stem from the function, the situation, and the topic. They are the language forms a speaker uses to express (to complete or realize) a message; to indicate an awareness of elements in the situation (social roles, for example, which will influence the formality or informality of the conversation); and to "keep to" the topic when it is important to do so, as in an interview.

The exponents we select in speaking depend not only on the situational elements mentioned above but on our personalities and on our level of linguistic competence. Let us look at the possible exponents in one example of a request:

Please open the window.

Open the window, please.

Would you open the window?

Would you mind opening the window?

I wonder if you would mind opening the window?

It might be a good idea to open the window.

Naturally, there are indirect ways of making a request to open a window, for example, as in, "It's very stuffy in here, isn't it?" (while remaining in your seat so that the other person will undoubtedly get up to open the window).

16

Everything said to this point can be diagramed very simply as follows (this diagram will be expanded below (p. 28)):

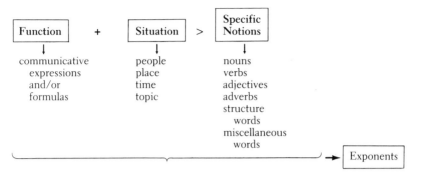

But other concepts in linguistics and sociolinguistics will have to be added to our discussion above. We cannot talk about people and places, for example, without mentioning *variations* of language resulting from such factors as *dialects*, the *formality* or *informality* we wish to or are required to maintain in a particular situation, and the *mode* (oral or written) that is being used to communicate. Moreover, under *notions* we will discuss— again very briefly—the universal notions found in all languages which come under the heading of general notions.

Before, however, proceeding to these finer definitions of terms, which you will find included under "Theoretical Bases" (pp. 22–39), it is worth emphasizing the reasons for the enthusiasm engendered by the functional-notional approach and explaining the accreditation system envisaged by the Council of Europe.

REASONS FOR OPTIMISM

The tremendous merit of the functional-notional approach to learning is that it emphasizes the fact that the students and their communicative purposes are at the very core of the teaching program. The learner's actual and foreseeable academic, social, and vocational needs will underlie all aspects of the program's linguistic and cultural content. While due attention is given to certain aspects of selection and grading of linguistic-cultural content, the primary consideration is those functions that persons of a particular age level, in a particular situation, would wish or need to express.

There are additional cogent reasons for the wide interest engendered by this innovative approach to language learning and teaching.

1. It sets realistic learning tasks in which full-class or individualized instruction may be utilized.
2. It provides for the teaching of *everyday, real-world* language use in a variety of sociocultural situations in which features of pronunciation, vocabulary, grammar, and culture are selected and graded according to their priority in actual communication, and intermeshed meaningfully from the first lesson at the beginning level of learning to serve the learner's immediate communicative purpose.
3. It leads us to emphasize the need for numerous, varied, receptive activities before rushing learners into premature performance. (*Receptive* is also called *interpretative* by some writers.)
4. It recognizes that while the language used in any speech act should be based on the situation or setting in which it occurs and be grammatically and semantically appropriate, the speaker must, above all, have a real purpose for speaking and something to talk about.
5. The act of communication, even at elementary levels, will be intrinsically motivating simply because it expresses *basic, universal communicative functions* of language and because it makes use of notions that are most appropriate to complete the specific function or functions being expressed.
6. It enables teachers to exploit sound psycholinguistic, sociolinguistic, linguistic, and educational principles. (This will be explained further below.)
7. It can develop naturally from existing teaching methodology. Curriculum writers and teachers may, thus, use an eclectic approach, taking what has been found best and most suited to their teaching personalities from direct, audio-lingual, structural, situational, or any other method and integrate relevant features of each into a functional-notional approach. Our discussion of methodology below will underscore the familiar elements in the teaching process while recommending several innovative techniques and strategies leading to effective communication within a functional-notional format.
8. It does not insist upon mastery of any body of material when it is presented. A spiral, expandable curriculum is envisaged so that grammatical and topical or cultural materials can be studied in greater depth whenever relevant during the course.
9. It makes provision through a unit and module system (which will be explained at length below) for admission to certain programs at any time during the year. The F-N[1] approach is designed for regular long-term school courses, in elementary and secondary schools and univer-

[1] From this point on, F-N refers to functional-notional.

sities, as well as for intensive courses (during the regular school year, in summer schools, or in evening classes). Hence,

10. It provides for the widespread promotion of foreign language learning at the very moment when other language learning methods and programs being publicized would restrict the number of persons in a classroom—some even suggesting a one-to-one pupil-teacher ratio. Bilingual or multi-lingual education for every member of society has never been as essential to mankind as it is today.

CURRENT THINKING ON A UNIT-CREDIT SYSTEM

Although discussion of a unit-credit system has centered mainly on the needs of adults who have fairly well-defined needs, the idea of such a system is fundamental to Council of Europe thinking and has great potential significance for school language work also. For this reason it is worthwhile to consider briefly how a unit-credit system might work, as envisaged in earlier international discussion.

So many countries throughout the world are expressing interest in a transferable credit system that the Council team plans to consult with educational representatives of all of the interested countries before issuing definitive guidelines. An excellent discussion of the problems and benefits involved can be found in Professor Trim's monograph, "Draft Outline of a European Unit-Credit System for Modern Languages Learning by Adults." (1980). Since we are convinced that a unit-credit idea will be a boon for immigrants or language learner's of all levels everywhere, we shall underscore those facets of the discussion which we consider universally applicable. Our summary and thoughts will, of necessity, be very briefly stated.

At the present time, it is felt that it will be motivating and productive to give formal recognition through tests or more informal measures to learners who have participated in regular school courses or crash programs in which particular or partial units have been studied. The units, including one or more functions for presentation and a coherent, cohesive set of learning tasks, will be constructed on the basis of an analysis of language use in actual or foreseeable situations; the social, vocational, or academic needs of students; and on a set of linguistic, sociolinguistic, and psychological principles.

A unit consists of a cluster of speech acts centered around a major language need; for example, learning formal and informal modes of asking for information, teaching the enabling skills students will need to encode or decode a chunk of discourse about a topic of specific academic or vocational interest, or helping them to render the equivalent of a passage or unit of discourse in their native language and in the target language. A study of the unit will enable learners to acquire the communicative *potential* to deal with one or more functions. Notice that "potential" and not immediate "mastery" is sought.

For special academic, professional, or vocational purposes, *modules* and not units can be limited to the functional, grammatical, notional, and cultural content needed to perform very specific duties, for example, to serve as a receptionist in a doctor's office or as a telephone operator. The services to be performed—as determined by a job analysis—will delimit the receptive and productive language the student will be expected to learn and the degree of skill he will be required to achieve.

To illustrate the differences between units and modules, let us take the modal "can." In a module, the operator or receptionist would concentrate on one meaning of "can"—that of possibility—"Can you hold the line? Can you wait five minutes?" In a regular course, the student would learn multiple uses of "can" in a variety of social situations, for example, "Can I have some cake/money/the car? Can you swim/speak English?" etc., in one or several *units*.

Modules for specific purposes can be placed in separate handouts or booklets or can be found in the back of regular textbooks. They should not be allowed to destroy the continuity of the text unless their content is relevant or can serve as an example of a linguistic or cultural element one is focusing on. We would hope, however, that the module with "can" would motivate the learner to discover other uses of it.

Units and modules can be written in great detail or they can be what has been called "abstract," that is, specific as to global content but free as to internal organization (we could start with any meaning of "can," for example, in any social situation) and mode of presentation. In harmony with the spiral or cyclical approach advocated in the F-N approach, a unit or a module need not present a completely new function or topic. It may review a familiar function or topic, but give learners the possibility to handle more complex concepts within a grammatical category or within notions centered about a specific topic; to process the material at a faster pace, more accurately, and consistently; and, of decided importance, to increase the *availability* of expressions, structures, and notions for recall—in other words, to enable learners to retrieve from their memory store and, thus, to remember previously taught linguistic items in a shorter period of time so that their oral or written production will become increasingly fluent.[2]

[2]Examples of modules will be found on pp. 81-3.

A unit will specify the general grammatical, lexical, notional-semantic (that is, the meaning and the appropriate use of a word in a specific context or social situation), the communicative function to be focused upon, the elements in the (social) situation, and the terminal behavior (see pp. 21–2 for discussion) which will be required of the learner. In a formal testing situation, it is expected that performance tests and not achievement tests will be required.

Related to the unit-credit system is the matter of cost-effectiveness, a factor which is of interest to all school systems. How can one enable a learner to achieve the highest levels of communicative potential with the resources—money and teachers—available? There are numerous variables in a learning-teaching situation especially when the learner needs to learn the target language to enter the mainstream of a school or of a community in which the target language is the dominant language of social and vocational (professional) communication. It is important therefore for educators to determine the learning cost for each level by asking such questions as, What precisely is to be learned? How much time might the learning be expected to take with different categories of students having quite varied social or vocational needs? In order to answer these questions effectively, it is necessary to bear in mind several factors which are designed to hasten the learning process and to enhance motivation. In selecting the communicative functions and notions, educators should carefully consider three components which are of undoubted utility in language teaching whatever the needs or the motivation of the learner. The first: How will *social* interaction be affected by the learner's ability to produce an utterance or a stretch of speech with the functions and notions within the unit? Second: How *frequently* will this function arise in various life situations? Should it, therefore, be introduced early at any particular learning level and practiced intensively at succeeding levels? Third: Is the structure, expression, or notion *generalizable* to other categories? For example, the question words "how long" can be appropriate in discussing universal notions of time, space, quantity, or matter. In other words, one should ask as noted above, Can the learners make good, perhaps even unlimited use of the limited language material we are presenting to them at any one time?

The *terminal behaviors* underlying the questions we have just listed will be set forth in the curriculum in behavioral terms. (Behavioral, incidentally, should not be confused with behaviorist.) For example, will the input (the varied stimuli) the learners are receiving from the material enable them to say and do what they desire to do through language? Will it enable them to enter the part of the foreign speech community they need to enter? Will it enable them to produce increasingly correct and appropriate language? Will it enable them gradually to develop the "Sprachegefühl" needed to monitor and correct their verbal behavior?

THEORETICAL BASES

Any language teaching approach generally reflects the principles its proponents consider valid within linguistic, psychological, sociological, and educational theories. The audio-lingual approach, as we have seen, resulted in great part from structuralism in linguistics and behaviorism in psychology. And so it will be with the F-N approach, which combines a "communicative grammar" with cognitivism and humanism.

Sociolinguistic Considerations

First and foremost, emphasis has shifted from the former overweaning preoccupation with structure and setting to the communicative purpose of the speech act. As we shall see, however, neither grammar nor situation is excluded or neglected, but these are no longer considered the primary focus of curriculum writers or teachers. The primary focus is the learner and the function or functions of language—the communicative purpose he wishes to express and to understand.

Since a speech act—communication—takes place in definite but varied sociolinguistic situations, both linguistic and extralinguistic factors have been taken into consideration. The approach takes cognizance of the fact that the social roles and the psychological attitudes of the participants toward each other in a conversation (employer-employee, teacher-pupil, doctor-patient, parent-child, for example), the place and time of the communication act, and the activity or topic being discussed will determine to a large extent the form, tone, and appropriateness of any oral or written message.

While communicative behavior is *always* situationally conditioned and therefore subject to infinite variations, we should like to single out three factors that underlie any speech act: a. the *functions* that language serves in real-world, everyday use; b. the *varieties* of language that are possible within each of the functions; and c. the *shared sociocultural allusions—* which some writers have called *presuppositions*—which not only are necessary to a complete understanding of the oral or written messages we receive, but also determine their acceptability or appropriateness. Let us examine these variables, each of which has decided implications for teaching and learning. We shall begin with the *functions* of language, the very core of the F-N syllabus.

Categories of Functions

There are numerous ways of labeling the major functions expressed in language. Wilkins (1973,1976) lists the following:

Modality (to express degrees of certainty, necessity, conviction, volition, obligation, and tolerance)

Moral discipline and *evaluation* (judgment, approval, disapproval)

Suasion (persuasion, recommendations, predictions)

Argument (relating to the exchange of information and views: information asserted or sought, agreement, disagreement, denial, concession)

Rational inquiry and exposition (authors' note: similar in sub-categories to argument and evaluation)

Personal emotions (positive and negative)

Emotional relations (greetings, flattery, hostility, etc.)

Interpersonal relations (politeness and status: degree of formality and informality)

van Ek (1980) distinguishes six main functions of communication:

imparting and seeking factual information (identifying, reporting, correcting, asking);

expressing and finding out intellectual attitudes (expressing and inquiring about agreement and disagreement, accepting or declining an offer or invitation, etc.);

expressing and finding out emotional attitudes (pleasure or displeasure, surprise, hope, intentions, etc.);

expressing and finding out moral attitudes (apologizing, expressing approval or disapproval, etc.);

getting things done (suasion) (suggesting a course of action, advising, warning);

socializing (greeting and leaving people, attracting attention, proposing a toast).

A convenient way of grouping communicative functions is to use five broad categories: *personal, interpersonal, directive, referential,* and *imaginative.*

The *personal* function refers to the speaker's or writer's ability to clarify his thinking, to arrange or classify material in his mind or to express his innermost thoughts as well as the gamut of emotions that every human being experiences: love, joy, disappointment, distress, anger, frustration, annoyance, sorrow. Moreover, it refers to the speaker's or writer's ability to clarify his purpose in speaking or writing and—in the case of speaking—to change the conversation or terminate it depending on the response he is obtaining from his listener.

The *interpersonal* function enables us to establish and maintain desirable social and working relationships. Within this category would be included expressions of sympathy; joy at another's success; concern for other people's welfare; the making or polite breaking of appointments; apologizing for errors or commitments not met; the appropriate language needed to indicate agreement or disagreement, to interrupt another speaker, or the change or avoid an embarrassing subject—all of which we use in everyday situations and which help make living with others possible and pleasant.

The language used in the *directive* function enables us to make requests or suggestions, to persuade, or to convince.

The *referential* function of language—the one which has been the most frequently practiced in language classes in the past—is concerned with speaking or writing about the present, the past, or the future; the immediate environment; and language itself. This latter function is often referred to as the *metalinguistic* function. Incidentally, we would include translation from one language to another under this function. (By translation is meant the rendering of an utterance in one language into its equivalent meaning in the other language and not a word for word rendition (see p. 165).)

The *imaginative* function refers, of course, to the ability to compose rhymes, poetry, essays, stories, or plays orally or in writing; to use the language creatively.

Varieties of Language

The general basis for the use of functions seems simple enough, but the *varieties* of language which can be used within each may sometimes either obscure the message or render it totally inappropriate. Language varieties are generally conditioned by three principal factors: geographical factors as in the case of dialects; social factors which depend not only upon social roles but also on differences related to social classes, status in the community or nation, and educational background; and the factors which underlie the elements contained in the term "register" as used by some writers. The term "register" is generally defined as variation of language which differs according to a) the *formality* or the *informality* of the situation; b) the *topic, activity*, *work*, or *profession* under discussion; and c) the *mode*—oral or written—of the discourse. But in addition, as Martin Joos has very aptly pointed out in his book *The Five Clocks*,[3] there are shades of informality and formality in speech and in writing ranging from casual or colloquial to frozen.[4]

Following is a brief summary:

Formal: in most writing and in giving public reports

Informal: the private, conversational language used in daily communication and in personal letters

Polite: with people one doesn't know well or people on different levels in terms of age or social position

Familiar: with people one knows intimately

Tentative: tactful language to avoid arguments or embarrassing disagreements

The following is an example of making a suggestion using different levels of formality: *casual* or *colloquial* or *familiar*: "How about (or What about) coming to the movies tonight?"; *informal*: "Would you like to come to the movies tonight?"; *consultative*: "Do you think there is a good film we might go to see tonight?"; *formal*: "Might I escort you to the movies tonight?"; *frozen*: "I would deem it a privilege if you would accompany me to the cinema tonight." (Frozen style could only be used in this context as a joke.)

Each of us varies his speech many times during the day depending upon the person or persons we are with and the situation in which we find ourselves. The phenomenon is so common that we have coined a term for it: "code-switching." "Code" is the name given to the shared language of a community of speakers as opposed to the word "idiolect" which is used to refer to a person's individual use of the language or dialect.

Let us give a brief illustration of code-switching. A doctor playing tennis with a friend would use a casual, informal, or familiar register. The same doctor at a formal, professional dinner party would use a consultative, formal, or perhaps even a frozen register. Now, let us assume for a moment that the doctor is talking about a patient who is not doing very well in the hospital. He will have occasion over a period of time to discuss the patient with various people. We might hear him say the following (depending on his personality) *to his wife* or other family member, "I'm really worried about that guy. I don't think he's got a chance." (familiar/colloquial); *to the patient*, "Well, you're looking fine today. We'll have you

---

[3] Adapted from M. Joos, *The Five Clocks*, (New York: Harcourt, Brace, 1967).

[4] For an excellent discussion, see also G. Leech and J. Svartvik, A *Communicative Grammar of English* (London: Longman, 1975), pp. 21–28.

out of bed in no time at all." (informal); *to the patient's family*, "He's not doing too well. We're doing everything we can." (informal); *to a fellow doctor*, "Joe, about that patient in (Room) 204. I've tried X, Y, and Z and he's not responding. Is there anything else I might do?" (consultative); *to the hospital board members*, "The patient whose charts you have just received has not responded to the medication prescribed and to intensive care therapy." (formal); *in a paper to be delivered at a conference*, "A male patient aged forty-two was admitted to the hospital on December 10. He exhibited the following symptoms: xxx. Examination revealed: xxx. We ran the following tests on him: xxx, etc. (formal/frozen).

There is still another aspect of code-switching which can exert a tremendous influence on the learning of a foreign language.

Most people speak nonstandard dialects in their homes, to intimate friends from the same town or even to strangers if they have never learned the standard language of the community. Because of this, many students may experience serious learning problems: a. They are forced, in school, to learn the standard form of their native language, so that the foreign language they are learning is in effect a third language, not a second one. b. When many of them return home from school, they speak and hear only their own dialect and not the standard language. But if the foreign language teaching is sensitive to language variation, as the F-N approach forces it to be, difficulties of this kind will be reduced, for multilingualism and multidialectalism will be welcomed as strengths.

Cultural Knowledge

While the linguistic forms within each of the functions and varieties could in principle be taught over a definite period of time—depending on the learners' ages, motivation, needs, and language levels—far longer time will be necessary to acquire enough knowledge about the culture of the target community to participate fully in a conversation at the beginning of a stay in a foreign country. Parts of messages in oral or written communication are misunderstood or given false values due to the fact that sociocultural experiences have not been shared by listener and speaker, or writer and reader. Sometimes gesture and facial expression may be especially difficult for the non-native speaker to decipher, and all language operates within a network of other meanings deriving from clothes, architecture, and other cultural conventions of all kinds.

Nor is cultural immersion—simply living in the target country— enough to overcome the gap (this is true of some native speakers as well). Unless newcomers receive a tremendous amount of varied input (stimuli) from near-native or native speakers of the target language and culture, they may spend years acquiring the significance of gestures, distances, or cultural allusions. *Explicit information* will be needed especially if the newcomers to the target country live and work in areas where they continue to hear their native language/dialect.

An F-N curriculum, like many approaches before it and others in use today, provides for the implicit and explicit learning of culture and language varieties through a multi-media approach and an active methodology based on creative use of language. Where feasible, radio broadcasts, television, tapes, cassettes, documentary and recreational films, and pictures of all kinds as well as short illustrated dialogs in a variety of everyday, real-life situations are recommended and exemplified in the curriculum. Because of financial and other considerations, many schools will concentrate on the use of pictures in association with mini-dialogs.

In the matter of cultural allusions, paralinguistic features of languages such as tone of voice, groans, sighs, and other unarticulated sounds which convey meaning to a listener, and kinesics (gestures and facial expressions), the curriculum sets realistic objectives. Learners—particularly prospective migrants—will be given *basic* cultural insights and facts for immediate recognition and use in their native tongue (with target language equivalents when necessary) and thus the *potential* for continuing their study through observation while studying, working, and living with native speakers of the new community. Modules centered around orientation to the new community are catered for as are longer units for regular school programs.

The chart on p. 17 can now be expanded, therefore, to include the additional elements we have discussed under sociolinguistic foundations.

Psycholinguistic Components

We would like to underscore three elements within psycholinguistics which are of primary interest to teachers and curriculum writers. (Others will be discussed under "Educational Principles".)

1. An F-N curriculum, as is true of other humanistic approaches, has taken cognizance of the basic needs of all human beings. It makes provision for teaching the appropriate language needed at the five levels of human needs recognized by most psychologists (Maslow 1970), beginning with the need for survival (exemplified in the *Threshold Level* (van Ek 1980) of the F-N syllabus) to the most elevated need of man—the need for self-realization or self-actualization. The Council of Europe plans eventually to recommend the following five levels

EXPANDED CHART

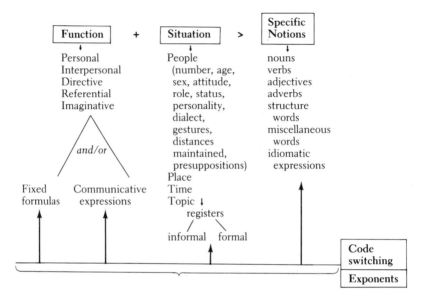

of training for which full or partial credit may be received depending upon the number of units or modules completed within each level and the quality of performance the learner can demonstrate: survival (the threshold level—considered a passport to step into the foreign situation and survive); basic; general competency; advanced and professional.

2. The curriculum is self-motivating since it is specifically designed to serve the actual social, cultural, or vocational needs of learners as determined by interviews and/or job analyses for adult learners and teachers' observations in the case of children.

3. Moreover, it has had written into it an awareness that each human being can have a different rhythm or pace of learning as well as a different mode or strategy for acquiring knowledge. The unit or modular organization of the curriculum materials, the multi-media and cyclical or spiral approach advocated and illustrated below, as well as the *alternative* linguistic forms—ranging from the very simple to the extremely complex—permit learners of different ages, of varying abilities, and at different language learning levels to express *all* the communicative functions of language. They may express these with

gestures and diverse exponents, however, in harmony with their personality; their immediate academic, social, or vocational needs; and their intellectual or linguistic capacity.

Most important, the placement of language items has been changed to conform to the actual real-world need for a particular item. In student materials being prepared, the teaching of the present perfect, for example, used extensively in actual speech, is included among the first units. In an F-N curriculum, priorities for teaching communicative expressions, structures, topics, and notions are determined primarily by the communication act the learners need to or wish to express.

Linguistics

Let us move quickly to linguistics. By linguistics in this book we refer only to what a person must know about or do with the language when he is a native member of a speech community or when he wishes to become part of a foreign speech community. The F-N approach will help the learner at each level acquire a reasonable, basic knowledge of the phonological, grammatical, and lexical subsystems of the language, as well as the ability to use these in actual communication. A variety of learning activities will enable students to encode or decode a message, either oral or written. Depending on the learning level, they will also learn to use gestures and other paralinguistic features to help convey meaning.

It is obvious that whatever linguistic school one "prefers," whatever the starting point—phonemes or utterances—students must learn the items within the various subsystems which are interrelated in any communication act of listening, speaking, reading, and writing. The meaning of any utterance is the combination of the sound, grammar, lexical, and cultural systems reflected in it.

LANGUAGE
(The code of a community of speakers)

Subsystems of Language

The Sound System	Intonations, stress, rhythm, pause, elision, vowels (full and reduced), consonants
The Grammar System	Morphology (*inflection* for plurality, tense, possession, etc.) (*derivation*—prefixes, suffixes, infixes) Morphophonemics (sound or spelling change, i.e., due to letter combinations): I walk*ed*/t/, I want*ed*/ɪd/, I comb*ed* /d/ Syntax—word order
Vocabulary (Lexical) System	Communicative expressions Fixed formulas Content words (nouns, verbs, adjectives, adverbs) Structure words (pronouns, prepositions, conjunctions, etc.)
Cultural System	Appropriateness of language to the social situation Gestures, distances maintained, unarticulated sounds (as in grunts or sighs) Values, mores, taboos, rituals, habits, art forms Social institutions

A conscious or unconscious knowledge of these subsystems is necessary in the skills of *listening* with understanding; *speaking* appropriately, fluently, and correctly; *reading* with comprehension and enjoyment; and *writing* both for practical purposes and to express original thoughts and ideas. Thus *encoding* (putting our thoughts into oral or written words, utterances, and exponents at all levels of formality and informality) and *decoding* (understanding what we hear and read) require knowledge and insight into the elements listed above.

Encoding requires other enabling (subsidiary) skills as well: control of perceptual (that is, acoustic and visual skills) and motor skills which will permit the speaker or writer to put his thoughts into *informational* sequence—into the correct forms and word order and into the sound or spelling patterns needed for comprehensibility. *Decoding* requires the hearer or reader to discriminate intonation, word and sentence stress, sounds or the sound-symbol relationships, as the case may be; to distinguish word order and structural differences; to recognize redundant features of language; to make full use of cognates, where feasible; to retain the first part of the message while continuing to listen or to read; to call to mind immediately—from the words he has stored in his memory—the meaning of the notions in the context of the particular message; and to deduce the meaning of a new word from its context. It is not necessary to remind ourselves that an insight into the social conventions of the speech community which will determine the social and psychological *appropriateness and acceptability of the speech act* is fundamental in both the encoding and decoding processes.

Decoding oral speech is generally more difficult than *encoding* (putting one's thought into words and placing them in logical, appropriate sequence). While we can simplify what we say, we cannot always ask someone who is speaking to us to speak more slowly (although many speakers do it automatically when addressing a language learner or a nonnative speaker) and to pause at points in the utterance which will not cause confusion. Notice the sentence, "He went in spite of the rain," which may often cause the listener or reader to put *went* and *in* together with consequent misunderstanding.

Neither is it often possible in face-to-face communication—as opposed to listening to a cassette or tape which can be stopped and turned back—to ask the speaker to repeat what he had said. Problems of timidity or fear (in class, in job interviews, in talks with persons in authority) will inhibit the listener. As we will note in the chapter on "Developing the Communicative Abilities" (pp. 135-56), it is recommended that much more class time than heretofore be devoted to the ability to *listen* with comprehension. Listening is no longer thought of as a "passive" skill. It requires as we all know the active attention and involvement of the listener.

The term "notions" which we have mentioned but which need further clarification would be placed under linguistics. Notions in the F-N approach are often placed under two headings. They may be *general*—referring to *universal* linguistic phenomena such as *time, space, quantity, motion, matter, case,* and *deixis*—Wilkins (1976) calls these semantico-grammatical categories—or *specific,* that is, the *structural* and *vocabulary items* which would be found within the general categories and which are needed to complete or to clarify and complete functional expressions of language. (For example, we regret *something,* we disagree with *someone* or with *some opinion,* we compliment *someone* on some achievement.)

Two terms above under general categories may need further illustration: *case* and *deixis.* By *case,* in Latin and in many spoken languages, we refer to the varied grammatical functions of nouns, for example (see also, Chapter 1, p. 4). Wilkins (1976, pp. 34–6) recognizes seven cases: agentive (the person who instigates an action); objective (the entity acted upon by the verb); dative (the person affected by the verb); instrumental (the inanimate means by which an action is carried out); locative (the location of an event); factitive (the object or being resulting from the action of the verb, e.g., the dinner is cooking); and benefactive (a person benefitting from an action).

Although of academic interest, these cases and subcategories need not concern us unduly as teachers. When we might have occasion to teach, "*He* went *to* London *by* train," or "*They* came *from* Chicago *by* car," we would simply point out that we use *by* before means of transportation and that we use *to* in order to indicate the location of a place (or destination) and *from* to indicate the place which was left.

The concept of *deixis* is useful (although we would certainly not use the term with learners, except perhaps with those at an advanced or professional level). Deixis refers to grammatical categories such as pronouns, demonstrative adjectives and pronouns, possessives, or articles and adverbials which link various parts of the same or different utterances together. For example, in the utterances, "I expect the doctor to come in any minute...Ah, *here he* comes now," *here* is a demonstrative pronoun which signifies that the person is approaching the place where the speaker is; *he* refers to "the doctor" in the previous sentence. This relationship of words and their referents should definitely be pointed out in the presentation of the parts of speech mentioned above and of any other linking words. The terminology should be simple, however, and descriptive, "What does *here* refer to? Where is the speaker? Where is the doctor? To whom does *he* refer?"

Finally, we should consider briefly the relationships between functions, notions, and grammar. A number of linguists, perhaps most notably the British linguist Halliday (1973,1978), have attempted to develop theories of language structure which show how the formal grammatical patterns reflect the functions of language, arguing that language use determines language structure. It is not necessary for this to be so, for the relationship between language use and grammatical form could be as arbitrary as the relationship between the meaning of a word and the form of the word (*pink* is not a particularly pink word). However, the attempt to determine ways in which language structure reflects the ways we think and the ways we use language is clearly worthwhile as a subject for investigation. It is also clear that this concern is very similar to that which has inspired the F-N movement in language teaching. But we are not in a position to make a close link between theory and practice, and none of the educational theorists have yet done more than produce lists of grammatical items and separate lists of functions and/or notions. It is of course possible to show (as Leech and Svartvik, 1975, do) that certain forms can often exemplify certain functions and, conversely, that certain functions will lead us to incline towards certain forms—but there is no *necessary* relation between the two. Any grammatical structure *can* be used to express any function, and the abstract functional categories of linguists like Halliday have no immediate pedagogical use, as currently formulated. It would not be too misleading to suggest that the relationship between linguists' functional grammars and the functions of the Council of Europe work is still only metaphorical. (For a discussion of Halliday's most accessible paper in this area, see Brumfit and Johnson 1979, pp. 25–44.)

The language teacher thus has a responsibility to provide language structure for learners, as well as responsibility to give them opportunities for using the language. We are not yet in a position to be able to say that, for second language learners in the classroom, language use will automatically produce a full, native-speaker grammatical system.

Psychological Bases

An F-N approach makes use of many of the basic principles of the psychological sciences. Among these, the following find applications in both the linguistic and cultural content and the methodology advocated in the approach:

• Learning generally results when unit and program content and activities are related to the needs and experiences of the learners. As we have noted above, an analysis of students' immediate and foreseeable needs is considered the first, indispensable step in curriculum planning.

• Student motivation is of primary importance in acquisition of knowledge and skills. Motivation—to use the terms of Gardner and Lambert

(1977) and their research colleagues—may be "integrative" or "instrumental." By "integrative" is meant the desire on the part of the learner to be accepted by and to enter the community of the target culture. By "instrumental" is meant the desire to learn a second language or culture in order to obtain a better education, a better job, or better grades.

In our view "instrumental" and "integrative" should not be considered as standing at different ends of the learning process. Both types of motivation should be fostered in the language classroom. Success, as demonstrated by good grades in language study, may lead to "integrative" motivation. Moreover, it is extremely difficult in many schools in communities where there are no target language speakers in the community, no films, and no other resources to achieve "integrative" motivation.

• Learning is enhanced when presentation and practice of language items are made meaningful through their use in real life (or even simulated) situations. The more associations made between communicative expressions and notions and a variety of situations, the greater the likelihood of retention and more immediate recall. The same structure, communicative expression, or lexical item should be reentered in as many different, appropriate situations as feasible.

• Students should become active participants in the learning process since, depending on the learning strategies they have developed since childhood, they will undoubtedly restructure what we teach them in their own way. A communicative methodology encourages this, and an F-N curriculum systematically promotes this encouragement. Generally, and with older learners especially, the more responsibility students are given, the more they will learn.

• Students should be helped to perceive the relationships among the elements in language, situation, and culture through simple diagrams, graphics, and visuals of all kinds. Often, clear oral explanations of the relationships (which can be elicited from the students through questions related to the diagrams) will guide them to an understanding of the "language in use." For example, "*John* loves to dance. *He*'s an excellent dancer."

• Activities in the classroom should take into consideration the fact that all individuals have different learning styles (listening, listening and reading, writing, etc.) and different rates of learning. Suggestions for group and individualized class work will be found below.

• Transfer of learning is not always automatic. Through many examples and learning tasks, students can be helped to recognize the shared elements of communicative expressions and of notions; the recurring rules underlying grammatical structures; or the permitted co-occurence of sounds or words. For example, we can say, "I enjoyed watching the man," "I enjoyed watching the film," but not, "I enjoyed watching the book."

Educational Principles

Sound educational principles underlie the construction of an F-N curriculum. Foremost among these are the following characteristics of an F-N approach:

• Transfer of learning is not always automatic. Through many examples and learning tasks, students can be helped to recognize the shared elements of communicative expressions and of notions; the recurring rules underlying grammatical structures; or the permitted co-occurence of sounds or words. For example, we can say, "I enjoyed watching the man," "I enjoyed watching the film," but not, "I enjoyed watching the book."

Since it is impossible to teach the whole of language at any learning level or in any one course, our aims should be rooted in reality: we should make every effort to give learners the *potential* ability and motivation to continue their studies, and to generalize from the communicative expressions, grammatical rules, and notions learned in one sociocultural situation to other appropriate ones.

• A *spiral or cyclical approach* is highly recommended. In this approach, the same sociocultural theme, structural category or language function is studied—in logical sequence always—in greater depth at successive levels of learning. The material studied previously is recalled, reviewed, and integrated with the new learning.

On the next page are examples of a spiral treatment of grammatical and situational (sociocultural) categories.

Comments on Figures 1 and 2 (Finocchiaro 1979, p.14) below:

In Figure 1, the person at the center is the learner moving in increasingly wider circles toward the target-language country and the world.

In Figure 2:
Starting with *I* and *you* makes possible immediate student-student and teacher-student communication and interaction in such activities as chain drills, questions and answers of all types, paired practice, and small group work.

Depending on the function and situation you are presenting, possessive adjectives (*my, your,* etc.) may be learned before direct or indirect object pronouns (*me, him,* etc.).
For example: I hurt *myself.*
For example: He did it *himself.*

Sociocultural Themes

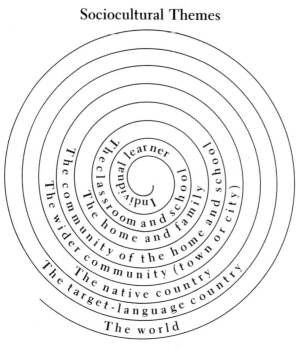

Figure 1

A Structural Topic
(Personal Pronouns)

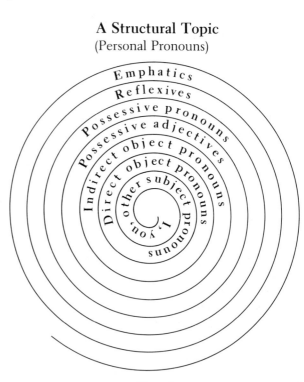

Figure 2

•   The curriculum is divided into units or modules which are in turn divided into teaching lessons—the number depending on such factors as the learning level and the material to be covered. The functions the learners would need or wish to express within a social situation form the nucleus of each unit and serve as the fulcrum around which the dialogs or reading passages, the communicative expressions or formulas, the relevant structures and notions, and the learning tasks and activities are developed. The starting point is the *communicative function* and the *social situation* in which the function or purpose is being expressed. The vocabulary and lexical items—that is, the notions—are centered around one or more functions and topics (complimenting someone, for example), making immediate communication possible.

•   A spiral approach is used in presenting the same or similar functions in different sociocultural situations. Following is an example that encompasses a number of units at one learning level and combines F-N and structural criteria. (Only a few of the notions [vocabulary items] possible within the unit are illustrated.)

Some characteristics of the F-N units illustrated below:

•   Notice that the title of the unit is often expressed in functional terms so that learners are immediately given the necessary mental "set" or readiness so essential for focusing their attention on the communicative purpose of the dialog, the mini-dialog, or the reading passage.

•   The same function (apologizing, for example) may be presented in different situations in two (or more) successive units, especially in intensive (short-term) courses. Different functions may be presented in the *same* or *in different situations.*

As you can see, the function *requesting directions* is presented in two different situations—at a bus stop and at a gas station. Even in the small sample above, the advantages of having learners understand the use of the same function in more than one situation are apparent: 1) Learners get insight into the fact that language makes "infinite use of finite means"— that is, of the unlimited use in actual speech of a limited number of communicative functions (as well as of sounds, verb forms, and other linguistic elements). 2) They also acquire a wide range of notions, relevant to the every day topics that most human beings have occasion to talk about.

•   The notions in the chart depend on and stem from the meshing of function and situation. The grammar and vocabulary to be taught in each unit result from the integration of function and situation.

A MINI-CURRICULUM

Unit	Date	Title and Function	Situation	Communicative Expressions or Formulas	Structures	Nouns	Verbs	Adj.	Adv.	Structure Words	Misc.	Activities
X	2/4	Apologizing	Theater (asking someone to change seats)	Excuse me. Would you mind...? I'm very grateful.	V + ing	seat place friend	move change					Dialog study Role play Expanding sentences Paired practice
XI	2/11	Apologizing	Department store (Returning something)	I'm sorry. Would it be possible...?	Simple past Present perfect	shirt	buy wear	small	too	you	dates	Aural comprehension Indirect speech Changing register
XIV	3/15	Requesting directions	At the bus stop	I beg your pardon. Could you tell me...?	Interrogatives (simple present) Modal—must	names of places	must get to get off take		how where	us	numbers	Reading questions and answers Cloze procedures Dictation
XVI	3/25	Asking for information	In a post office	Excuse me. Where would I find...?	Modal—can	stamps savings account	sell buy open					Expanding sentences of previous dialogs Role playing with these

Unit	Date	Title and Function	Situation	Communicative Expressions or Formulas	Structures	Nouns	Verbs	Adj.	Adv.	Structure Words	Misc.	Activities
XVIII	4/5	Expressing frustration	Home (Dinner guests late)	How inconsiderate! Why couldn't they have telephoned?	be + Ved It's (time)	food dessert roast	ruin spoil serve	late	so		time & numbers	Any of the above Dicto-comp
XX	4/25	Requesting directions	Gas station	I beg your pardon. How would I . . .?	Imperatives (affirmative) (negative) tell . . . to	high- way traffic light	reach get on turn off say tell			me	ordinal numbers	Any of the above Reported speech (e.g., car passenger wants to know what attendant has said)

COMMENTS

Some of the structures may be: a. taught for receptive use only.

b. presented for the first time.

c. reintroduced after having been taught earlier.

It is desirable to indicate on the right side of the chart several of the major learning activities the students would engage in within the unit. (You should also list these activities under the dialogs in a separate notebook. Nearly every activity suggested can be engaged in within any unit (Finocchiaro 1979, p. 15).

ADDITIONAL CHARACTERISTICS OF THE CONTENT IN AN F-N APPROACH

Some of these may already have been touched upon in our discussion above. Since it is an innovative approach, however, and since some points are controversial (for example, the recommendation that the students' native language be used when necessary and wherever feasible, see pp. 57–9 for further comments), reemphasis is warranted.

• In each unit and at each level the learner is helped—through oral discussion with a teacher or through an introductory paragraph in his *native language*, where feasible[5]—to understand the social roles and psychological attitudes of the speakers toward each other, and thus the rationale for the formality or informality and/or appropriateness of the language in the particular situation.

• Since it is patently impossible to teach the whole of language and culture in any one unit, year, or level, curriculum planners have come to the conclusion that, particularly in regular courses, selection and gradation of language items or notions within the communicative functions is imperative. This selection and gradation is more flexible than in the past; for example, *to have* or *the simple present* may be deferred until much later in the units but will nonetheless be presented in logical sequence. The selection will depend on such factors as the functions and notions the learners need, the linguistic knowledge they already have, the complexity of the grammatical structure they are about to learn, and the length of the stretch of speech necessary to express their communicative purpose.

The curriculum generally provides for learners in any one unit or module to be given only a passive or receptive awareness of alternative forms by which a function may be expressed. The term "receptive" is gradually being replaced by "interpretative," which is closer to what the mind does when hearing or reading a new linguistic element or a previously unfamiliar fact. Not only does the mind *receive* the impression but it generally *associates* the new element with related concepts stored in its memory bank. Learners may thus decide to make an alternative form part of their active vocabulary because its expression is more in harmony with their way of speaking.

• In addition to having a communicative function rather than a situational topic or structural item as its starting point, the F-N curriculum differs from a structural or situational syllabus in several respects. For one thing, the structures in the various utterances of a dialog may be dissimilar,

[5] This is "feasible" where the students all understand the same native language and where the teacher can speak it (unless there are bilingual teachers, parents, or student aides available).

as they would be in real-world communication. For example, a suggestion such as, "Let's go over the engine," may elicit a reaction of disagreement followed by an alternative suggestion, such as, "I don't feel like it now. It's late and I'm sure it's too complicated. We can do that tomorrow."

• Moreover, in the F-N curriculum, a number of different functions may be clustered in one unit. For example, an invitation may be extended, accepted gracefully, arrangements made about time, place, and transportation, and thanks extended before conventional parting remarks are made. A refusal of the invitation would force the use of an entirely different range of functions and notions.

Look at the units outlined below. You will note that the three units may be presented separately but that they are all clustered around the interpersonal function of extending an invitation or making an appointment which may be accepted or refused. (The first unit is considered the "core" unit; the others—following the core—are called "extensions." There can be as many extensions as you and your students wish to devise.)

A "Core" and Possible Extensions
(beginning and intermediate levels)

Motivation: Related to students' lives and perceived needs

Situation: Speakers (attitudes, roles), place, topic, time when the conversation may be taking place

Function: Making an appointment; persuading, refusing

I	II	III
A,B. Greetings	⟶	
A. Asking for an appointment	⟶	
B. Accepting	B. Refusing	B. Refusing
A,B. Making arrangements	A. Persuading	A. Persuading
	B. Accepting (for a future date)	B. Adamant refusal
A,B. Leavetaking	A,B. Making arrangements	A. Angry interchange
	A,B. Leavetaking	A,B. Cold leavetaking

NOTE: At the beginning levels, weeks may elapse between the presentation of formats I and III. At more advanced levels, all three—created by groups of learners themselves with teacher help—could be prepared and dramatized in one lesson by pairs of students.

• Most important, in the F-N approach grammatical structure and function do *not* overlap. As we have already seen, function may be expressed directly or indirectly through the use of any number of different structures. There is *no obligatory one-to-one relationship* between structure and function. For example, a request may be worded as, "May I have a glass of cold water? Could I have...? Would you get me...? I wonder if I might have...?" The same function (requesting something) may be expressed indirectly, but with the same meaning, in a question such as, "Is there (or Would there be) a glass of cold water?"

By the same token, a *directive* might be expressed as, "Pick up your coat and put it away," or (in an angry tone) "Is that *your* coat on the floor?"—an interrogative which obviously does not ask for information.

Notice some other negative interrogatives which do not ask for information but which express other emotions.

1. Why aren't they here?
   (anger, frustration, concern)
2. Aren't they a handsome couple?
   (admiration)
3. Aren't you coming to the beach?
   (disappointment, surprise)
4. Won't you have some of my cake?
   (hospitality)
5. Couldn't you wait a while longer?
   (a plea)
6. Why don't you stay home for a change?
   (disappointment, plea, anger)
7. Why can't I come with you?
   (suspicion, jealousy, discontent)

Conversely, the same structure may be used to express more than one function of language. An utterance such as, "You don't really like . . . " may be used to find out about someone's moral or intellectual attitude, or to persuade someone to change his mind. Utterances can be multifunctional. Notice: "Could you tell me (polite request) how long it will take (information wanted) to get to New York City?"(location).

• The curriculum places emphasis first on making the students *aware* of the functions found within the complex, diversified, sociocultural situations of our daily lives, and *then* on enabling them to express these functions correctly and appropriately in the language they are learning.

• Attention is given to ways in which students' knowledge of their native language can be utilized in the presentation of the new material. (This facet of the approach presents some problems which will require teachers' collaboration and further research. For example, will the expression of functions and notions which contrast markedly in L_1 and L_2 be deferred to a higher level? They should *not* be if we are to give the learners' communicative purpose priority.)

• Selection and gradation of grammatical structures within the function to be expressed will depend—as in all curriculum planning—on the age of students; their linguistic-cultural needs; the complexity of the grammatical item; the knowledge students already have, not only of their native tongues but also of the target language structures and notions which will clarify the new structure. As we have seen on p. 17, nearly all functions can be expressed on a continuum—from very simple terms in brief utterances to longer ones of great complexity.

• The approach makes provision for the teaching of the notions and expressions needed in other disciplines (curriculum areas in a school situation) both in a second language (where the target language is the one spoken in the community) and in a foreign language situation (where the target language is learned in one's native land). Concepts and language needed in social studies, geography, mathematics, art, music, and the native language and literature, as well as those needed for professional or vocational use, are interwoven in the curriculum at all appropriate levels. (These will be discussed in Chapter 5, p. 131-2.)

• In programs for adults (who may range from functional illiterates to professionals) units contain linguistic, and cultural materials they will need immediately for *sociocultural* or *sociovocational* purposes.

• Finally, although this does not apply more to the F-N curriculum than to other approaches, it is worth emphasizing the role of the teacher, by reference to two quotations. The humane basis for F-N work requires a recognition of the central role of human relationships.

"I have come to a frightening conclusion. I am the decisive element in the classroom. It is my personal approach that creates the climate. It is my daily mood that makes the weather. As a teacher I possess tremendous power to make a child's[6] life miserable or joyous. I can be a tool of torture or an instrument of inspiration. I can humiliate or humor, hurt or heal. In all situations it is my
[6] You may substitute "learner" or "student."

response that decides whether a crisis will be escalated or de-escalated, a child humanized or dehumanized."

from the *New York State Bulletin of Foreign Language Teachers* (1979)

"Let people realize clearly that every time they threaten someone or humiliate or hurt unnecessarily or dominate or reject another human being, they become forces for the creation of psychopathology, even if these be small forces. Let them recognize that every man who is kind, helpful, decent, psychologically democratic, affectionate, and warm, is a psychotherapeutic force even though a small one."

from the *New York State Bulletin of Foreign Language Teachers* (1979),
reprinted from
Abraham H. Maslow (1970)

SUGGESTIONS FOR DISCUSSION

1. Observe a friend or a family member over a period of a week and note down the number of times and the circumstances in which he uses nonlinguistic gestures to communicate in his native language.
2. Explain what is meant by self-realization or self-actualization. What qualities would a person need to attain a state of self-realization? Do you feel that you have attained it? If not, what do you think is impeding you?
3. Select five expressions in your native language which are expressed very differently in the target language. a. What difficulties would your students experience in learning them? b. How could you help them to overcome the problems?
4. Do you think that giving learners the "potential" to continue their studies is a more realistic objective than expecting mastery? For what age levels? For students with which needs? In which linguistic and cultural areas might "mastery" take longer to attain?
5. Give ten different ways of inviting a person to visit you or to go to specific places. Use informal and more formal language. Explain the elements in the situation briefly.
6. What are some of the major advantages that the F-N approach has over the strictly situational or structural approaches?
7. Do you think a unit-credit system would work in your state or country? If not, why not? What problems do you foresee?
8. What is the major difference between a module and a unit?
9. Which criteria should be kept in mind in selecting and grading teaching items?
10. What guidelines would you consider in writing terminal objectives at your teaching level in your state or country?
11. In talking about the persons engaged in conversation, which variables should be taken into consideration?
12. Give several presuppositions you had about people who spoke your second (or third) language before you developed insight into their culture.
13. List ten additional emotions/thoughts you would include under the personal function.
14. In what ways can the same language vary at one time (in the present)?

15. Make a suggestion to various persons using four different levels of formality. Why did you have to change the levels?
16. Why might living in the foreign land not be enough to learn to function in the new language?
17. Prepare an example of how you switched codes on any one day. Talk about the persons with whom you spoke, the place, the circumstances, etc.
18. Give the steps a learner has to go through in *decoding* and *encoding* oral language.
19. What are the universal notions of language? Give several examples of case and deixis.
20. Which psychological bases do you consider essential in teaching? (Think of yourself as a former student and as a teacher.)
21. Prepare a spiral approach diagram for any structural category in your *target* language.
22. In which circumstances should the students' native language be used?
23. Prepare a core functional format related to breaking an appointment with your dentist. Now expand it in two ways.
24. Give as many ways as possible of helping a learner from another region, state, or country retain pride in his language and culture.
25. Explain the implication of Maslow's statement. How could you as a teacher ensure that you not let a student feel hurt or rejected? Give practical examples.

3 Planning the Curriculum Content

INTRODUCTORY REMARKS

Constraints on the Curriculum

As we saw in the previous chapter, the F-N curriculum starts not from the question, "What is the grammar of the language?" but from the questions, "What do learners need to do with the language?" and "What kind of meanings do learners need to express in the language?" Consequently, a well-designed curriculum will start with an attempt to specify the *needs* of the learners. This is not always easy to do, but it is usually possible to give approximate answers to certain basic questions.

1. Will learners be mainly concerned with listening, reading, and conversation or reading and writing?
2. What kinds of situations will they probably encounter? (Formal or informal? Professional or friendly or casual? and so on.)
3. How many of the situations they will encounter will be fairly predictable, where knowledge of conventions and fixed phrases may be helpful, and how many will be unpredictable and free?
4. What are the main topics, or subject areas, which they are likely to encounter in the foreign language?
5. What kind of general functions (see p. 32) are they most likely to have to perform in the language being learned?
6. Where will learners need to use the language?

The answers to these basic questions will provide guidance about the kind of curriculum to be developed; however, even when such questions can be answered specifically, the answers will not provide us with the teaching program. They will provide us with a checklist, though, which we can refer to in order to clarify whether the general balance of the program is right and whether important aspects of language use have been neglected.

Translating these general needs into the basis for effective teaching requires that we should do two things:

a. Construct a program which is realistic in terms of the physical and administrative conditions in which it will have to operate.

b. Adapt the program to be consistent with what we understand to be the most efficient ways of learning languages.

To do a. well we need to ask questions like:

1. What type of program are we concerned with? Is it intensive or regular over a long period? How old are the students? What is their language level?
2. Will students need the language for immediate use? In school and/or out of school? Or will they only require it at some unspecified time in the future?
3. Are there particular social, political, religious, or economic factors which will affect relations between students and teachers (for example, are the teachers local or foreign, from backgrounds similar to or different from the students, and so on)?
4. Are there resources in the school and the community which could affect the implementation of the curriculum?
5. How much training and experience will teachers have? How overworked are they? How committed?

To do b. well we need to make our program responsive to three basic requirements:

1. Does it provide systematic exposure to the basic systems of the language, so that students have enough data available to enable them to build up for themselves the basic patterns of the language?
2. Does it provide enough opportunities for all students to experience use of the language for themselves over an extended period ("use" here may include listening, speaking, reading, or writing)?
3. Is it organized in such a way as to motivate students to make the maximum use of the opportunities provided through a. and b. above?

It is always difficult to answer these questions, simply because we are talking primarily about human beings—teachers and students—and they all have different backgrounds, personality traits, needs, and motivations. But, because we teach classes and not individuals and because language is a means of operating within a large social group, our curriculum must be based on generalizations about the social process of learning and using languages.

48

Let us start our discussion by stating what a curriculum should provide:

1. An analysis of the general aims of the program (in other words, the terminal behavior to be achieved by students at the end of the course).
2. A progression of units which guides the teacher by indicating what aspects of the language are to be concentrated on at any given stage.
3. A list of items (functional, notional, or grammatical items, as well as points of pronunciation or of relevant cultural information) to be isolated within each unit.
4. A description of the situations, tasks, and activities through which language items and skills will be introduced and practiced.
5. Suggestions for evaluation (testing) of the pupils' growth.
6. Sources for teacher reference and pupils' texts.

A curriculum, therefore, specifies the knowledge, skills, and insights the student will be expected to acquire through a series of in-class or out-of-school tasks and activities designed to foster learning. It will also specify the degree of performance the student will be expected to demonstrate through various oral or written measures. A syllabus, on the other hand, generally provides a listing of content to be learned but does not suggest methods, activities, and measures for evaluation.

And now, let us turn to a brief discussion of our questions.

• In an F-N approach, the unit-credit system makes it possible to envisage several types of courses: *extensive* (regular) courses in elementary, secondary schools, and universities lasting perhaps three to five years; *intensive* (crash) year-round courses of two weeks to five or six months duration or *intensive* vacation courses; and *self-study* courses—residential, correspondence, or tutoring. All of these can be provided either in the learners' native country or in the target country.

• While our aims and some techniques for achieving the aims may be similar when we are teaching the target language as a foreign language or as a second language, factors within the students and in the community in which the teaching is taking place will have a decided effect on our program. A glance at the charts below gives a brief idea of the factors to be considered in either situation.

1. FACTORS IN CURRICULUM PLANNING: A BRIEF OVERVIEW[1]

The Participants in the Learning Teaching Process

I.

Who/What:	Possible Characteristics:	Insights from the Sciences:	Discoveries Through Such Measures as:
THE LEARNERS	*Attitudes toward:* The target language and its speakers Their peers Learning *Motivations:* Intrinsic (integrative) Extrinsic (instrumental) *Needs:* Not predictable in the case of young learners in native country Foreseeable: All learners in new country Adults - vocations; professions *Previous language learning experience:* With target language With other languages *Proficiency:* In L_1 In L_2 Strategies, styles, rhythm of learning or acquiring knowledge	Psychology Psycholinguistics Sociolinguistics Sociology	Interviews Questionnaires Observation Language tests Attitude and value scales Job analyses (Knowledge and skills needed in specific vocations or professions) Talks with target language educators and visits to target language country

[1]We are indebted to a lecture by Sophie Moirand, of Université de Paris III for the idea for this chart.

	Possible Characteristics:	Insights from the Sciences:	Discoveries Through Such Measures as:
THE TEACHERS	*Attitudes toward:* Other ethnic groups Teaching profession *Educational background:* Level of schooling Courses taken Visits to country of immigrants *Linguistic competence:* Conscious knowledge of target language system Experience in learning a foreign or second language Proficiency in language (non-native speakers) *Teaching competence:* Pre-service training In-service training Membership in professional associations	Education Linguistics Psycholinguistics Sociolinguistics Sociology	Interviews Classroom observation Questionnaires Attitude and value scales Language tests Tests on methodology and learning and teaching theory Publications: articles, reviews, units, modules Attendance at relevant conferences Observation of rapport with colleagues; parents; learners
THE INSTITUTIONS	Political or social constraints Public, private, business Resources available Objectives Philosophy Attitudes towards ethnic groups Hiring and promotion policies for staff Evaluation procedures	Education Psychology Philosophy Sociology	Study of constitution, statutes, by-laws Financial statements, programs, curricula Visits Talks with students; parents; teachers; administrators; community agency personnel

II. Instructional Objectives

Objectives:	Learning Situations:	Skills and Competencies To Be Developed:	Through:
GLOBAL (personal–social–cultural)	Short intensive courses Long term regular courses; *All* learners	The integrative skills: listening speaking reading writing communicative competence	An interdisciplinary approach The use of authentic material Carefully selected texts Study of units Study of modules (for vocational or professional purposes) Group work
ACADEMIC	For each learning level Long and short term courses; *All* learners	Subsidiary (enabling skills under each of the above) e.g., communicative competence:	Individualized instruction Study of school records (units, credits completed) Job analyses Learning through formal
SPECIFIC (sociocultural; vocational; professional)	Intensive courses vacation regular session Adult immigrant tourists or guest workers Language/orientation courses for all learners in the target country	Awareness of people, place, time, topic Appropriate language and paralanguage needed in the specific situation Focus on functions, grammar, lexicon, pragmatics Emphasis on reading and understanding as well as speaking, talking and listening, interacting; writing skills depending on learner needs Fluency	intensive study and through a variety of relevant stimuli and activities Use of spiral approach (expressions, items, materials, to be recycled continuously)

III. Determining the Linguistic and Cultural Contents

Need for:

Analysis of learners needs
Selection
Sequencing
Grading
Choosing relevant topics

Criteria, e.g., Linguistic Content:

Distance between L_1 and L_2
Frequency of occurrence; need in real life for items in the community, academic, or vocational program
Generalizability to other situations
Complexity of structures
Importance of and interest in topics

Cultural content:

Learning site (native or target) country of learners
Comparison between L_1 and L_2 culture
Contrasts between L_1 and L_2 culture
Emphasis on appreciation of cultural pluralism

Based on the Sciences:

Anthropology
Education
Linguistics
Psycholinguistics
Psychology
Sociolinguistics
Sociology

Through:

Analyses of speech acts and events
Contrastive analyses
Observation of target language interaction; situations
Research on learners' errors and interlanguage

IV. Selecting Classroom Methods and Strategies

Bases:

Age of learners
Learning rhythm
Learning styles
Native land or target country
Needs of learners
Personality and experience of teachers

Approach Determined by:

Linguistic school preferred
Method favored, e.g.,
    situational
    audio-visual
    audio-lingual
    functional-notional
    communicative
    functional-grammatical
    notional
    eclectic

Gleaned from:

Descriptive linguistics
Didactics
Education
Linguistics
Psycholinguistics
Sociolinguistics

Strategies:

Interactions between students and teacher and among students
Group work
Paired practice
Activities such as role playing
Problem solving
Playing games
Manipulative exercises
"Free" communication

IV. Selecting Classroom Methods and Strategies

Bases:

Resources available (lab, projectors, authentic target language material)

Approach Determined by:

Philosophy, e.g., humanistic
Psychology: operant conditioning; cognitive code

Gleaned from:

Strategies:

Translation (equivalents)
Listening, talking activities
Dialog study
Continous recycling of content in warm-up activities, tasks

V. Program Evaluation

What:

The program objectives, the curriculum, the materials, the in-and-out-of-class learners' activities, teachers, texts, tests, strategies

When:

Formative (daily, weekly) and summative (after each unit or large segment of material)

Who:

Teachers, supervisors, administrators, research personnel (universities, foundations, special centers)

How:

Discrete point and integrative written tests; oral interviews; classroom observations of teaching strategies, student interactions and learner production (quality, quantity); learner success (upper academic levels and jobs)

2. VARIABLES IN A SECOND LANGUAGE SITUATION

Within the School and Community	Age Level				Type of Program		
	5–9	10–12	13–15	16 and above	Continuing Education	Literacy	Special Purpose
Types of organization available in the school or community for newcomers (e.g., integrated, pull-out, bilingual, ESL)							↑
Number of learners involved in the school or community second language program							↑
Variety of languages and cultural backgrounds in the same class; in the community							↑
Linguistic distance between L_1 and L_2							↑
Cultural background of learners (education, customs, students of both sexes in the same class)							↑
Literacy in L_1							↑
Previous schooling in native country (years, subjects, foreign languages learned)							↑
Schooling in host country (subjects taught in L_1 and in L_2)							↑
Availability of bilingual personnel; training and qualifications							↑
Resources, interest, and involvement of community							↑
Time of entry into L_2 program (beginning of academic year?)							↑
Age of entry into L_2 program							↑

COMET
C — Curriculum
O — Objectives
M — Methods and Materials
E — Evaluation Procedures
T — Teachers (Preparation and Skills)

Second Language Migrant Settings

Despite the formidable list of variables that are particularly significant in second language work, there are several advantages in a second language situation (cf. "Variables Chart" on p. 55). The language taught in the classroom will have more meaning for the learners since they can use it immediately outside of class; learners can acquire language incidentally as they read signs, listen to conversations on the street or on trains or buses, go to the movies, watch TV, or get different kinds of "input" from many sources in their environment.

The pace of learning will have to be quickened since teachers will want to help younger learners enter the mainstream of the school. Moreover, an interdisciplinary approach will have to be used by the teacher of the second language. Concepts and notions needed in the other curriculum areas of the school will have to be given priority within the general framework of the target language curriculum. By the same token, older learners will need to receive intensive instruction in those skills they will require if they are to enter the vocational-professional world as quickly as is feasible.

Foreign Language Settings

Where the target language will be taught as a foreign language (for example, in the native country of the learner), the teacher alone will have to prepare intensive continual listening, speaking, and reading activities which the learner will not find outside the classroom. He will have to make provision in his lesson planning for frequent reviews in order to counteract the learners' natural tendency to forget the language which they may hear and practice only in the classroom situation for two to five or six hours a week depending on the school or community policy.

On the other hand, the needs of our learners are many and varied depending upon their age level, their sociocultural desires or vocational/professional aspirations, and the degree of skill they will have to reach in order to satisfy these aspirations. But there are additional problems too, which go even beyond the variables indicated on the charts. Some will have to learn new alphabets and writing systems; some (especially those over the age of ten or eleven) will experience difficulty in hearing and producing the sounds of the target language, perhaps because of conflict with sounds and sound sequences in their native tongue; younger learners may not be highly motivated because they are being forced by parents or guardians to leave their friends and a known way of life to move to a foreign environment or to speak a foreign language in their native environment.

The learner's attitude toward the target language and its speakers will influence his motivation. In schools especially, where learners do not experience success because of poor placement policies and where—in the mistaken belief that this is for their benefit—pupils are not permitted to use their native tongue at all, motivation is very difficult to sustain.

The learner's literacy in his native language will affect classroom organization and teaching techniques. Intraclass grouping and individualized instruction will be essential components of a heterogeneously organized class. (A class may be heterogeneously organized as chart 2 indicates with respect to the number of ethnic groups clustered together, or to the wide age span of the students, who may or may not know the same native language.) Moreover, socioeconomic level, parent encouragement or lack of it, and out-of-class time that can be devoted to study all play a part in determining what will be learned and the time it will take to reach an acceptable level of performance.

School and community policies and resources are of paramount importance in the implementation of a curriculum. Ministerial "decrees" and the educational philosophy of the supervisory staff often give teachers a feeling of insecurity, which is reflected in their attitude toward their students. The school-wide program, the physical plant itself, and the quality and quantity of instructional materials cannot help but affect teaching practice.

The community in which the learning center is located has become increasingly important in recent years in curriculum planning and textbook writing. The socioeconomic level of the community often influences the aspirations or lack of aspirations of parents. The resources in the community (in the native land or in the "new" country)—people, places of interest, services, and facilities—can, when utilized effectively, enrich the experiences of the learners and engender motivation. Lack of target language resource people and facilities will force the teacher to prepare activities in which real interaction is simulated or severely limited.

In our discussion, we have focused on young children and adolescents. Older learners generally enter language learning programs with high motivation, definite purposes, and specific needs. It will depend on the program and especially on the teacher to sustain such motivation and either to meet the learners' specific needs or to channel them to sources where they could be met more effectively.

But above all else, the teacher is the most important single element in the learning process. Teachers should not only serve as models of the target language, but should be willing to prepare a wealth of instructional materials for group and individual instruction, to learn about group dynamics, and to plan lessons which are balanced and varied. They need not know the native language of the learners—although it would be an added asset—but they should have the security to consult native speakers or bilingual persons whenever they need help. Above all, the teacher must be committed to the principle that all normal human beings can learn— although they may not all learn at the same rate.

Criteria in Curriculum Planning

Long-term Courses

Before proceeding to the core of this chapter—the linguistic-cultural content of a curriculum—it may be desirable to make several additional comments on curriculum planning.

- The starting point of each unit or module is the study of one or more functions of language exemplified in situations which will clarify their communicative use.
- The material in each unit should be graded—where feasible—with respect to the functional category to be presented. The function and necessary structure and notions which can be expressed more simply, e.g., "*Can you* have dinner with us on Sunday?" should precede something like, "*Would it be possible* for you and your wife to have dinner with us on Sunday?" The previous knowledge of the student, for example, is the function of invitation with "can" being introduced for the first time; the grammatical complexity of the structures, the degree of their generalizability, their possible early subsequent use with other situations and topics, and the possible lack of familiarity with other notions such as "have dinner" or "Sunday" should be included among the criteria for the selection and grading of material. Moreover, within the same unit, some material should be graded (structural forms, for example) while other items, such as communicative expressions and formulas—which should be given priority, can be ungraded and learned for their immediate communicative value.

From the first unit at beginning levels, both *formal* and *informal* language should be used and explained or exemplified with relation to the people in the situation (age, social roles, status, etc.).

- There should be systematic provision (in dialogs, language drills, reading passages, and dictations, for example) for the constant reintroduction of all material which has been presented previously with the new material being taught.
- A spiral approach should be used in the presentation and practice of

any linguistic or cultural item. (In a spiral approach we return to a topic, a functional category, or a structural category one or two months or even a semester after its initial presentation. *After reviewing* what the students had already learned about it, we proceed to go into the category or topic in greater depth—presenting one or more additional facets of it.)

Intensive Courses

In intensive crash programs, however, learners may be guided to select units or modules for study which they need immediately in a new community or in a new work situation.

In extensive-type lower school programs, the curriculum should provide integrative experiences in which all students on a level learn a given body of content. The curriculum, however, should also provide for the inclusion of differentiating experiences which recognize the uniqueness of each individual. Not all of the students need to understand or produce various intonation patterns unless they are going to be broadcasters or teachers. It is imperative, however, that enrichment experiences be offered to individuals who have potential and will be engaged in teaching, broadcasting, playwriting, or the like.

The curriculum should provide for flexibility in methodology. It is unrealistic to expect that all students will profit from any one method or technique. Since we do not really know how learning takes place in the human being, we do students an injustice when we adhere strictly to unproved language-learning assumptions, practices, or clichés such as those advocating that students should never talk *about* the language; that reading should be deferred for X number of hours; that dialogs need to be memorized; that the use of the student's native language may be harmful; that a prescribed sequence of learning must be followed without deviation; that rules or generalizations should never be given; that all grammar should be taught only through transformation rules, etc. Flexibility in methodology also requires adaptation based on the known experiences of students beyond the classroom. Improvisation should be encouraged so long as it has a language-learning focus. Outside visits, use of self-teaching material, or language laboratory work should be integrated into the classroom period; television viewing, work experiences, or participation in sports should be woven into the lessons.

The curriculum should make provision for continuous evaluation not only of the students' growth but also of the curriculum itself (activities and experiences, related instructional materials) and the testing procedures.

THE CONTENT OF THE CURRICULUM

Attention to Students' Needs

Since the learner is at the center of the F-N approach, his needs should take precedence in organizing the curriculum. The problem is, of course, as Richterich (1972) explains so clearly in his Council of Europe monograph, that where adults are concerned, there are generally two kinds of needs: a. objective (foreseeable), those that can be deduced from a job analysis, or from a study of a person engaging in the duties of his profession; and b. subjective (partly or not at all foreseeable), depending upon the people one meets or the events that occur in an unexpected situation. Moreover, even objective needs will differ widely as one thinks of the individual concerned, e.g., a pop composer-singer who wants to learn to sing a popular tune in another language, a doctor who has accepted a research assistantship in a large hospital, a young woman who has been asked by a relative in another country to come and help him as a receptionist.

The needs will have to be met in distinct ways in crash (intensive) short term programs and in extensive, regular school programs particularly if the unit-credit system will operate. Texts, workbooks, audio-visual materials, and measures for evaluating the successful completion of any unit or module will have to be prepared—and not only for courses given in a learning center but also for possible residential and correspondence courses.

All individuals will have similar sociocultural needs—the need to live and to survive in an unfamiliar community through such means as a. learning to say the basic formulas or expressions of greeting, for apologizing, and for requesting information or directions to shop, for example; and b. learning to recognize signs which may spare them embarrassment or save their lives. Other linguistic and cultural knowledge will be imposed by the realities and special circumstances of the situation for which the knowledge is needed.

The needs of children and youngsters can be foreseen particularly when they are already living in the target country. Every effort will have to be made to enable them to enter the mainstream of the school and community. Where feasible, all the mass media resources of the community will have to be deployed in order to allow these youngsters to receive input (stimuli) from as many sources as possible. It is most important that all teachers in a learning center be encouraged to feel that—where the linguistically handicapped children are concerned—they are teachers of their native language first and then teachers of their particular subject area. For more discussion on this topic you may wish to look at another book[2] written specifically on this subject.

CATEGORIES OF FUNCTIONS

As noted above (Chapter 2) several persons have subsumed the categories under different headings and elaborated them in diverse ways. The purposes are similar, however, as you will see. We are listing possible functions first since the content of the unit will stem from the function, the situation, and the topic being discussed. As we have seen (chart, pp. 38-9) the same function can be used in a nearly endless variety of situations. Since at nonvocational or professional levels especially, the topics can also be varied under the same function and within the same setting, it is desirable as you plan materials to a. specify the function; then b. to decide in which situational setting the particular function would be most interesting and relevant to learners; c. to consider topics that would be appropriate with the function that persons of a particular age level and with specific sociocultural or sociovocational (professional) needs will have; and then, finally, d. to list tentatively the structures and notions you will want to use. The number, selection, internal gradation of the structures and vocabulary items will depend—let us emphasize this point again—on the age and needs of the learners, their previous knowledge, and the formality or informality of speech required by the social roles of the people in the situation. An example will be given below.

Wilkins' Categories of Communicative Functions[3]

NOTE: The main headings and subheadings are stated in his words but some of the nouns have been turned into verbs and some of those which overlapped slightly have been omitted for reasons of space (Wilkins 1972, pp. 14-23).

1. *Modality*
   A. Certainty. Degrees of objective certainty (total certainty, probability, possibility, nil certainty—negation impossibility, impracticability)
   B. Necessity, i.e., social necessity

[2] Mary Finocchiaro, *Teaching English as a Second Language,* rev. ed. (New York: Harper and Row, 1969).

[3] In order to assist curriculum developers, we include a number of lists of functional categories. Readers who may be familiar with these lists may turn to p. 68.

C. Conviction, i.e., personal conviction regarding the truth of a proposition, less than objective certainty or necessity (strong position: believe; intermediate: think; weak: doubt; negative: disbelieve, deny)

D. Volition, i.e., the speaking intent with regard to a proposition (will, choose, (to) be inclined, want, prefer, etc.)

E. Obligation incurred, i.e., speaker's admission of an obligation in force as a result of either a present or a past event ((to be) a duty, promise, assure, guarantee, etc.)

F. Obligation imposed, i.e., utterances intended to impose an obligation on someone else (command, order, prohibit, forbid, etc.)

G. Tolerance, i.e., no hindrance offered to a proposal (grant, allow, permit, consent)

2. *Moral discipline and evaluation*

A. Judgment, i.e., accepted (yield, confess), favorable (justify, defend), valuation (estimate, value, appreciate, overestimate, prejudge), delivered (condemn, convict, rule, find, award)

B. Release from blame or accusation (release, excuse, pardon, absolve)

C. Approval, i.e., expression of approval of another's behavior, performance, etc. (approve, commend, deserve, merit, give credit)

D. Disapproval, i.e., expression of disapproval of another's behavior, performance, etc. (blame, reprimand, accuse, condemn, deplore, etc.)

3. *Suasion*, i.e., utterance designed to influence the behavior of others.

A. Suasion (persuade, suggest, advise, recommend, beg, urge)

B. Prediction (caution, direct, warn, instruct, etc.)

4. *Argument*, i.e., categories relating to the exchange of information and news.

A. Information
   a. asserted (tell, inform, assert, etc.)
   b. sought (request, question, ask)

B. Agreement, i.e., agreeing with a statement or proposal made— (agree to, assent, consent, agree, approve, etc.)

C. Disagreement (dissent, disagree, dispute)

D. Denial (deny, refute, reject, protest, decline)

E. Concession, i.e., argument ceded or case withdrawn (concede, grant, admit, retract, allow, confess, etc.)

5. *Rational enquiry and exposition*, i.e., categories relating to the rational organization of thought and speech. Clearly much of the content of argument and suasion will be taken up with utterances from these

categories (imply, conclude, demonstrate, result, interpret, explain, define, illustrate, classify, compare, contrast).

6. *Personal emotions*, i.e., expression of personal reactions to events.
   A. Positive (enjoy, satisfy, wonder, amaze, surprise, fascinate, etc.)
   B. Negative (displease, shock, annoy, grieve, anger, exasperate, resent, scorn, disdain)
7. *Emotional relations*, i.e., expression of response to events usually involving the interlocuter.
   A. Greeting (welcome, salute, farewell)
   B. Sympathy (regret, sympathize, console)
   C. Gratitude (to be thankful, to be grateful, thank, acknowledge)
   D. Flattery (compliment, flatter)
   E. Hostility (curse, abuse, threaten, scorn, show coolness)
8. *Interpersonal relations*, i.e., status (frozen, formal, consultative, casual, intimate); politeness (to be rude, cool, polite, impolite, civil, uncivil).

van Ek's Categories of Language Functions

These cover most of the communicative functions that would be included in a regular, basic course of three years duration at the secondary school level. In harmony with the spiral approach advocated, the language beyond a three-year program may be more complex and sophisticated but the communicative purposes to be uttered or written—while expressing perhaps finer, more subtle nuances—would be very similar to those expressed below. In this listing, we are using Professor van Ek's words but stating some together (for reasons of space), *expressing* and *inquiring* for example (van Ek 1980).

1. *Imparting and seeking factual information*: identifying, reporting—including describing and narrating, correcting, asking.
2. *Expressing and finding out intellectual attitudes*:
   - expressing agreement and disagreement
   - inquiring about agreement or disagreement
   - denying something, accepting an offer or invitation
   - declining an offer or invitation
   - inquiring whether offer or invitation is accepted or declined
   - offering to do something
   - stating or inquiring whether one remembers or has forgotten something or someone
   - expressing or inquiring whether something is considered possible or impossible
   - expressing or inquiring about capability or incapability

- expressing or inquiring whether something is considered a logical conclusion (deduction)
- expressing or inquiring how certain/uncertain one is (others are) of something
- expressing or inquiring whether one is/is not obliged to do something
- expressing or inquiring whether others are/are not obliged to do something
- giving and seeking permission to do something
- inquiring whether others have permission to do something
- stating that permission is withheld

3. *Expressing and finding out emotional attitudes:*
   - expressing and inquiring about pleasure, liking
   - expressing and inquiring about displeasure, dislike
   - expressing and inquiring about surprise, hope, satisfaction, dissatisfaction
   - expressing or inquiring about disappointment, fear, or worry
   - expressing and inquiring about preferences
   - expressing gratitude and sympathy
   - expressing and inquiring about intention
   - expressing and inquiring about want and desire

4. *Expressing and finding out moral attitudes:*
   - apologizing
   - granting forgiveness
   - expressing and inquiring about approval and disapproval
   - expressing appreciation
   - expressing regret
   - expressing indifference

5. *Getting things done (suasion):*
   - suggesting a course of action (including the speaker)
   - requesting, inviting, or advising others to do something
   - warning others to take care or to refrain from doing something
   - instructing or directing others to do something

6. *Socializing:*
   - to greet people
   - when meeting people
   - when introducing people and being introduced
   - when taking leave
   - to attract attention
   - when beginning a meal
   - to propose a toast

Finocchiaro's Functional Categories

Mary Finocchiaro has preferred to place the functional categories under five headings as noted above: *personal, interpersonal, directive, referential, and imaginative.*

Specific functions under each heading include:

1. *Personal* (clarifying or arranging one's ideas; expressing one's thoughts or feelings): love, joy, pleasure, happiness, surprise, likes, satisfaction, dislikes, disappointment, distress, pain, anger, anguish, fear, anxiety, sorrow, frustration, annoyance at missed opportunities; moral, intellectual, and social concerns; and the everyday feelings of hunger, thirst, fatigue, sleepiness, cold, or warmth.

2. *Interpersonal* (enabling us to establish and maintain desirable social and working relationships).
   The Interpersonal category includes:
   - greetings and leavetakings
   - introducing people to others
   - indentifying oneself to others
   - expressing joy at another's success
   - expressing concern for other people's welfare
   - extending and accepting invitations
   - refusing invitations politely or making alternative arrangements
   - making appointments for meetings
   - breaking appointments politely and arranging another mutually convenient time
   - apologizing
   - excusing oneself and accepting excuses for not meeting commitments
   - indicating agreement or disagreement
   - interrupting another speaker politely
   - changing an embarrassing subject
   - receiving visitors and paying visits to others
   - offering food or drinks and accepting or declining politely
   - sharing wishes, hopes, desires, problems
   - making promises and committing oneself to some action
   - complimenting someone
   - making excuses
   - expressing and acknowledging gratitude.

3. *Directive* (attempting to influence the actions of others; accepting or refusing direction):
   - making suggestions in which the speaker is included

- making requests; making suggestions
- refusing to accept a suggestion or a request but offering an alternative
- persuading someone to change his point of view
- requesting and granting permission
- asking for help and responding to a plea for help
- forbidding someone to do something; issuing a command
- giving and responding to instructions
- warning someone
- discouraging someone from pursuing a course of action
- establishing guidelines and deadlines for the completion of actions
- asking for directions or instructions

4. *Referential* (talking or reporting about things, actions, events, or people in the environment in the past or in the future; talking *about* language. This is often termed the metalinguistic function.):
   - identifying items or people in the classroom, the school, the home, the community
   - asking for a description of someone or something
   - defining something or a language item or asking for a definition
   - paraphrasing, summarizing, or translating (L_1 to L_2 or vice versa)
   - explaining or asking for explanations of how something works
   - comparing or contrasting things
   - discussing possibilities, probabilities, or capabilities of doing something
   - requesting or reporting facts about events or actions
   - evaluating the results of an action or an event

5. *Imaginative*
   - discussing a poem, a story, a piece of music, a play, a painting, a film, a TV program, etc.
   - expanding ideas suggested by others or by a piece of reading
   - creating rhymes, poetry, stories, or plays
   - recombining familiar dialogs or passages creatively
   - suggesting original beginnings or endings to dialogs or stories
   - solving problems or mysteries

Categories of Situations

As we have already seen, people, time, setting (place), and topic discussed in a particular speech act are included in the term "situation." Situation is extra-linguistic but still helps determine the language used in the exponents; context is linguistic. Richterich and van Ek go into each of the components of a situation in great detail, but in writing units, the setting— the place where the conversation may be taking place—can often be nonspecific; that is, on any street, in anyone's home, in any park. The setting becomes significant when we are in places which will affect what we say at a particular time; a post office, a railroad station, or a museum that is having a special exhibit which you are visiting with a friend, for example.

Both Richterich's and van Ek's situational elements refer primarily to adults. You will, therefore, find several differences between these below, and the example of a curriculum for secondary schools you will find later in this chapter.

Richterich

(We are unfortunately forced to condense or omit many of his examples because of lack of space):

1. *Agents*
   A. Identification (occupation, age, sex, name, place of residence, civil status)
   B. Number in the situation (one, two, three to five, etc.)
   C. Roles:
      a. social: old/young, parent/child, asker/giver, friend/friend, stranger/stranger, etc.
      b. psychological: respect, obedience, admiration, antipathy, disdain, etc.
      c. language: one single speaker; one speaker + one addressee, etc.
2. *Time*
   A. Time of day
   B. Duration of the speech act
   C. Frequency—first time, occasionally, regularly
   D. Events—prior (to the) meeting, present, subsequent
3. *Place*
   A. Geographical location (country, region, locality)
   B. Place—outdoors (square, street, beach, building site), indoors: private life (flat, villa, room); public life (shop, hotel, school, station, theater, office); work (office, workshop)
   C. Means of transportation (car, bus, train, plane, subway, boat)

D. Surroundings (family, friends, acquaintances, learning, anonymous)

E. Environment (relevant to the language act)

In *van Ek's specification of situations*, again, we shall have to condense or omit overlapping items. Professor van Ek makes very clear that he has limited the elements within the situations to conform primarily to threshold level needs; that is, adults leaving for or already arrived in a foreign country, where he should not only be able to "survive" but "cross the threshold into the foreign language community."

1. *Social roles* (stranger/stranger, friend/friend, private person/official, patient/doctor, etc.)
2. *Psychological roles* (neutrality, equality, sympathy, antipathy)
3. *Settings*
   A. Geographical location (foreign country where the target language is the native language, foreign country where the target language is not the native language, one's own country)
   B. Place
      a. outdoors (park, street, seaside)
      b. indoors: private life (house, apartment, room, kitchen); public life (purchases, eating and drinking), accommodation (hotel, camping site, etc.), transport (gas station, lost and found), religion, physical services (hospital, pharmacy or chemist's), learning site, displays (museum, art gallery), entertainment, communication, finances, work, means of transport
4. *Surroundings* (human) family, friends, acquaintances, strangers

GRAMMATICAL CATEGORIES AND CLASSES[4]

Following is a brief alphabetical listing of grammatical categories, and transformation operations found in many languages. It is placed here for your convenience in preparing dialogs and drills and as a reminder to you of material you may have presented which should be reintroduced wherever and whenever logical and feasible. Some of these categories and operations may not exist in the language you are teaching while others not included here may exist. Add; delete; combine. Use this list in the way it best suits you.[5]

[4] For another list, see L.G. Alexander in van Ek (1975, pp. 185–233).
[5] A few examples are given when the grammatical term may not be well-known.

ADJECTIVES (e.g., comparative, indefinite, interrogative; used as complements)

ADVERBS (e.g., of frequency, manner, place, time; words, phrases, clauses)

ARTICLES (e.g., definite, indefinite, partitive: e.g., I don't need *any* apples)

AUXILIARY VERBS *(be, do, have, will)*

CLAUSES (e.g., conditional, coordinate, subordinate) cause, condition, purpose, result

COMMANDS AND REQUESTS

COMPARISONS (adjectives, adverbs)

COMPOUND SENTENCES (with *and, but, or*)

CONDITIONAL SENTENCES (with *if* and the *present* or "contrary to fact") e.g., *If I get* the money, I'll buy that suit;/*If* I *had* some money, *I'd take* a vacation.

CONJUNCTIONS (coordinating, subordinating)

CONTRACTIONS

DEMONSTRATIVES (adjectives and pronouns)

DETERMINERS (e.g., articles, indefinites, possessives) demonstratives, quantifiers

DIRECT OBJECTS OF VERBS AND PREPOSITIONS

DO —as a full verb. (e.g., What do you *do* all day?)

DURATION (with *during, for, how long, since, while*)

EMPHATIC STATEMENTS OR UTTERANCES (e.g., I *do want* to see him now.)

EXCLAMATORY STATEMENTS OR UTTERANCES

FAMILY NAMES

FREQUENCY ADVERBS *(always, never, often, sometimes,* etc.)

FUTURE (with present, present progressive (the *ing* present) *going to* or *will*)

GERUNDS (as subject, object, after prepositions or certain verbs) e.g., Swimming is enjoyable. I enjoy swimming.

HAVE —as a full verb (to eat or drink; to possess)

IMPERSONAL —*it* as subject; or with *be* + adj.

INDIRECT OBJECTS (with verbs like *give, show, tell*)

INDIRECT SPEECH (e.g., commands, questions, statements)

INTENSIFIERS *(quite, too, very, rather, a little, a lot)*

INTERROGATIVE SENTENCES, UTTERANCES, AND WORDS

MODALS *(can, may, should, ought to, have to, must,* etc.)

MODIFIERS (adjectives, adverbs, nouns: e.g., Where is the *bus* station?)

NOUNS (e.g., as modifiers of nouns, countable, non-countable, expressing possession, proper names, compound nouns)

NUMERALS (cardinal, ordinal)

OBJECTS (direct, indirect, of prepositions)

PARTICIPLES (present, past) in the present and past perfect; passive voice; as adjective

PARTITIVES (*a bottle of*, etc.)—In French and Italian, *of* + the article

PASSIVE (present, past, present perfect, future)

PAST TENSE

PHRASES (adjectival, adverbial)

PHRASAL VERBS (intransitive, e.g., *stand up*; transitive, e.g., *turn the light on*)

POSSESSIVES

PREPOSITIONS (e.g., accompaniment with direction) to, toward, from, across

PRESENT (continuous, perfect, simple)

PROGRESSIVE (present, past)

PRONOUNS (e.g., demonstratives, indefinite, interrogative, personal, (subject, object) reciprocal, reflexive, relative)

QUANTIFIERS (all, any, many, some, etc.)

QUESTIONS (e.g., attached, inverted, *Wh*)

RECIPROCAL WORDS (*each other*)

REPORTED SPEECH (e.g., He said that...; I told them that...)

REQUESTS AND SUGGESTIONS

SHORT ANSWERS (yes/no tag answers, a word, a phrase, noun + *be*/auxiliary/or modal)

STATEMENTS

SUBJECTS (e.g., agreement with verbs, contractions)

THERE (unstressed (existence or fact); stressed as adverb of place, e.g., *There's* a plane in the sky; I'd like you to go *there* quickly.)

TIME

TITLES: e.g., *Mr., Mrs., Ms., Miss, Rabbi, Father, Your Honor, Excellency,* etc.

VERBALS (e.g., gerund, infinitive, participle)

VERBS (e.g., aspects, moods, orthographic changing, sequence of tenses, two-word, three-word (separable or inseparable))

WORD ORDER (basic pattern but see also below: subject, verb, object, manner, place, time)

YEARS (spoken, written)

ZERO ARTICLE (no article in some languages with abstract nouns, mass nouns, names of places, languages, meals, possessive adjectives and pronouns, titles and proper nouns)

CATEGORIES OF TOPICS

Since the topics adults discuss often depend on social roles, occupation, background, and numerous other factors, we have thought it desirable to focus on topics for younger learners in the secondary schools. Among them, you should use only those that are relevant in your teaching situation. Topics—more suitable perhaps to adults—can be found in van Ek. Professor van Ek makes use of the situations listed above but adds what he calls "behavioral specifications," i.e., what a person should say or do in the situations. For example (in talking about persons), learners should be able to give and seek information about themselves and, if applicable, others with regard to name, address, etc.

You will notice that in listing the topics we are following the spiral approach of the diagram on p. 36.

A cyclical list

1. Introductions and identification
   A. Greetings, leave-takings, introductions
   B. Identification of self and others
   C. Address, age, phone number, where feasible
2. The immediate classroom
   A. Names and location of parts of the room
   B. Names of instructional materials
   C. Identification of activities (reading, writing, etc.)
   D. The program (hours for various subject areas, activities in and out of class)
   E. Common classroom expressions
3. The school
   A. Location of rooms and special places in the building
   B. People in the building (names, functions, special services)
   C. Rules and regulations (fire drills, time of arrival, use of stairs)
   D. School activities such as club programs, general organization, assembly programs, newspapers, magazine
4. The family
   A. Members
   B. Relationships and ages

C. The home
    a. Rooms and their uses
    b. Furnishings
    c. Cleanliness (how, who)
    d. Safety
D. Occupations of various members
E. Meals (table setting, formulas)
F. Daily health routines
G. Clothing (including seasonal changes necessary)
H. Recreational activities
5. The immediate community of the school and home
    A. Homes
    B. Nonresidential buildings (offices, movies, library, etc.)
    C. Transportation facilities (directions, tickets)
    D. Communication facilities (telephone, mail, newspaper, radio, television)
    E. Consumer services (stores, banks, etc.)
    F. Local government agencies (post office, police station, firehouse)
    G. Places of recreational interest (parks, libraries, community centers, movies, theaters, outdoor cafés)
    H. Educational opportunities (for parents as well)
    I. Places of worship
    J. Formulas used in telephoning
    K. Current events
6. The wider community
    A. Health services
    B. Transportation and communication
    C. Government—city, state, national
    D. Nearby centers—rural and urban
    E. Current events
    F. Places of recreation
7. Cultural heritage
    A. Holidays
    B. Heroes and history
    C. Historical documents and speeches
    D. Songs, rhymes, proverbs
    E. Music, literature, and art forms
8. The culture of the *target* country
    A. As above with attention given to similarities and to possible differences

9. Personal guidance (This topic is treated in greater detail because of its importance to adolescents and adults, both in one's native country or in a foreign country.)
   A. Social:
      a. Recreational facilities (addresses, special features, fees or qualifications for admission)
      b. Social relations—living together, working together, and playing together with others in the school and community.
      c. Customs:
         • Greetings and leave-takings (with peers, elders, children, family members)
         • Foods—time for meals, types of restaurants, special holiday foods
         • Holidays—dates, gifts, visiting, greeting cards, other customs
         • Dress—seasonal, formal, informal, special occasion
         • Communication—letters, telegrams, telephones
         • Transportation—reservations, importance of arrival time
         • Business forms and legal practices
         • Courtship and marriage
         • Behavior patterns in various situations—social, educational, vocational
         • Consumer education—installment buying, credit borrowing
         • Social amenities in different situations (going to the home of strangers or friends, applying for a part-time job)
   B. Educational:
      a. Opportunities for advanced study (college, university, other)
      b. Requirements for admission to institutions of higher learning (physical, educational, other)
      c. Scholarships
      d. Training for specialized careers
      e. Adult education
      f. Library, museum, and other facilities
   C. Vocational:
      a. Opportunities for employment after graduation (part-time employment)
      b. Requirements for various types of employment
      c. Means of finding employment (agencies, newspapers, governmental agencies, letters, friends, etc.)

d. Filling out forms such as applications for employment, social security, pension
e. Getting a job (dress and conduct at interview)
f. Holding a job (punctuality, performance, human relationships)
g. Labor laws, taxes, pension, rights and responsibilities
h. Specialized vocabulary
D. Leisure-time activities:
a. Community facilities
b. Hobbies—kinds (indoor, outdoor)
c. Arts, crafts, dancing, sports—where to learn, cost, etc.
d. Private recreational facilities and clubs
e. Popular sports in the community or city (as participant or spectator)
f. Club programs in schools
E. Moral and spiritual values:
a. Principles of human dignity
b. Individual rights and responsibilities
c. Places of worship—addresses, denominations, special language services (if these exist)
10. Miscellaneous
A. Expressions of time
B. Days of the week
C. Months of the year
D. Weather and safety
E. Seasons
F. Weights, sizes, measurements, money
G. Formulas and communicative expressions of courtesy, agreement, disagreement, regret, surprise, excitement, pleasure, etc.

The topics above could be used either in the native country or in the target country of the learners. One more should be added in either situation:

11. The relation of (name of country) to the world.
A. Membership in international organizations (UN, UNESCO, FAO)
B. Commercial relations (imports and exports)
C. Tourism
D. The influence of our language on others (cognates, special terms, expressions)
E. The influence of our literature, art, music, technological advances on other nations.

WRITING THE CURRICULUM

Setting a curriculum down on paper generally benefits from the collaboration of teachers of foreign language and related subjects, school supervisors, and anyone else in the city, region, or nation concerned with the teaching of foreign languages in the school system. The writing presupposes that the students' special needs have been analyzed; that some factors within the students (e.g., their present knowledge of the target language) have been evaluated; that topics of interest to learners of the approximate age group concerned will have been selected.

The overall curriculum for the entire program should be tentatively set down; the items selected for learning in the regular courses will be included within the appropriate levels for courses; materials for presentation will be selected from existing materials or those especially prepared; and measures for evaluating the curriculum will be decided upon and changes will be made when learning results do not prove satisfactory.

To summarize, in order to plan a curriculum the writer(s) should do the following:

Analyze   Learners' target language proficiency and present communicative needs

Survey   Resources in the school and community (people, places, materials)

THEN

1. *Select* — Language functions for emphasis
2. *Choose* — Relevant social/academic/vocational situations
3. *Identify* — Topics of interest to students at different age levels
4. *Specify* — Appropriate communicative expressions and formulas, structural patterns and notions (stemming from 1–3)
5. *Determine* — Exponents
   a. of high frequency;
   b. generalizable (stemming from 1–4)
6. *Gather/Prepare* — Audio-visual materials
7. *Provide for use of* — School, community, other resources to ensure an interdisciplinary approach
8. *Prepare/Adapt* — Dialogs and mini-dialogs for unambiguous

	presentation and oral practice of exponents, functional expressions, structures, and notions
9. *Grade (text or teacher-prepared)*	Tasks and activities for learner interpretation and performance in class—for whole class, group, pair, or individual work
10. *Evaluate*	Student growth (as *one* clue to the efficiency of your plan and the strength of your materials)

THEN

Divide 1–10 into units and/or modules.

Units

Let us look first at some aspects of units.

Comments

•   The units to be included in each level could be centered around a story or each could stand alone with respect to topic or theme.

•   The functions within a unit should be those we use most frequently in real-life communication. Some could be introduced for receptive (interpretative) use only; some aspects of a function could be presented for active learning; some could be extensions of known functions, for example, alternative ways of expressing them.

•   The structures chosen for presentation and practice are generally arbitrary. Communicative functions usually have no special grammatical realization nor are they used in unique situational occurrences. Other structures appropriate for use with the particular function and with the topic could just as easily be selected for inclusion in any given unit *provided they are frequently used in the real world and applicable in other situations and build upon elements of a familiar structure, grammatical category, or lexical class* (foods, for example).

•   The notions will depend, as we know, upon the function(s), the situation (people, place, time), and the topic.

•   Units are, in turn, divided into teaching lessons. How long it will take to complete a unit should not be stated although a time limit could be suggested. With some classes, it may take ten teaching lessons, with others twelve or more, and with more able pupils, fewer than ten.

The unit sequence which follows is taken from an actual textbook series. After the sequence, we shall go over the basic segments generally included in a unit and last, but most essential, we plan to *suggest* one way of dividing a unit into teaching lessons.

Remember as you read the following pages that each one of us writing a curriculum could have "juggled" the components differently producing quite different units. The important point is that at some logical time in the course of an intensive or extensive program the most essential functions, structures, and notions are presented and practiced in a variety of appropriate social situations with diverse topics. It is impossible to teach all of a language at one time but it is possible to teach what we do with enthusiasm and with the innate concern for the feelings of our learners.

A Brief Example of a Unit Sequence[6] Level III
(Secondary school, Adult education, University levels)

Unit	Function(s)	People	Situation Setting	Topic	Communicative Expressions and/ or Exponents
I	Reacting to an emergency Reporting the circumstances Asking and answering questions about treatment	Patient, Relative, Doctor, Nurse	Doctor's office or emergency room of a hospital	Illness or accident	Where's a hospital... What's wrong? (informal) Tell me where you feel the pain. How did it happen? Does it hurt when I touch you here? Could I... I'm sorry. You have... We'll have to put you in a plaster cast. I'd like to call... Nurse, please prepare the patient. How long before I can move? Get this prescription filled. Take these pills three times a day. Call me in a week or before if the pain gets worse.

[6] We are grateful to Ms. Cheryl Elliott for her creativity and help in working on this example.

Unit	Function(s)	People	Situation Setting	Topic	Communicative Expressions and/ or Exponents
II	Receiving visitors from abroad Greetings Introductions Reporting about the trip. Asking for information and confirmation	Relatives arriving Friends and relatives meeting	Airport (past the customs area) Bank at airport	The trip The need to change money	It was a great... You look (fine) How the children have (grown)! Where can (we) ...change... We heard that... What is the rate of exchange? What do you want to change, money or traveller's checks?
III	Apologizing to someone in a crowded store Buying food and drinks for a party	A mother and son Another customer	A supermarket (Causing boxes to fall off a shelf) (Bumping someone's cart)	Buying food for a welcome party	I'm so sorry. Joe, please help the lady. How clumsy of me! That's all right. Excuse me, where do you keep...? It's right there. They're in Aisle 6. They're next to the... Do you carry...? Please sell me two shopping bags.
IV	Visitors recounting the events of the day Introductions Passing foods, complimenting the hostess	Visitors, family, other guests	At the dinner table in a home	Telling about visiting the museum and the zoo	May I present...? I'm so happy to meet you We've heard so much about you Boy, was that great! (familiar) What a fabulous exhibit! Could you pass the...? Thank you for inviting... (Everything) was (delicious). Jim, you're a lucky guy. You married a wonderful cook. (familiar)

Unit	Function(s)	People	Situation Setting	Topic	Communicative Expressions and/ or Exponents
V	Explaining how something works	The older relatives	Workshop (in a garage)	Hobbies	This is a great workshop. I enjoy...ing. How does...work? Look, first you...then you... I wonder if I could make one like it. It's easy. All you do is... Thanks. I'll let you know how it turned out.
VI	First denying responsibility, then admitting guilt reluctantly	Some young people	In the street (playing ball)	A ball has broken a window	I wasn't even (here). Look at this window. Which one of you did it? If you don't tell me, I'll have to... You should have been more careful. Well, Dad, you see... OK, no allowance for you this week. (familiar) Get the window fixed immediately.

Unit	Function(s)	People	Situation Setting	Topic	Communicative Expressions and/ or Exponents
VII	Making promises Discussing likes and dislikes	Young people	Library	Likes and dislikes of authors, books, magazines	Would you mind if...? I'll return it... He's not my favorite... Why not? Well, I think... Now, if you really want to read something good, get... I'm sorry, could you repeat that? I'm very sorry, would you mind (spelling), etc. I hope you'll enjoy it. I'm sure I will. You and I usually like the same things, don't we?

Modules

Modules may be included in units and texts or may be self-contained and completely separate from the regular course material.

As noted above, if self-contained modules appear in the regular text, they should be so prepared that if they are taken out of the text, they do not affect its continuity.

Modules are generally used in intensive courses for special purposes and thus can be introduced in the native country or in the target country for immediate use. Modules are similar to units in that they include one or more functions, all the elements in the situation and notions, and exponents. Exponents depend on the function, situation, topic, and notions needed to clarify or complete the functions.

Generally, modules differ from units however, in two principal ways:

A. *At the time of introduction,* they are used in only one specified situation.

B. Generally only one use of the communicative expression or grammatical structure is taught in the module, whereas in a unit, we could include two or three uses of *could,* for example, or alternative exponents for similar ideas. Nothing would prevent us, if necessary, from using *could* or any other structure, formula or communicative expression in subsequent modules—or depending on the student's language program—in other units.

Following are two examples of modules based on the two vocational needs we talked about above: the receptionist in a doctor's office (the doctor's patients are all English speakers), and the pop singer who wants to record his most popular song in an English-speaking country.

Core module
RECEPTIONIST

NOTES:
A = Active use
R = Receptive knowledge on the part of the receptionist

	Receptionist	*Known patient*
A	Greetings	Greetings
A	How are you feeling this week?	Not too well.
A	I'm sorry.	
A	The doctor is waiting for you in Room 2. Here is your card.	Thank you.

Expanded module
RECEPTIONIST

NOTES:
A = Active use on the receptionist's part
R = Receptive use on the receptionist's part

	Receptionist	*Known patient*	
A	Greetings		
A	Your appointment is for four o'clock.	Yes, is the doctor free?	A
A	No, I'm sorry.		
A	He's been delayed in the hospital.		
A	I expect him at four-thirty. Can you wait?	I'll have to. I must see him today. I don't feel well at all.	R

RECEPTIONIST

Receptionist	*New Patient*
A Please sit in the waiting room.	
A You'll find some new magazines there.	
A I'll call you as soon as he comes in.	Thank you. A
A You're welcome. Make yourself comfortable.	

Expanded module
RECEPTIONIST

Receptionist	*New Patient*
A Greetings	Greetings
	I'd like to see Dr. X. A
A Are you a patient of Dr. X's?	No. I've never been here before. R
A Who recommended you to Dr. X?	My doctor, Doctor Y. A
A The Doctor will be free in a half hour. In the meanwhile, could you give me some information about yourself?	Yes, of course.
A What is your full name?	Mrs. Beth Rhodes.
A Will you spell your last name, please?	R-h-o-d-e-s.
A Where do you live?	7 Park Street.
A What is your telephone number?	321-0475
A Can you repeat that please?	Of course. 3-2-1-0-4-7-5.
A When were you born?	On January 12, 1930.
A What are your symptoms?	I have a constant pain on my right side.
A Thank you. Please wait in the waiting room.	

This could be expanded even further by asking about illnesses in parents or other close relatives, date of last examination, childhood illnesses, operations, etc.

Core module
OUR POP SINGER[7]

NOTES:
R = Receptive use on the singer's part
A = Active use on the singer's part

PEOPLE: *Receptionist, Studio Director, Singer*
PLACE: A recording studio

Receptionist:	You're Mr. X. I've seen your picture. The Director will be with you in a few minutes.	R
Singer:	Thank you.	A
Director:	Hello. It's good to see you. I like your song and your voice.	R
Singer:	Thank you. You are very kind.	A
Director:	Do you have a translation of your song?	R
Singer:	I do not understand.	A
Director:	Do you have English words for your song?	R
Singer:	No. You will do that. Yes?	A
Director:	We have to call our translator. Can you come in tomorrow at two o'clock?	R
Singer:	Yes.	
Director to Receptionist:	Please call Rod and ask him if he can be here at two o'clock tomorrow.	R
Receptionist:	Yes, he can make it (informal).	
Director to Singer:	Fine. We'll see you here tomorrow at two o'clock. (Leave-takings)	R
Singer:	Good-bye, thank you.	
Director and Receptionist:	See you tomorrow. (Informal)	

[7] You will note that the Pop Singer uses very brief exponents and sometimes forms that indicate an incomplete knowledge of English. His messages, however, are clear to his listeners.

The *extended modules* can be devoted to the translation and changes required by the singer; to his learning the stress and pronunciation of the song in English; to the day when the recording will be made for which he will have to learn specific language, e.g., stand closer to the mike, stand within this circle; and specific gestures, e.g., two fingers raised means there are two minutes left, finger across the throat—there are thirty seconds left.

You will have noted that this module can focus upon comprehensible intonation, pronunciation, stress, and rhythm. The teacher may wish to use these same techniques to have native language songs translated into English by the more creative students and learned by the entire class.

General Basic Segments of a Unit

1. *Title*—stated in terms of the principal function or as a situation. The subsidiary functions can be listed immediately below with accompanying pictures to clarify them. The students' native languages (in a homogeneous class) can be used at beginning levels followed by a brief, simple summary in English, or in any other target language.
2. *Situation*—a brief explanation in the target language.
   • Dialog of ten to fifteen utterances which can be broken into normal mini-dialogs of two to three utterances each.
   • Questions or other tasks on the dialog (True/False, Multiple Choice, Wh questions).
3. *Pronunciation practice* (intonation, sounds in words and in utterances, stress).
4. *Study of communicative expressions*— in illustrated mini-dialogs followed by guided repetitive practice and paired practice.
5. *Study of the grammatical structures* and student discovery of underlying rules followed by guided and freer real communicative practice.
6. *Types of oral activities*—listening to and answering questions; directed practice ("Ask me, him, us, etc."); practice in pairs, role playing, adding one or more sequential sentences to an utterance.
7. *"What would you say?"*—A situation is given which will elicit the use of the communicative expressions in context by a number of students.
8. *Reentry* of familiar with new material in reading, writing, listening, and speaking activities and tasks.
9. *The unit vocabulary*—notions and communicative expressions.
10. *A unit summary*—"We have learned how to (e.g., ask for information)"

Dividing a Unit of Work

(One way but remember that there are as many ways as there are teachers.)

Session I

•   Introduction of the major communicative function in a context (motivation) (situation)
•   Listening to the entire dialog. (If a long dialog starts the unit, you may prefer to leave it to the end as a culminating activity)
•   Learning of four or more sentences of the dialog or learning two mini-dialogs containing the function through listening, repeating, and dramatizing
•   Questions and answers based on the dialog itself and dialog personalization (asking questions within the students' experiences related to the topic, where feasible)
•   Some intonation or pronunciation practice

Session II

•   Reviewing the dialog segment or the mini-dialog previously studied
•   Learning four or more sentences of the dialog or other mini-dialogs clarifying the function
•   Questions and answers based on the new dialogs
•   Pronunciation practice (intonation or stress)
•   A communicative expression (presentation, "rule generalization," and oral practice)

Session III

•   Dramatization of the known dialog segments or mini-dialogs
•   Alternative(s) of the communicative expression where feasible; presentation, in context
•   Practice in pairs and groups
•   Pronunciation practice (new notions in context)

Session IV

•   Language items: notions/structures—one or more depending upon their relationship to previously taught structures or to the students' native language

Session IV (cont.)

- Repetition and simple conversion exercises of the new items
- One or more appropriate guided tasks (expansion, integration, see p. 165)
- A related game; questions and answers on the dialog and dramatization of the dialog or mini-dialog by groups of individuals
- Role-playing

Session V

- Language structures and notions—one or more
- Repetition and creative exercises of the new items (practice in pairs with free responses)
- One or more activities based on items taught during the preceding sessions
- Dramatization of the new dialog and of other related ones part of which may be integrated with the new dialog

Session VI

- "Free" conversation exercises in which new items are combined with others previously taught in chain drills or other types of interaction exercises
- Introduction of the reading selection (motivation and clarification of difficulties of the first segment)
- Oral reading and intensive study of the reading selection
- Group recombination of dialog with other familiar ones
- Role-playing

Session VII

- More difficult free tasks and activities related to the items taught in the unit
- Review of the reading selection (e.g., student-formulated questions, word study exercises, oral summary, practice on note-taking)

Session VIII

- Oral activities—e.g., "What would you say?"
- Directed practice—ask X (why) when/if/whether/how, etc.

Session VIII (cont.)

- Listening comprehension activity
- Role-playing

Session IX

- Dramatization of the dialog
- Group work—completion and/or preparation of an original dialog centered about the major functions of the unit
- Cloze test; dictation or listening—writing task
- Role-playing

Session X

- Test (oral and written)

SUGGESTIONS FOR DISCUSSION

1. Which are basic questions that should be asked before a curriculum can be prepared?
2. What "direction" does a curriculum guide generally provide?
3. What are some of the school variables which will affect the curriculum?
4. How will teaching differ in a foreign language and in a second language situation?
5. What is meant by communicative competence? What is the relationship of linguistic competence to communicative competence?
6. What are the major aims of a language learning program?
7. Discuss several criteria for curriculum planning.
8. Why should methodological techniques be flexible?
9. Can learners' needs be fully analyzed? Why not?
10. Wilkins' categories start with *modality*. Give several utterances using modals or alternative structures which exemplify modality.
11. In van Ek's list, prepare several other subcategories under "Expressing and Finding out Moral Attitudes."
12. Which additional interpersonal functions can you think of in the Finocchiaro list?
13. Which people and elements does Richterich include under situation?
14. Under grammatical categories, which others would be needed in your target language?
15. Which topics do you consider most important under personal guidance? Why?
16. In which ways—other than those mentioned in this book—can you use the cyclical list of topics?
17. Using any one of the *functions, situations,* and *topics,* prepare a brief outline for five units at a *beginning* level.
18. Use one of your student texts and tell how you would divide a unit of work into teaching lessons. (Use only the material within the actual unit.)
19. What would you add to the unit? What would you discard? What would you adapt? Give the reasons for your decisions.
20. Write out a "core" module for a specific job to be done in a particular situation.

21. Suggest four possible expansions of your core module.
22. Discuss your modules with members of a small group.
23. Do a role play on the modules in this chapter or on one selected by your group.

4 Methodology

GENERAL CONSIDERATIONS
A Functional-Notional Methodology

Discussion in Europe of F-N approaches has concentrated on defining the contents of syllabuses. Methodology has been seen as a secondary consideration. But for most teachers, of course, methodology is crucial, for this is the area which they can control most effectively. While we recognize that procedures for the presentation and practice of learning material are personal and individual matters which rely heavily on the relationship the teacher has built up with the class, there are nonetheless basic principles which are compatible with the objectives of the F-N approach. These principles underlie what has been described as the communicative approach to language teaching (Widdowson 1978; Brumfit & Johnson 1979), and they can be related to two main assumptions. The first assumption is that we are concerned in the classroom with language *use*, not language knowledge; the second is the view that we learn language most effectively by using it in realistic situations. Most F-N discussion has been concerned with the implications for syllabus design of the first assumption, but attention is now turning to the implications for methodology of the second.

The suggestions which we make in this chapter result from our attempts to relate our years of practical teaching experience to the discussions of language teaching that have emerged in the last decade. As with any suggestions of this kind, we would expect the good teacher to adapt, enrich, improvise, rearrange, create, and discard according to local requirements. These suggestions are simply ways of enabling teachers to engender the motivation and enthusiasm that must be constantly sustained in learners.

The F-N approach is committed to organizing the course content in the most highly motivating way possible for students. But skilled organization is useless without effective classroom activity. The procedures outlined below will all enable teachers to lead learners to appropriate use of the language. At the same time, we should make it clear that many of the techniques recommended have been in the repertoire of good teachers for decades, if not centuries. Methodologically, the F-N approach demands more emphasis on certain techniques than in the recent past, but it does not claim to overturn all our traditional expectations and offer a new panacea which will solve any problems overnight. The task of teaching well will always be long and difficult. If it was not, we should not require skilled professionals to perform it, and we should not find successful achievement of our task so rewarding.

The methodology of the F-N curriculum evolves out of, and goes beyond, many of the language learning principles which have developed over the past century. It may be helpful, however, to specify how the audio-lingual method, used intensively in the United States since about 1945, differs from F-N methodology. In order to clarify the comparison, we shall treat the audio-lingual method in its strongest form.

	Audio-lingual Method	*Functional-Notional Methodology*
1.	Attends to structure and form more than meaning.	Meaning is paramount.
2.	Demands memorization of structure-based dialogs.	Dialogs, if used, center around communicative functions and are not normally memorized.
3.	Language items are not necessarily contextualized.	Contextualization is a basic premise.
4.	Language learning is learning structures, sound, or words.	Language learning is learning to communicate.
5.	Mastery, or "over-learning" is sought.	Effective communication is sought.
6.	Drilling is a central technique.	Drilling may occur, but peripherally.
7.	Native-speaker-like pronunciation is sought.	Comprehensible pronunciation is sought.
8.	Grammatical explanation is avoided.	Any device which helps the learners is accepted—varying according to their age, interest, etc.

Audio-lingual Method	Functional-Notional Methodology
9. Communicative activities only come after a long process of rigid drills and exercises.	Attempts to communicate may be encouraged from the very beginning.
10. The use of the student's native language is forbidden.	Judicious use of native language is accepted where feasible.
11. Translation is forbidden at early levels.	Translation may be used where students need or benefit from it.
12. Reading and writing are deferred till speech is mastered.	Reading and writing can start from the first day, if desired.
13. The target linguistic system will be learned through the overt teaching of the patterns of the system.	The target linguistic system will be learned best through the process of struggling to communicate.
14. Linguistic competence is the desired goal.	Communicative competence is the desired goal (i.e., the ability to use the linguistic system effectively and appropriately).
15. Varieties of language are recognized but not emphasized.	Linguistic variation is a central concept in materials and methodology.
16. The sequence of units is determined solely by principles of linguistic complexity.	Sequencing is determined by any consideration of content, function, or meaning which maintains interest.
17. The teacher controls the learners and prevents them from doing anything that conflicts with the theory.	Teachers help learners in any way that motivates them to work with the language.
18. "Language is habit" so errors must be prevented at all costs.	Language is created by the individual often through trial and error.
19. Accuracy, in terms of formal correctness, is a primary goal.	Fluent and acceptable language is the primary goal: accuracy is judged not in the abstract but in context.

Audio-lingual Method	Functional-Notional Methodology
20. Students are expected to interact with the language system, embodied in machines or controlled materials.	Students are expected to interact with people, either in the flesh, through pair and group work, or in their writings.
21. The teacher is expected to specify the language that students are to use.	The teacher cannot know exactly what language students will use.
22. Intrinsic motivation will spring from an interest in the structure of the language.	Intrinsic motivation will spring from an interest in what is being communicated by the language.

At the same time, we wish to insist that most sensitive teachers have been moving away from any strong audio-lingual position whenever they have interacted with their classes as people. The features of the F-N methodology outlined above derive from the practice of many teachers who would not consider themselves adherents of any particular method—but they combine to form a coherent position which is a long way from that being advocated twenty years ago. In particular, there are two major differences. The first is that the claims of F-N methodology are more modest theoretically than audio-lingual claims. We are by no means certain how people learn languages, though teachers have developed a great fund of experience to draw upon when they assist learners. However, because teachers are often successful does not mean that we can describe clearly *why* they are successful. Consequently an F-N methodology has to leave more to the practical expertise of teachers. It does not claim to tell a teacher how a particular student will or ought to learn a language. Secondly, the F-N methodology allows greater initiative not only to the teacher but to the student. Since the F-N curriculum is centrally based on students' needs and purposes, the student must have the opportunity to use the language for purposes which the teacher may not have anticipated, and in ways that the teacher may not expect. In this respect the student is being allowed to do what all language learners do in natural conditions—to try to say what is needed by whatever linguistic means are available, even if that means making mistakes. The idea that every mistake made by a student makes a repetition of that error more likely has been rejected—in practice it has simply meant that many students have grown up terrified of ever speaking at all. This is not to say that the need for accuracy has been rejected, but simply that the way to achieve it has been redefined to include a great deal of language use in meaningful situations—but still with the support of correction for some of the time.

The Role of Fluency Work

The role of "natural" language activity may appear somewhat controversial, for most teachers are understandably unwilling to encourage their students to make errors without good reason. But many of the points listed above in the comparison with audio-lingual methodology do lead to a demand for fluency work (for example nos. 7, 9, 13, 14, 18, 19, 20, and 21). For this reason we would like to justify our emphasis on fluency work in this section.

Foreign language syllabuses in the past have tacitly assumed that students learn small units one by one and gradually create a language system by separate attention to each item in the system. Sometimes the language has been presented in the separate units for students to learn, as in the strong audio-lingual approach (Wilkins 1976, p. 2 refers to this type of syllabus as "synthetic" because the student has to synthesize the separate elements to form a grammar). Sometimes much of the grammar is presented through fairly natural chunks of language, as with reading methods and grammar-translation, so that the student has to analyze the elements of the grammatical system out of the total and confused picture presented by the natural language (Wilkins calls this an "analytic" syllabus). Both approaches have in the past restricted the student's *production* of the foreign language for much of the early learning period, and the former approach has restricted—often severely restricted—the language provided to learn from. Learning, it has been assumed, should be based on accurate reproduction of items presented by a model source, such as the teacher or the textbook.

When we decide that accurate reproduction occurs we base ourselves on the criteria that descriptive linguists use when they make a model of the grammar of a language: we judge students' production in terms of sound, lexical, grammatical, or (in the case of whether the language is appropriate or not) communication systems. But while these considerations may be important in testing a learner's performance, or in linguistic description, it does not follow that they will be significant in helping the process of learning. Indeed, too, much emphasis on these aspects will probably result in our producing linguists and language testers rather than language users.

Consider what happens when we hold a natural conversation in our native language. We attend to the content of what is being said, and rarely to the message form, unless there is something deliberately bizarre about the form. If someone does correct us, for example by interrupting us with remarks like, "Hold it, that sentence isn't correct," or "Repeat that word with the correct pronunciation, please," we shall rightly interpret the interruption as a rude attempt to ignore what we say by concentrating on how we say it. Outside the teaching context, we object to people not being interested in us and our views or ideas, and simply scoring points off us by ignoring the message and concentrating on the form. Inside the classroom, we cannot afford to do nothing but accuracy-based work, for if we did we should never allow learners to act as genuine language users at all. There is, of course, a role for correction and for the presentation of language forms. But the learners, especially at the early stages, have a major problem, for no one can communicate naturally and at the same time concentrate on the form rather than the content of their speech—and even with writing the same difficulty can apply: too much concern for accuracy impedes fluency. The kinds of rules we are really using in a conversation or discussion are rules of interaction. We want to know how much information we already share with the other participants, so that we can tell how much we need to say to establish our point; we need to establish that we are in fact both taking part in the conversation with the same intention and, if not, to adjust it to an agreed purpose. Altogether, we prefer not to waste effort on providing too much information, nor to waste effort by providing so little that we shall need to repeat it all more clearly because we were not understood the first time. We do not normally want to draw attention to the way we speak and distract attention from the message. All in all, we negotiate the purpose of conversations to reach agreement with the other participants, and we negotiate about the meanings and significances of the language items we use in order to achieve our agreed purposes.

We do of course obey linguistic rules while we are doing all this, but even these may be subject to some adjustment. In practice, where there is good will, we tend to converge on the accent of the people we speak to, we tend to select structural and vocabulary items which we perceive will be understood—in short, we cooperate as far as we can by adjusting to their expectations. And they are also doing it, at the same time, for us. (Where there is ill will, we may use the same strategies to confuse and obscure communication, but teachers are not concerned with encouraging ill will.) The most important point to note is that we do not need to teach language users to make these small adjustments, for they are making them all the time in their mother tongues, but we do need to provide plenty of opportunity for students to practice such adjustment in foreign languages.

Furthermore, many scholars (see, for example, Halliday 1975; Krashen 1981) will argue that language *learning* will best take place through such use of language, through the struggle to adjust to the expectations of other users.

What we are in fact saying here is that each user's language differs slightly and that language use involves a constant process of adjustment to slightly new meanings and, indeed, structural patterns. And this applies as much to nonnative speakers as to native speakers. There are generalizations to be made of course, and they have been made by linguists, but they only provide us with a basis so that we can start negotiating the meanings appropriate to particular situations.

Adaptation and improvisation are thus not advanced abilities, but essential and central characteristics of language use which must have a place in an efficient classroom.

We may distinguish three methodological positions, showing varying degrees of acceptance of this argument:

1. The view that our formal teaching may continue but more emphasis should be given to opportunities for improvisation (advanced, for example, by Wilga Rivers—"Talking off the tops of their heads" in Rivers 1972).

2. The view that language teaching should retain some concern with accuracy but that the true learning will take place only when there is a great deal of improvisation and invention by students from the very beginning (Brumfit 1979, 1980).

3. The view that activities using a language, either the teaching of other subjects (Widdowson and Brumfit 1981) or a sequence of problem-solving tasks (Prabhu and Carroll 1980) should in themselves be enough to enable students to learn a language effectively, because improvisation and adjustment will be goal-directed and natural.

The third position, the most radical, is of great interest to many people and is currently being evaluated in a research project in Bangalore and Madras in India. But for general use the first two positions seem at the moment more acceptable. What is clear is that the traditional classroom procedures (presentation, drilling, and practice) will make *available* to students the tokens with which they must conduct linguistic negotiation. But these procedures are concerned primarily with availability, not with learning. We would not consider that a student has learned an item unless it can be used appropriately *without conscious thought,* and we all know that presentation, drilling, and practice do not lead us to that happy position. What they are intended to do is to enable students to store the items so that they are available for future use. But until what is stored has become activated by use (either in recognition activities like listening and reading, or in production) we cannot say that it has been fully learned. "Natural" language activity in the classroom provides the opportunity for such activation, and it must by definition be unpredictable linguistically.

The unpredictability is necessary because we cannot predict any relation between teaching and genuine use by students. The time lag between teaching and use will vary between language item and language item, and between student and student with the same item. Some items, like new pieces of vocabulary with clear-cut technical meanings, may be used effectively almost at once. Others may not surface for six weeks, six months or more after being taught, or may not surface at all, simply being understood receptively. But it will be when students are engaged in fluency activities, that is when they are negotiating with language and adjusting and improvising with the limited language that they know, that they will both internalize and extend their understanding of the linguistic system. Language is created *by* learners, not given *to* them.

If we accept this communicative view of language learning, we shall be willing to accept as central to our methodology the many forms of fluency activity that teachers have always recognized as useful but peripheral. Any kind of talking activity, in which students work in pairs or groups with all the groups talking at once, will have some elements of fluency discussion. Many improvisational role-play and simulation activities and many language games will involve elements of oral fluency. In these, as in other activities, the criterion for fluency will be the learners' relationship with the language. If they are operating in the same ways as they would with their own language, without obviously thinking about formal features, then it is a fluency activity. Thus exercises in listening, speaking, reading, or writing can be either accuracy exercises, in which formal features are being concentrated on, or fluency exercises, when the activity is natural. It does not matter what mistakes the students make during these exercises, providing errors do not prevent them from being able to perform the activity naturally and comprehensibly. If errors do have this effect, the exercise is too difficult for the students. But if they can somehow struggle to success, while thinking about the task performance and not about the linguistic forms, the effort will have helped their language learning without diverting attention from communication.

There are many books of communication exercises available to assist the teacher in devising communicative activities. But it is not necessary to base fluency work on games or meaningless competitive tasks, and different types of exercise will be appropriate to different educational situations.

Any kind of language exercise can be discussed in small groups in class, either in preparation for writing or to help students correct what they have already written. There are no textbooks suitable for individual work which cannot be used for cooperative work in order to develop fluency practice. All that is needed is a teacher willing to commit a substantial proportion of time (anything up to two-thirds of class time) to such activities.

For fluency work to be successful, the teacher should explain to students why it is being encouraged and why they will benefit from not being corrected all the time. At the same time, teachers should provide specific sessions when correction of widely occurring errors (perhaps by very traditional procedures) will be made, and—above all—teachers must ensure that good spoken and written models of English are provided. Without such models and opportunities for correction, fluency practice runs the risk of producing nothing but a fluent classroom pidgin. While this risk may be worth taking in preference to the inhibiting effect of entirely accuracy-based teaching, there is no reason to encourage weak English, for fluency-based procedures should, over a long-term course, lead to just as accurate English as an accuracy-based one. The argument is over means, not ends.

With these thoughts in mind, we can turn to the basic responsibilities of the teacher.

THE TEACHER'S RESPONSIBILITIES

Since, then, the learning and teaching strategies suggested in the F-N curriculum will be incorporated into the normal procedures of a language lesson, it may be desirable to review briefly some of the basic responsibilities of the language teacher in relation to F-N teaching. What are they?

Among others:

1. To know the interests of the students; their linguistic and cultural needs; their learning styles, and, with older learners, their social and vocational aspirations.
2. To ascertain at what points on the continuum of each of the communication skills (listening, speaking, reading, writing, and communicative interaction) in the target language the students are if they are not beginners.
3. To learn about the resources—people and places of the community—which could be utilized in possible real communicative or simulated activities.

4. To broaden the experiences of learners through listening, viewing, reading, and other visual, acoustic, or tactile activities in order to provide them with a wide range of concepts and notions to think about, discuss, and write about.

5. To enrich their vocabulary not only by providing them with such varied experiences but also by including—in dialogs and other oral or written materials—the communicative expressions, the formulas of the language, and (in speech) the hesitation words, the exclamations and the appropriate, unarticulated sounds which are authentic and typical of normal communication.

6. To present the communicative function or functions, the structures, notions, and cultural insights in appropriate realistic situations which would not only *clarify* their meaning but would also exemplify the dimensions of human experience in which they are generally used. For example, would we use the functional expressions of warning, "Look out," and "Be careful," in similar situations? In our dialects and those of many others, we would use, "Look out," when a car or a truck, for example, is about to crash into the person we are warning. We would use, "Be careful," to inform someone that a traffic light has changed to red (indicating stop) or that a snowfall has made the streets very slippery.

7. To modify the order of presentation in student texts in order to teach high-frequency, appropriate, feasible, and functional expressions and notional items needed in actual communication situations. These should be presented *before* those which would be of less use in the particular environment of the school and in the probable present and foreseeable experiences of our students.

8. To reintroduce; that is, to reenter previously taught linguistic or cultural material with newly acquired material in always *more extended contexts.* This consciously introduced teaching step (a component of the spiral approach) would help learners internalize rules of grammar and use as they restructure and integrate linguistic forms and concepts in gradually longer stretches of speech.

9. To introduce linguistic material which has been presented under one function within a specific sociocultural situation in a *totally different one* so that learners become aware of the fact that language makes unlimited use of limited means. (You will find the chart on pp. 38–9 helpful in illustrating how this objective can be reached.)

We cannot underscore this point strongly enough. Students derive essential feelings of achievement and success when they perceive that the same functions and notions can be used not only in multiple utterances but also in diverse sociocultural situations. It is also of tremendous benefit in helping learners "internalize" linguistic items, word order, and other features of the target language system.

10. To offer both controlled or guided activities leading to fluency, accuracy, and habit formation (e.g., the ability to move lips and tongue quickly in forming a sound or to use the *present perfect* instead of the *simple past* with *many times*) and those more creative tasks in which students can make and are encouraged to make free choices. The F-N curriculum provides for the important steps of conscious selection and the use of alternative utterances to express the same idea. This, in fact, is one of its great strengths, and fluency activity gives students the opportunity to do this.

    Moreover, the curriculum content and activities give learners practice in making responses when either they have no prior knowledge of what they will hear, or they are asked to make inferences from partial or nonexplicit information in a dialog or other passage.

11. To use *both* the operant conditioning and the cognitive-code theories in presentation and practice, as appropriate. Learners are thus enabled not only to perceive—in model examples—the recurring features and therefore the rules which govern the communicative *use* of functional expressions and language structures—a feature of the cognitive-code theory—but also to achieve fluency and accuracy in understanding and interacting with others and in reading and writing through guided practice activities and tasks. Such fluency and accuracy may result from applying the operant conditioning or habit-formation theory in a formal learning situation. The procedures chosen will depend on students' past experience and expectations.

12. To prepare realistic activities which have some relevance to the students' everyday life and communication needs and which use the learners' school and probable home and community experiences as a starting or "jumping-off" point for motivating the study of a conversation, a reading passage, or whatever.

    For example, if the dialog in the students' textbook refers to a supermarket or an open-air food market in the target culture, it is desirable, before talking about the situation in the dialog, to guide the students to talk about where they go shopping for food, when, the kinds of things they generally buy, with whom they might go, etc. Psychological research tells us that an unfamiliar concept is learned and retained when it is associated with an actual remembered experience one has already had.

13. Not to intervene when students are expressing themselves creatively

during fluency activities unless there is a complete breakdown in understanding. A corollary to that suggestion: to praise learners afterwards for all efforts—however minimal the contribution—which indicate a real desire on their part to communicate and interact with others.

14. To encourage students to discuss their culture and their values in the language they are learning. This strategy has two principal advantages: a. It will convince learners that the new language is an instrument of communication which permits them to use the communicative functions and talk about all the topics they talk about in their native language. b. Even more essential, it will give them a feeling of pride in their culture. (*Culture* is used in the anthropological sense to denote the language, customs, mores, taboos, art forms, and social institutions of any society or community of people.)

It is important that students be helped to feel that culture is generally the result of geographical factors and of historical events, that all people have culture, and that "different from" does not mean "better than" or "worse than." To develop in our learners an appreciation of *cultural pluralism* is one of the many worthy goals of the F-N curriculum.

THE TEACHER'S MORE SPECIFIC TASKS

To all the activities advocated under language learning theories and methods used to date has been added—as has been noted—the emphasis on functional, real-world use of language. This would include, as it should, the central role assigned to a speaker's or writer's communicative purpose and the concepts or appropriateness and social acceptability in the situation in which a conversation is taking place or is referred to in a reading passage. Attention to communicative purpose and function—and particularly to the interpersonal function—should start from the first day of the first level of learning. In the elementary, junior, senior high school, afterschool center, or university, students might learn to say, for example, "Hi, John," but "Good morning, Mrs., Ms., Mr...." or to respond, "I don't remember," when asked, "What's his/her name?" in referring to another student. Certainly, learners should also be encouraged to say, "I'm sorry, I didn't understand" (and not, "Huh," to a teacher, school principal, or stranger, for example) and after a very few lessons to ask, "How do we say X in (the target language)?" or "What does X mean (in our native language)?"

What additional knowledge, skills, or attitudes, then, will teachers have to help students acquire? We shall mention several in random order since these will be illustrated in later chapters. Teachers should help learners

1. Recognize communicative functions as well as formal, informal, familiar, polite, appropriate and inappropriate, acceptable and unacceptable speech in listening and reading activities.
2. Gain insight into all aspects of the culture system of the target language including the paralinguistic (gestures, intonation, etc.) features of language.
3. Use either appropriate paralinguistic features or paraphrases or alternative utterances to convey their meaning when they cannot recall specific communicative expressions, structures, or vocabulary items.
4. Gain a conscious awareness of the *redundant* features of language as an invaluable aid not only in listening and reading comprehension but also in speaking or in writing. Redundancy, a phenomenon of natural languages, is the term used for the multiple clues contained in an utterance or a series of utterances which will *eventually* make it possible for the language learner to hear a partial message or to skim lightly through a reading passage and still understand—at least globally—what has been said or written. We have used the word *eventually* because extensive, continual training will be needed by the learners in listening for and recognizing the multiple clues before they can grasp these immediately in a listening or reading task, and in making use of them in writing tasks.

   Let us look at an example of redundancy for *plurality*. (Redundancy, however, touches *every* aspect of language).

   (English) *Those two* boys *are* going to get *their* notebooks.
   (French) *Les deux* garçons *vont* prendre *leurs* cahiers.
   (Italian) *I due* ragazzi *vanno* a prendere *i loro* quaderni.
   (Spanish) *Los dos* muchachos *van* a coger *sus* cuadernos.

   In English, the first word (the demonstrative adjective or the article) and the number *two* immediately signal plurality obviating the necessity of hearing *are* (in English) which might have been reduced to a scarcely audible sound in fluent speech.
5. Be willing to guess from the context in listening and reading. (By "context" we mean the clues provided by all the language surrounding the item which has not been understood.)
6. Recognize that familiar words will vary in meaning as we encounter them in new situations. It is important to remind learners both that new meaning will occur, and of the original meaning and use.

7. "Monitor" their own speech—listen to themselves, watch the reactions of their listeners and check that they are communicating effectively.

8. Recognize language varieties and be able to discuss the reasons for their use. We would recommend, however, that normally dialectal variations should only be introduced after the basic corpus of linguistic material has been learned. As with all other decisions, however, this will depend on the needs of particular learners.

9. Become aware of cognates that may exist between words or expressions in their native tongue and in the target language. All factors we have noted elsewhere—homogeneous classes, teacher's knowledge of the students' native language, etc.—will have to be considered. Three other points, however, should be mentioned: a. Please do not allow your concern about the very few false cognates which may exist in the first and second languages (L_1 and L_2) to keep you from taking advantage of the large number of cognates which may be available to your students. b. It is a good idea to write the cognates on the chalkboard *under* each other to facilitate comprehension. For example, students might not recognize "national" orally unless they see it above "nazionale" (Italian) or "nacional" (Spanish). c. Cognates—in feasible circumstances— will permit you to use a word like "difficult" (a cognate in several commonly used languages) instead of "hard"— shorter but definitely ambiguous.

10. Enunciate clearly.

11. Note and learn the differences in pronunciation, form, and position (slot) in utterances of word families, for example, *ability, able, ably, inability, unable.* It is very helpful to have students devote a small section of their language notebook to keep a chart like the following:

Noun	Verb	Adjective	Adverb
happiness	(to) be happy	happy	happily
satisfaction	(to) satisfy	satisfied	satisfactorily

At the beginning levels, when learners are asked to perform some task with these word families, you should indicate—in a fill-in activity—exactly which form belongs in the blank space:

EXAMPLE: (to) be happy   He was_____ ___to feel well again.
                                                  (adjective)

         or   He went there_____.
                                                  (adverb)

(To say instead, "Go home and write ten original sentences," becomes a frightening, frustrating experience.)

A chart such as the above, although not in alphabetical order, lends itself to a variety of learning activities particularly after you start focusing on the use of prefixes and suffixes.

ENSURING BALANCE IN A PROGRAM

We shall now turn to steps generally taken in order to ensure a balanced program, and to present and practice a linguistic element. After outlining these two aspects of program implementation, we shall briefly discuss "grouping" in heterogeneous classes.

The definition of the needs of students, as discussed in Chapter 2, will provide answers to many of the fundamental questions of balance. It will determine, for example, the relative importance of reading, writing, and conversation abilities and the nature of the settings in which these abilities will be used. However, questions of how much time should be spent on each of these aspects will still depend on effective learning procedures— we cannot simply move back from a definition of needs to a teaching program. Language learning is a complex process and there will be no simple relationship between needs and teaching.

The approach to be taken to problems of balance will depend on the length and nature of the course. Let us illustrate some of the difficulties with specific examples. Supposing we have to deal with a group of students who require English primarily for conversation in English-speaking countries as tourists. Does this mean that we should exclusively teach conversational English by oral methods? In an intensive course which is mainly intended to activate English which has already been learned this might be the solution. But a longer-term course, or one for beginners or near-beginners, might proceed somewhat differently. Students might need to be able to write down some of what they learned because they found that the process of writing helped to imprint items in their memories, or they might want to extend their vocabulary by extensive reading, or to have reading and writing exercises as a basis for group discussion (conducted in English) which would provide a focus for natural, genuine language use. Students' needs will not simply be the abilities they will most obviously use when they have finished the course, for they will have needs which assist the process of learning. Furthermore, they may want to use language for many purposes which are not essential to their objectively perceived needs, yet these—subjective—desires will be far more important to the learner, and consequently far more important to the teacher, than the instrumental needs of the course as a whole. The task of translating a curriculum specification into materials, and of translating materials into effective teaching, is never an easy one.

But the teacher is responsible for using available materials so that there is a systematic, orderly development, as well as the variety, enjoyment, and surprise necessary for motivation. Haphazard development only means that students, and very often teachers also, do not know exactly what is to happen next, or why. In most institutions, students need to know whether notebooks and other necessary materials are needed for a particular class. They should know, also, roughly what kind of work to expect in a particular class. From such routines they develop a sense of security and confidence in the teacher. Even during unpredictable fluency activity students should feel secure in the knowledge that the teacher fully understands the purpose of the activity and could explain how it helps language learning.

Below, we offer some guidance on allocation of time for the teaching of particular aspects of language. These must not be considered inflexible schedules. They are simple guidelines to help those who have not developed their own strategies by trial and error. Suggestions like these can only be a starting point for the necessary adaptation to each particular group of learners.

A possible weekly schedule
(This example assumes a four hour schedule in a regular school program which may be of five years' duration.)

Task	Level I	Level II
Specific contextualized presentation of new items through role-playing or dialog. (These may be new linguistic or cultural or functional items.)	1–2 hours	1–2 hours
Basic reading for fluency	½ hour	½ hour
Fluency conversation/discussion/free role-playing, etc.	½ hour	½ hour
Writing	¼ hour	½ hour
Gaining cultural insight	¼ hour	¼ hour
Specific pronunciation work	½ hour	¼ hour

Task	Levels III, IV, and V
Structured input of new items through role-playing, etc.	½ hour
Reading (intensive and/or extensive)	1 hour
Oral preparation and follow-up to writing (writing often to be done out of class)	1 hour
Specific remedial accuracy work	¼–½ hour
Projects; involving fluency discussion, reading, and writing	1–1¼ hours

The structured input will include formal listening, reading, and improvisation activities at different times, and as far as possible all activities should be integrated into natural spoken and written language work wherever this can occur spontaneously.

Preparing a Varied Daily Schedule

There are no absolute rules about how a lesson should proceed, but experienced teachers find that they select from a standard collection of routines and use these increasingly flexibly. These routines will include (in an approximate order of use):

Warm-up, casual conversation with the class or a few students on any appropriate topic, carefully adjusted so that it will be comfortably comprehensible to all the students who are being talked to.

Correction of homework, where appropriate and normally very briefly.

Pronunciation practice, perhaps a drill or remedial exercise on intonation, rhythm, or stress.

General motivating discussion to introduce new material. Perhaps a few questions, or a brief story or factual background, depending on the nature of the material.

Presentation of new material by means of student activity, based on a text, teacher demonstration, recording, or any other activating device.

Student practice of new materials, often in groups or pairs.

Free fluency activity to enable students to use their own language on any interesting activity—again, often in groups.

Summary of lesson.

Brief reference ahead to next lesson to ensure continuity.

BASIC STEPS IN PREPARING LESSON PLANS

In this section, we shall underscore the stages in presenting a communicative expression or a related structure. Other recommendations have already been given in Chapter 2 (pp. 13–46), and those related to development of communicative ability (reading comprehension) for example, will be found in Chapter 6 (p. 145).

After the introductory part of each lesson (exchange of greetings, warm-up activities, pronunciation, 30-second written quiz, and homework correction—if homework had been assigned), you should move ahead to the suggested steps below. The steps are not rigidly defined. They are *not* prescriptive. Please feel free to make any changes necessitated by your learning-teaching situation.

Let us make the assumption that you, the teacher, will present the material live to an entire class. This does not preclude the use of the tape or cassette recorder, language laboratory, film, or other audio-visual aid *after* your initial presentation. It is desirable, however, for the students to see the movement of your lips and your gestures as you present the new material. Let us also make the assumption that the students have a textbook and that the textbook will be open (as soon as the students have learned to read) to the main dialog, the mini-dialogs, the reading passage, or whatever you are using for initial presentation and practice. Since we do not really know as yet how learning takes place and what the learning styles of your learners are, it is generally safer to have the eye reinforce the ear.

A Possible Lesson Outline

Level:	Beginning—Secondary School
Function:	Making a suggestion
Steps:	(Each of these are illustrated further on pp. 122–3 and 125–7)

1. Presentation of a brief dialog or several mini-dialogs, preceded by a motivation (relating the dialog situation(s) to the learners' probable community experiences) and a discussion of the function and situation—people, roles, setting, topic, and the informality or formality of the language which the function and situation demand. (At beginning levels, where all the learners understand the same native language, the motivation can well be given in their native tongue.)
2. Oral practice of each utterance of the dialog segment to be presented that day (entire class repetition, half-class, groups, individuals) gener-

ally preceded by your model. If mini-dialogs are used, engage in similar practice.

3. Questions and answers based on the dialog topic(s) and situation itself. (Inverted, *wh*, or *or* questions.)

4. Questions and answers related to the students' personal experiences but centered around the dialog theme.

5. Study of one of the basic communicative expressions in the dialog or one of the structures which exemplifies the function. You will wish to give several *additional* examples of the communicative use of the expression or structure with familiar vocabulary in unambiguous utterances or mini-dialogs (using pictures, simple, real objects, or dramatization) to clarify the meaning of the expression or structure. As Dell Hymes has said, "There are rules of use without which the rules of grammar would be useless" (Hymes 1971). He was referring to such aspects of communication as attitudes of the speakers, their purpose in speaking, the frequency with which an expression is used, its feasibility, and its appropriateness in the situation.

6. Learner discovery of *generalizations* or *rules* underlying the functional expression or structure. This should include at least four points: its *oral and written forms* (the elements of which it is composed, e.g., "How about + verb + ing?"); its *position* in the utterance; its formality or informality in the utterance; and in the case of a structure, its *grammatical function* and *meaning*. (It is helpful to put two model examples on the chalkboard and to underline the important features, using arrows to referents where feasible.)

7. Oral recognition, interpretative activities (two to five depending on the learning level, the language knowledge of the students, and related factors.)

8. Oral production activities—proceeding from guided to freer communication activities.

9. Copying of the dialogs or mini-dialogs or modules if they are not in the class text.

10. Sampling of the written homework assignment, if given.

11. Evaluation of learning (oral only), e.g., "How would you ask your friend to _____. And how would you ask me to _____."

As you will have had occasion to notice in this chapter, the F-N approach presents innovations in the focus on communicative purpose and on the meshing of functions and social situations which give rise to communicative expressions and notions.

More important, however, it underscores the fact that language is a system but a *dynamic* system. It is never static, and its users can modify and recreate it, enrich and adapt it in consonance not only with changes in the real world around us, but also in the attitudes and responses of the persons with whom they interact.

MAKING PROVISION FOR GROUP INSTRUCTION

In some teaching circumstances, you may be forced to provide for the teaching of more than one group during the same class hour. The groups may differ for a variety of reasons; e.g., some are native speakers of your country's language while some have no knowledge of the language at all, some may have come from other school systems in your country where the curriculum content bore little or no resemblance to yours, some may be illiterate in their native tongue. Any of these factors—found in countries like the United States, Great Britain, Canada, or Australia which receive many non-English-speaking immigrants and their children during the school year—create difficulties for school personnel.

Individualized instruction would be the ideal solution if the school could not only press community members, older learners, paraprofessionals, and others into service but also provide materials such as individual worksheets for their use. This is often impossible because of the lack of bilingual assistants, or the dearth of materials which should be prepared and shared by all the schools in a region or nation.

What measures might alleviate your tremendous work load? On the basis of our many years of experience as teachers and supervisors of such classes, allow us to make some practical suggestions:

1. Do not try to create more than two large groups in your class. You could then—as the need arises—provide individual help and tasks to learners within the two groups as often as feasible.
2. The division into two groups can be made on several bases depending on the circumstances in your school: younger and older learners, literate and illiterate learners, native speakers and nonnative speakers, those with different writing systems, or whatever grouping will be most *logical* and *effective*.
3. Depending on your program and the type of class organization for newcomers in your school, try to spend at least one-half hour with each group on alternate days.
4. Make sure that the entire class meets together as often as feasible.

For example, the entire group can meet together for the warm-up, pronunciation, and summary sections of the lessons. Then the teacher will work intensively with Group I on Monday and Wednesday and with Group II on Tuesday and Thursday. Wherever feasible, the class should meet as a group during one hour to sing songs, take dictations, listen to tapes, dramatize dialogs, or develop cultural insights.

A few additional suggestions may not be amiss with relation to this type of needed group work. It is desirable to

- Write the assignment for each group on the chalkboard.
- Select a group leader and a group reporter from among your most able students within the group. (Occasionally, you may ask someone from the other group who has completed his work, or a student from another class, or a community member to assist the group leader.)
- After presenting the new material to that day's group, circulate between the two groups. Occasionally, you may prefer to sit at your desk and invite the group leaders to come up with questions or problems. You may also ask latecomers to your program, persons who have been absent for a period of time, or those who need remedial help to come to your desk for help at this time.
- Take time to spot check the written work that each group may have been asked to do.
- Occasionally, provide an audience situation before the entire class for members from either group to dramatize an original sustained dialog or mini-dialog, to engage in a role play of modules, or to talk about a book read in the native language or in the target language. The report to the class and the ensuing discussion should be in the target language.

SUGGESTIONS FOR DISCUSSION

1. Discuss the major differences between an F-N methodology and audio-lingual methodology.
2. Name five major responsibilities of teachers in implementing an F-N curriculum.
3. How could the teacher learn about the resources of the community if he is not a native of the community?
4. How could a teacher broaden the experiences of learners? Name at least ten activities that would lead toward that goal.
5. Identify some formulas which exist in your native and second languages.
6. How could learners be enabled to speak in increasingly longer contexts?
7. What do we mean when we say that "language makes unlimited use of limited means"?
8. Which two theories of learning should be used in language teaching?
9. How should practice activities be graded?
10. What should be the starting point of the presentation of new material? Why?
11. Should all student errors be corrected? Why not?
12. Why should learners be encouraged to talk about their culture?
13. Why is it essential to engage learners in fluency work?
14. What are some ways in which a teacher could develop awareness of different language varieties used in communication?
15. Explain *redundancy* with examples from your native and second languages.
16. What are the differences between context and situation?
17. How can learners monitor (control) their speech?
18. Do cognates exist between your native language and your second language? Try to give ten of them.
19. How could balance in curriculum planning be achieved?
20. To which communication skills is more time devoted at advanced levels?
21. Are the listening-speaking skills ever entirely put aside? Why not? What are some ways in which they can be integrated with reading and writing?

22. Mention five additional warm-up activities.
23. What should be included in the main steps of a daily lesson?
24. In heterogenous classes, how can you provide for group instruction?
25. Can you write a lesson plan around the function of complimenting someone? (Include the main dialogs, mini-dialogs, and recognition and production activities.)

5 Teaching the Discrete Linguistic-Cultural Features

Three strategies form the basis of the F-N approach: first, the teaching is centered around a situation; second, the essential elements of this situation are identified and analyzed; and third, these elements (the communicative expressions along with the structures and notions related to the situation) are introduced, at the beginning of the unit, in short dialogs. The task of the teacher is to present these elements, associated with a particular situation, at a pace appropriate to the class, taking into account age, ability, learners' needs, and any other relevant variables. In this way, the elements are presented and practiced within a specific context.

The F-N approach does not, however, necessarily exclude the teaching of specific points when and where the need for this arises. Problems may occur in connection with distinct sounds, word-forms, structures, or other linguistic or cultural items which—in authentic communication—would be closely integrated. These would normally be integrated also by the teacher, as outlined above, but it may sometimes be necessary to isolate certain items from the dialog both in order to ensure that students understand how and when these items are used, and also—when appropriate—in order to provide the students with additional practice. Students may, for example, be asked to reinsert items into the original dialog(s), or to insert them into "real-world" utterances or written text.

It is important that material presented and practiced within the F-N approach should be ordered in sequential, logical steps. Suggested below are four steps (none of which is necessarily unique to the F-N method):

1. *Understanding*
    This may be aided if students are encouraged to perceive
    A. a similarity with, or contrast to, an item in their own language (not of course always possible);
    B. a similarity with, or contrast to, an item in the target language already learned (and which is now being further developed, using the "spiral approach"); and/or

C. a connection with a familiar concept or situation—which needs to be associated with the new target language item.

In order to facilitate understanding, teachers may draw upon dramatized situations, where the use of an item is clearly exemplified and illustrated; they may bring into the classroom real objects or other visual aids; and they may paraphrase (i.e., use familiar words to explain new items) or explain how and when a new item is used. Explanations will usually be in the target language, but may on occasion be in the students' mother tongue—provided that this is both economical and feasible (i.e., provided that close equivalents between the two languages are not implied where they may not in fact exist).

2. *Formulation of rules*

Preferable, however, to any explanation by the teacher is the discovery and formulation of rules *by the students themselves*. On the basis of sample model utterances presented either orally or, when necessary, on the blackboard, students above the age of ten or eleven should be encouraged to formulate underlying linguistic rules. In order to draw out a point, teachers may underline relevant features on the blackboard or provide oral clues by questioning, but it will always be preferable for pupils to discover—rather than be told—the underlying rules. Students should be encouraged to formulate these in their own words.

3. *Repetition for fluency*

Fluency will be encouraged if students repeat after a native, or near-native, speaker. The teacher as model may proceed from eliciting whole-class (choral) repetition, through repetition by half the class at a time, followed by the use of smaller groups, finally to repetition by individuals—starting with the more able, who will be likely to provide the better models. In this way choral repetition will give way to individual work through a series of carefully controlled stages.

4. *Practice in fluent, spontaneous expression*

Following on from repetition will come other, more spontaneous, tasks. Closely guided exercises which allow little possibility of error will lead on to a "freer" use of the target language—such as, for example, adding to existing dialogs (first with, and then without, assistance by the teacher). The final goal will be spontaneous creative use in a "real-world" context.

There now follows a short survey of standard teaching procedures for each of the main subsystems of language. Many other works on English as a second language or foreign language methodology will provide further examples and elaboration.

THE SOUND SYSTEM

The sound system is made up of the following elements: individual sounds (or phonemes); liaison (or elision) between these sounds; and stress, intonation, and rhythm (including pause)—all of which are closely interrelated. Your voice, or that of a native-speaker[1], either live or recorded, should provide the students with a model for imitation.

Phonemes

Included below[2] is some nontechnical information about the positions for tongue and lips in the production of various English phonemes. It should be noted that technical description and phonetic script are not suitable for younger learners, except as recommended on page 118. Older students, however, may be shown in a simple way how to articulate the different sounds by placing or moving their tongues or lips as shown on the following diagrams:

Making the Consonant Sounds

Passage of air	Vibration of Vocal Cords	Two Lips	Lower Lip-Upper Teeth	Tip of Tongue-Upper Teeth	Tip of Tongue-Back of Upper Teeth	Front of Tongue Front of Palate	Back of Tongue-Soft Palate	The Vocal Cords
Completely stopped	No—Voiceless	p			t		k	
	Yes—Voiced	b			d		g	
Two sounds: A stop followed by a continuant	No—Voiceless					tʃ		
	Yes—Voiced					dʒ		
Through a narrow opening	No—Voiceless		f	θ	s	ʃ		
	Yes—Voiced		v	ð	z	ʒ		

A "native speaker" in this context may include anyone who is fluent and has a native or near-native accent in the target language, whether or not the target language is a mother tongue.

The charts and diagram are reprinted from *English as a Second Language: From Theory to Practice* by Mary Finocchiaro (1973) with permission from Regents Publishing Company, Inc., 2 Park Avenue, New York, NY 10016.

Passage of air	Vibration of Vocal Cords	Two Lips	Lower Lip-Upper Teeth	Tip of Tongue-Upper Teeth	Tip of Tongue-Back of Upper Teeth	Front of Tongue-Front of Palate	Back of Tongue-Soft Palate	The Vocal Cords
Through side of tongue	No—Voiceless Yes—Voiced				l			
Through nose	No—Voiceless Yes—Voiced	m			n	ŋ		
No stoppage	No—Voiceless Yes—Voiced	w			r*	y		h

*Tongue curls back.

The Vowel Sounds in American English

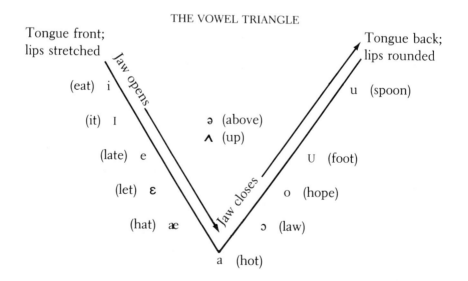

THE VOWEL TRIANGLE

Tongue front; lips stretched

Tongue back; lips rounded

Jaw opens

Jaw closes

(eat) i
(it) ɪ
(late) e
(let) ɛ
(hat) æ

ə (above)
ʌ (up)

u (spoon)
ʊ (foot)
o (hope)
ɔ (law)

a (hot)

The following chart, although in another form, gives you the same information about the tongue position of the significant vowels and will help your students make the sounds.

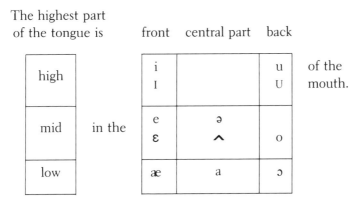

The highest part of the tongue is — front / central part / back — in the ... of the mouth.

		front	central part	back	
high		i, I		u, U	of the
mid	in the	e, ɛ	ə, ʌ	o	mouth.
low		æ	a	ɔ	

Older students should be made aware of the distinction between a phoneme and an allophone.

A phoneme is a sound upon which the *meaning* of a word depends. For example, /b/ and /p/ are separate phonemes in English because in the words *ban* and *pan*, which have totally different meanings, the meaning difference is signaled by the distinction in sound between /b/ and /p/.

An allophone, on the other hand, is a variation in sound which makes no difference to meaning. For example, the /p/-sounds in *pull* and *cup* are perceptibly distinct (varying mainly in the amount of aspiration, or breath, involved), and speakers of languages such as Hindi, to whom this distinction is significant for meaning, will readily perceive a difference between these two forms, or allophones, of /p/. A native English speaker, however, will probably not be aware of any distinction, as for him no meaning difference is signaled: in English the difference between these /p/-sounds or allophones will depend mainly upon the position of /p/ within the syllable and will thus be predictable, i.e., in no way significant for meaning. In other words, different allophones are interchangeable: substituting one for another would produce a foreign-sounding accent but would not affect meaning.

A teacher using F-N procedures will need at times to exploit standard procedures which have no particular F-N base. Below we outline some of the basic points to consider.

• In pronunciation drills, familiar words from previous units should always be used unless—in order to illustrate a phonemic contrast—no

familiar word is available. (Any new words introduced for illustrative purposes of this kind should be explained.)
• Pronunciation work on sounds (or sound combinations) should always be systematically reviewed and should incorporate any new vocabulary which has been learned since the initial presentation.
• Your students may find particular problems which stem from the difference between the sound system of their native language(s) and that of the target language. It may therefore be advisable to practice some sound contrasts, e.g., /θ/ /ð/ or /ʃ/ /ʒ/, *before* words containing these sounds occur within the teaching texts. Wherever possible, use high-frequency items as examples rather than rare ones.
• After practicing individual sounds, students should practice both recognizing and producing minimal contrasts (e.g., *man/men, hat/hut*, etc.) If the contrasting sound system of the students' first language(s) seems to cause special problems, additional practice material should be devised by the teacher as a supplement to the drills already contained within the text.
• Any practice of sounds in isolation should be followed immediately by use of these same sounds in continuous speech, and preferably in a variety of different positions. The quality of many vowels, for example, will change according to whether they occur in stressed or nonstressed sylla-bles. In the expression, "How do you do?" the first *do* will contain a weak (unstressed) form of the vowel, while the second *do* will contain a long, fully stressed vowel form.
• There has been considerable debate over whether students should be expected to learn a phonemic script. In general, this would not seem advisable for beginners, especially if they are also being expected to learn to cope with a new writing system at the same time. Older students, on the other hand, often enjoy learning a phonemic script and will benefit from it. The system can always be simplified by teaching only selected parts, e.g., the symbols for those sounds which cause special difficulty to particular groups of students. The sounds /i/ and /ɪ/, /ʌ/ and /ə/ are examples of vowel contrasts in English which often cause problems, and which can be dealt with effectively and economically once students have learned to recognize the relevant symbols. Then, if difficulties in recognition or production reoccur, the teacher can point back to these symbols on the blackboard.

One symbol which is specially useful in languages like French and English (both of which make frequent use of vowel reduction) is the symbol /ə/—called the *schwa*—as it has no regular alphabetic equivalent.

Failure to "weaken" unstressed vowels to /ə/ where appropriate will mean that students retain an unnecessarily foreign-sounding accent.

Liaison

Liaison (the process of linking separate phonemes, either within or between words) is a feature of many languages. Adjacent phonemes, for example, may show assimilation (where the articulatory features of one sound influence those of another) of various different kinds: a) with modification of one phoneme, e.g., ten cups→teŋkʌps; b) where a phoneme may disappear entirely, e.g., postman→posmən; or c) where two adjacent phonemes become fused into a third, separate phoneme, e.g., would you→wədʒyu. Contractions may vary quite considerably from the corresponding full forms, e.g., will not→wont.

The Stress System

There are in English two separate kinds of stress: word-stress and sentence-stress. Word stress may occur on any syllable of a word, and is fixed, i.e., speakers are not free to vary it (except within certain very restricted situations). The position of stress within a word therefore needs to be learned as part of the pronunciation of that word. Word stress may be phonemic (e.g., in the *meaning*-difference between 'present (always a noun or adjective) and preśent (a verb), or else—as is more usual—it may be non-phonemic (in which case there is no meaning-significance in the fact that 'always and 'sometimes have first-syllable stress, whereas a'gain is always stressed on the second syllable).

Sentence-stress, on the other hand, is not (in English) fixed and may be placed anywhere in the sentence according to the speaker's intention, attitude, emotion, etc. This may be well exemplified by the contrast between

Where did *you* go yesterday?—with focus on the person,
Where did you go yesterday? —with focus on the place,

and Where did you go *yesterday?* —with focus on the time,
where the "nucleus," or main stress, of the sentence varies according to the speaker's intended emphasis. Contrasts of this kind are best left to intermediate and advanced level teaching.

Intonation

Intonation is phonemic, and knowledge of its use is of primary importance in an F-N curriculum since attitudes of speakers are often interpreted incorrectly when there is insufficient insight into the culture patterns of native speakers of the target language. It is the term we use to designate the levels of pitch (the relative height of the voice) in a sentence, including the fading of the voice into silence at the end of an utterance. In English, for example, we use *rising-falling* intonation in statements, commands, or requests; in question-word *(Wh)* questions; and in attached/tag questions asking for *confirmation* and not for information.

We use *rising* intonation in questions requiring a yes/no answer (that is, questions beginning with a form of *be*, the auxiliary *do*, or with a modal—*can, may, should*, etc.) and in attached/tag questions when we are seeking information.

Following are brief examples:

Rising-Falling Intonation:

Statement: I didn't enjoy that |mo|vie.

Command: Don't leave the |ho\use.

Request: Please come to the |de\ sk.

Wh question: Where are you |go|ing?

Why are you |go|ing there?

Attached/tag questions asking for confirmation:

You're not |go|ing, are |y\ ou?

Rising Intonation:

Yes/No questions: Is he |here?

Do you want to |go?

Modals: Can I go |out?

Should you be |smoking?

Attached/tag questions asking for information:

You're not |go|ing, are |you?

Pause

Internal pause is phonemic in English and in some other languages. Notice the difference in meaning between /ais + krim/ (ice cream) and /ai + skrim/ (I scream).

Rhythm

Rhythm is often difficult for learners of English and, while not phonemic, can often distort speech and thus comprehension. Rhythm depends on the stressed syllables in an utterance, which tend to be regularly spaced in English. For example, English speakers try to maintain the same time between one stressed syllable and the next. This means that the unstressed syllables are spoken quickly and many of the unstressed vowels are reduced to /ə/.

There are three basic steps in presenting and practicing all the features of the sound system. After students are guided to understand the meaning of the word or utterance to be practiced, they are given many models of the sound, contrasting sounds, intonations, etc. Thus they *hear* the feature several times. In step 2, they are helped to *distinguish* between sounds, intonations, etc. This second step may be done by using contrasting features in the native and the target language or in the target language alone and having students indicate comprehension by using gestures or numbers or by saying "same" or "different." In step 3, the learners are asked to *produce* the feature *after* listening to the teacher's model (or a tape or cassette recording) first in isolation and then in an authentic (real) context.

Features of the sound system are the most difficult to acquire particularly if the learner is over about the age of eleven and if he has few opportunities to hear the target language either live or in films, recordings, or broadcasts. Today, teachers and other educators accept the fact that absolute mastery of the sound system (except for future teachers or broadcasters) should not be required since it may not be possible, and that comprehensibility, fluency, and situational appropriateness (in other words "communicative competence") are the primary goals the teacher should try to help learners achieve.

PRESENTING THE GRAMMAR SUBSYSTEM

When we use the word *grammar* we refer to its *two* principal subcategories as seen in the diagram on p. 30:

1. *Morphology*—the changes in *word form* produced by two linguistic phenomena: a. *inflections*: for plurality, gender, verb tenses or aspects, possession, possessives, etc. b. *derivation*: resulting from the addition of 1. *prefixes, suffixes* (and *infixes* in some languages such as Turkish or Spanish), and 2. changes made to a word root when nouns, verbs, adjectives, or adverbs can be derived from it through prefixes or suffixes, e.g., *sadness, sadden, sad, sadly.*
2. *Syntax*—the ways in which words combine to make sentences—which may be fixed, rigidly fixed in some languages like English and freer in others, as in Italian, for example.

The grammar subsystem is presented by following the sequence of the basic steps below and in much the same way as we would present communicative expressions. The practice tasks and activities are quite different, however. These will be the subject of Chapter 7.

Let us review the procedures for presentation and follow these with some comments which are particularly relevant to structures.

Steps in Presenting Items of Grammar

• Motivate the teaching of structures by showing how they are needed in real-life communication. Dramatize a situation (shopping for clothing, for example) by reminding students of something they have read or heard, or by deepening their knowledge of something already taught (e.g., the name of students' clothing) "What would you have to know (ask) if you went into a store to buy a (shirt)?" Pupils may answer size, material, price, color, style, etc.

• State the aim of the lesson.

• Review the familiar items, e.g., calendar, time, name of objects, auxiliary verbs in the target language that will be needed to introduce, explain, or practice the new item.

• Use the new structure (adjective of color, for example) in a brief utterance in which all the other words are known to the students.

• Model the utterance several times.

• Engage in full class, half-class, group and individual repetition of the utterance.

• Give several additional sentences in which the structure is used. Class and groups will repeat after you.

• Write two of the sentences on the chalkboard. Underline the new structure and (where relevant) use curved arrows to the other words in the utterance to which the structure is related.

• Point to the underlined structure (and the arrows) as you ask questions which will guide learners to discover the sounds, the written form, the position in the sentence, and the grammatical function of the new structure. ("What does it tell us?")

• Help students of about eleven and over to verbalize the important features of the structure. A chart such as the following can be very helpful with verb tenses and aspects.

• Engage the students in varied guided oral *practice*.

• Require them to *consciously select* the new grammatical item from contrasting ones they had learned in the past.

Verb Tense and Aspect Chart

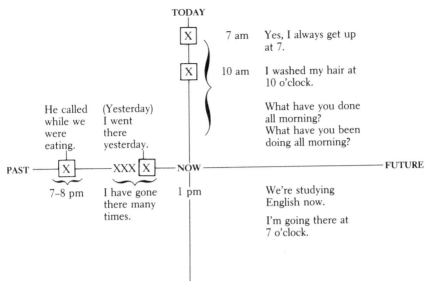

NOTES:

With *now*, we generally use the-*ing* present.

With *later*, we generally use *going to* or *will* if determination is expressed.

With the future, we generally use *going to* or *will* to express certainty or determination (I'll certainly see him tomorrow. I'll go there no matter what it costs.)

X = one *specific point* in time to indicate the present or the past tense.

} = duration aspect; present perfect.

XXX = present perfect or present perfect progressive with relation to now. The action of the present perfect may be repeated in the near future.

X = an event that interrupted an activity that was going on in the past.

• Help them to *use* the structure with communicative expressions and familiar (or new) notions.
• Where feasible, do a translation exercise.

Some Comments Related to Grammar

One of the major differences between the F-N method and the structural (audio-lingual) method is that the grammar introduced in the units is not sequenced or graded according to any linguistic theory. We use instead a communicative grammar, one which takes cognizance of authentic real world speech as recorded from live, spontaneous speech acts.

The structures flow from the communicative function, the setting and the topics. We no longer necessarily begin with *be* or *have* or the *simple present* unless these are logical and appropriate with the immediate communicative purposes of the speakers. That is not to say that a text cannot start with *identification,* forcing the use of *be,* e.g., "I'm John Smith." "Hi, John. I'm Rose Segal." (Most texts do so as a matter of fact.) We could, however, start with, "Pardon me. May I smoke here?" or "Can I have some water?" or (at a gas station) "May I have five dollars of gas?" or "Could you check the oil?"

Where we start depends on the communicative (social, academic, or vocational) needs of the learners, their age, their knowledge of English, if any, and the creative efforts of the curriculum or textbook writer.

Selection and gradation *within* structural categories are extremely important, however, in the presentation of grammar. Let us look at two obvious examples in English. The starting point will depend on you but, in teaching regular plurals of nouns, you should start either with /z/ as in boys and girls or with /s/ as in books or with /əz/ as in watches. In a regular course you should teach and practice all the nouns you intend to teach during that lesson with one /s/sound only. (Naturally, in reviewing at advanced levels or in "crash" (intensive, short-term) programs, the three sounds might be taught in one day but they should still be grouped *separately.*) The same caution holds true for the teaching of the regular simple past tense. Start with /d/, /t/, and /əd/ but keep them separate for presentation and practice.

• It is desirable in textbooks to mark, with different colored crayons, the sentences in exercises which should be practiced together. If you will be using a recording in which the sentences are not selected with awareness of difficulties in sounds, first go over with the students what they will hear on the recording.

• When you teach a verb aspect like the *present perfect* in English (which need not be deferred for a given length of time) it should be presented in the simplest way. (We generally use a calendar and present it with *many times.*) The present of *have* should be reviewed before the presentation.

When you come back to the present perfect (using the spiral approach), remind the students that they have learned one use of the present perfect (you don't have to use the term if your learners are not used to grammatical terminology); review the use and proceed to teach the present perfect with *just* or *ever/never* or *for* or *since*, etc., each separately but integrating them later in oral or written tasks or activities.

• Whenever there is even a remote possibility that your students will make a false analogy, you should be very clear and precise in your explanation (and practice) about the restrictions and limitations of the structure you are presenting. Two obvious examples in English: *want*, *need, know*, and *like* (verbs you will undoubtedly have taught early in the course) are not used in the *-ing* present, that is, in the present progressive. Some verbs are followed by the marked infinitive, "I like *to* ___; I prefer *to* ___;" others are followed by the *-ing* form, as in, "I enjoy swimming".

EXEMPLIFYING THE FUNCTIONAL APPROACH: THE FUNCTIONAL CATEGORIES

The communicative expressions you will wish to focus upon will have been embedded in the main dialog of the unit and/or in a number of mini-dialogs in your textbook. If they are not, you should prepare brief contextualized utterances and, preferably, mini-dialogs of two or three utterances which will clarify the meaning and use of the expression(s) in a variety of social situations. The number and types of social situations will depend on the age and language levels of the learners; for example, in making a suggestion which includes the speaker, we may wish to present *let's*. The simple, informal mini-dialogs might be as follows:

A.	Children:	Let's feed the fish now.
		O.K.
B.	Adolescents:	Let's play football after school.
		Good idea. Let's meet at my house.
C.	Adults:	Let's go to the movies tonight.
		Great. I'd like to see the film at the Z. Would you?
		Sure. Let's go there.

You should dramatize the dialog or mini-dialog using simple pictures or stick figures on the chalkboard to clarify the ages of the participants in the dialog and the topic or activity being discussed. Above in A. two children of either sex and a fish, in B. two adolescents of either sex and a football, in C. two adults of either sex and a movie theater. Make sure to point to the picture or figure of the person who is speaking. With children you may wish to make puppets out of paper bags and to have the speaker "nod" as he plays his role.

Use *let's* in other situations with other topics or activities. For example, Adolescents: "Let's go bike riding, swimming, climbing, etc."

Except for the new concept expressed by *let's*, all or most of the notions (expressed through the lexical items) in the mini-dialogs or utterances should be familiar to the pupils.

Before presenting the new communicative expression you should motivate the need for it and the use of it by relating it to experiences of the learners. For example, with the mini-dialog with adolescents above, you might ask one or more students, "Do you like to play football?" "You can't play football alone, can you?" "You want to invite a friend. What would you say?" (You would ask another student near him to stand; you would indicate the two of them by placing them closer together.) "Listen," you would say, "Let's, etc."

You will give (or read from the text) many similar examples.

Two of them will be written on the chalkboard (if students can read).

Say the examples on the board.

Underline *let's*.

Guide the students to tell you that *let's* comes first in the sentence; that it expresses an idea, thought, or suggestion that one person has; and that this person would like someone else to share in an action with him. (This step would be omitted with children. On the other hand, children would be encouraged—after you yourself had invited several children to do so—to "invite [ask] X to go to the door with you." Real actions clarify meaning and give the children the opportunity to move around.)

Engage in guided practice and in freer communication activities (see Chapter 7 pp. 157–66).

A few other remarks may be desirable at this point.

With adolescents and adults, guide students to understand whether the language in the expression is formal or informal, appropriate or inappropriate in the particular social situation. You can do this through pictures, stick figures, or other visual aids, or by telling the students explicitly what the situation is about—preferably in simple words in the target language (depending—as always—on their level of language learning), or in a brief explanation in their native tongue (where feasible) followed by the same explanation in the target language.

Before presenting the communicative expression, review the notions which will follow the expression. All new communicative expressions should be taught with familiar vocabulary items which have appeared in preceding units or modules.

Also review relevant concepts of time (days, months, etc.), and any other items which will be needed to express the function and to clarify the type of situation (people, places, etc.) in which the expression could be used appropriately.

When you reintroduce the communicative expression, do so in still other social situations and with other topics. This will ensure that you use a new range of notions which have significance for your students because they are related to the resources in the community in which they live; their school; their likes and dislikes; and their cultural values, mores, or taboos.

Your students should be made constantly aware of the fact that they are learning a language which can be used in any real-life situation. An F-N curriculum, you will recall, is an ideal instrument to prove again and again that language makes "infinite use of finite means."

TEACHING THE SPECIFIC NOTIONS THROUGH THE LEXICAL SUBSYSTEM

The notions, as we have learned, stem from the integration of communicative function and situation while centering about the topics or activities being discussed within the situation(s). Notions are expressed through *function* or *structure* words and *content* words. The *function* (structure) words are a closed class; that is, additions cannot be made to them, consisting as they do of prepositions, auxiliaries, conjunctions, and other words which have little or no referential meaning but which link words in an utterance together. The *content* words—the nouns, verbs, adjectives, and adverbs—can always be added to as technological advances or new ideas make such addition necessary.

Whereas all the structure words of a language have to be taught for active use, content words may be taught either for production or for recognition only. Naturally, a word taught initially for recognition only can later be made part of the learners' active vocabulary.

The *notions* are presented and practiced, as are all the other discrete elements of the language, underscoring the facts of *how* a particular notion is needed to complete a communicative function and *why* it is appropriate in the situation and with the topic under discussion.

Some additional comments may be in order with regard to notions:
- All the different uses of each structure word should be taught—one at

a time over a flexible period of time (except for adults in crash courses). Depending on the unit, the word *to* may be taught in simple directions, "Please go *to* the door; Come *to* the desk please"; then, in a later unit, "Please give the book *to* John"; and then in a still later unit, "I want *to* go," etc.

• Content words which are needed to talk about the immediate environment of the school should be given priority even if some of them are not included in the textbook and are not high frequency words.

• At elementary school levels, only about three to five new words should be presented for active use in one lesson; in the secondary schools, ten to fifteen. Student motivation and other factors will often determine the number of words which learners will internalize and be able to recall easily.

• Notions should always be introduced through *context,* that is, in authentic utterances that help to clarify their meaning and use.

• New vocabulary items should always be presented with *known* communicative expressions and structures.

• The F-N approach makes it possible to present vocabulary items around a topic or center of interest. This makes immediate, logical, conversational interchange possible.

• Content words should be introduced and practiced together with those words with which they generally occur, for example, the President *of* the United States, the Congressman *from* New York, a cup *of* tea.

• The same notions should be reintroduced as often as feasible with all the communicative expressions, structures, and situations in which they fit logically and appropriately.

• Where understanding a word depends on knowledge of other items in the context, this should be explained, e.g., *ruler* can refer to *a measuring stick or to a person who governs.* (An utterance like, "He's got *the ruler,*" can be really ambiguous unless the context and situation is made clear.)

• A file of pictures and a box with real objects are invaluable in teaching meaning. (See pp. 166, 177.)

DEVELOPING CULTURAL INSIGHTS

Aspects of culture (customs, mores, taboos, rituals, art forms) are taught incidentally as they arise in a dialog or reading passage and, more explicitly, through films, broadcasts, lectures, newspaper study, or student group projects. In programs designed for persons (children or adults) who are to move to another country within a short time, the insights which should receive immediate attention are those needed for "survival" in the foreign situation.

As we have already noted, the explanation of cultural insights should be both "incidental" and "systematic." As an aspect of culture is encountered in the students' various learning experiences it should be discussed. The level of detail required will depend on questions like the following:

1. What is the overall importance of this aspect of culture? Do you need to be aware of it when you visit the foreign country or when you meet native speakers of the target language?
2. Will this particular aspect of culture be taught in greater depth later in the semester?
3. If there exists a curriculum guide in your school, at which learning level has the aspect of culture been allocated for more intensive study?

The "spiral" approach is particularly suitable for the teaching of cultural items. We have found that—in regular courses particularly—students return pleasurably to a cultural topic and integrate their knowledge with some point of information they have already acquired or an experience they have already had. This is preferable to trying to treat a topic exhaustively all at once.

For example, holidays in the foreign country can be discussed when the issue arises, as can current events. Another method of motivating students to learn about the target culture is to encourage "pen pals" and use the letters as they are received as a basis for class discussion.

Many of the topics listed in Chapter 2, however, should be presented systematically. Contemporary topics, close to the students' lives, should come first. Topics should ideally coincide with the "evolving interests" of the students. If this principle of "evolving" interests is not written into the curriculum, a record card provided by the school should include the titles of all topics you have covered in some depth with any one class. Learners could then earn credits in your or another school system which may be using a similar curriculum.

In order to develop cultural insights, a variety of techniques should be used depending upon whether we are talking about one facet of a category, of eating habits, for example, in the target country (places, e.g., outside of the home, room in the house where meals are taken etc., special foods, holiday foods, hours, etc.); or of a period of history; or—at more advanced or professional levels—of "schools" of art or literary trends or aspects of medicine (anatomy, physiology, pathology, differential diagnoses, etc.).

The techniques below are listed in no particular order. Some are possible at every learning level. Some, such as the reading of literary masterpieces or professional journals, will be possible only at the fourth or fifth level, if at all. Some are especially appropriate for the beginning levels. Notice that all the techniques lend themselves to presentation and practice of communicative expressions.

1. The classroom should reveal the target culture through the use of charts, maps, pictures, books, and artifacts. We realize that this is not always possible, of course, and that it depends upon whether the school allocates special rooms for language. In the literature, this is termed "creating a cultural island."
   A. Parts of this room may be labeled in the foreign language (especially suitable for beginners).
   B. On a bulletin board may be displayed newspaper clippings about current events in the target country, taken from either target-language or native-language sources. Advertisements, comic strips, proverbs, pictures, etc., will all be of interest. A group of students should be given responsibility for changing items on this board at regular intervals.
   C. The classroom may also contain objects related to the target culture, e.g., money, menus, costumes, stamps, etc.
   D. Books and magazines (at appropriate levels of language and interest) should be provided. These should include material about the target country written both in the student's own language and also in the target language. Bilingual texts, if available, are also of great value.
      Newspapers in the target language can be used at a number of levels; they can be studied from the point of view of style, format, attitude, and so on. All reading material should be chosen bearing in mind the students' interests (e.g., adventure, love, science). Students will then be motivated to learn the language while at the same time familiarizing themselves with the culture of the target-language country.
   E. If possible, the room should also contain records of contemporary music and folks songs, and the equipment for playing these.

2. Projects are of great value. Individuals or small groups may undertake projects related to the foreign culture. These can then lead to class discussion. According to the students' learning level, projects may include work on:
   A. maps of all kinds
   B. timetables and itineraries

C.   floor plans of buildings, appropriately labeled

D.   menus, both typical ones and for banquets, etc.

E.   basic language information about the foreign language compared with the mother tongue

F.   a class newspaper

G.   a scrapbook of current events, etc.

H.   play readings, perhaps rehearsed with movement

I.   original, rehearsed skits or plays

J.   a book fair

K.   study of any appropriate aspect of the culture and customs of the target country, for presentation as a broadcast, or exhibition, or guidebook (depending on the level and interests of the students)

3.   Where feasible in long-term regular programs, the foreign culture may be learned and/or experienced in

A.   a language or culture day (songs, dances, stage backdrops, talks by community resource people or experts)

B.   a festival to which community members are invited

C.   hearing and learning songs and dances of the country

4.   The showing of visual materials and a cassette or tape should be used for

A.   listening to readings by contemporary writers

B.   listening to commentaries on museum exhibits as students view works of art or artifacts

C.   seeing short films or interviews with people in the news

D.   listening to illustrated talks on medicine and nursing

5.   Literary masterpieces (if necessary, adapted or simplified) should be studied, since literature reflects all that is included in the term "culture": the people's customs, values, and beliefs; their character; and the historical/geographical background to their behavior. Also, authentic use of language registers, dialects, and idiolects are ideally exemplified through works of literature and can provide excellent bases for class discussion.

There is disagreement on this point, but we think that works in translation are better than nothing—for those students who would otherwise have no access to the foreign literature.

6.   An interdisciplinary approach should be used wherever feasible. Planning areas of cooperation with teachers in other departments will be of tremendous help to your students as they listen to another point of view, or to some aspect of a subject in greater depth. For example,

teachers of science and social studies may give brief talks in the native language. These can be followed by oral discussion in the target language. Moreover, music teachers may be asked to encourage your learners to sing songs in the target language during their class period; art teachers may be asked to help students make posters or drawings of places, people, or impressions of the the target country.

7. People in the community who have visited the target country may be invited to come to the class or school— when time permits—to talk about and perhaps illustrate with photographs, film strips, and other realia—some aspects they considered significant in the country.

    These people may be speakers (native or nonnative) of the target language. The necessary letter of invitation and thanks to the visitor cannot help but reinforce not only communicative expressions of invitation, compliments, and thanks but forms of address, dates, salutations, and closing formulas.

In developing cultural insights our goal should be not merely to give learners a piece or body of information but, more importantly, to foster a positive attitude toward, and an appreciation of, the target country's inhabitants' way of life. This appreciation should be extended to embrace peoples the world over. This objective—termed cultural pluralism—can be more long-lasting and far-reaching than that of learning the target language. Whereas the language may—in some circumstances—be partially forgotten through disuse, the positive attitudes and empathy engendered through helping students appreciate another "life style" will undoubtedly prepare our learners to meet people of still other nations in possible future contacts. The important feeling to be promoted in cultural "discussion" is, "These people are human beings like me and share with me and my countrymen similar values, customs, hopes, and desires."

SUGGESTIONS FOR DISCUSSION

1. Explain the basic steps in presenting any linguistic or cultural element. Add examples.
2. Of what elements does the pronunciation system consist?
3. What makes the difference in the pronunciation of consonants?
4. What is a phoneme? Give examples in your native and second languages.
5. Which are the principal intonation patterns in your native and second languages?
6. What are the three principal steps in teaching pronunciation?
7. What is the difference between a phoneme and an allophone?
8. Indicate the stress of ten words in the target language.
9. Give examples in English or in your target language of utterances with rising-falling intonation and with falling intonation. Label the examples.
10. Give examples of intonation units in your target language.
11. Prepare several mini-dialogs that might be said by children, by adults, by adults talking to children.
12. How can students be guided to discover the underlying rule of a communicative expression or structure?
13. What do we mean by morphology?
14. What do we mean by syntax? Is syntax rigidly adhered to in your native and in your second language?
15. When and how would you engage in the step of conscious selection? (Use two or three actual items in your second language.)
16. Indicate three ways in which you could use the verb aspect chart.
17. What do we mean by function or structure words? When and how should they be taught?
18. Which content words should be given priority of presentation in *your* school? Why?
19. Give a definition of culture.
20. What do we mean by cultural pluralism?
21. Which aspects of culture can be taught incidentally?
22. In your classroom, what possibilities do you have to set up a "cultural island"?

23. How could you work with other subject teachers in your school to enrich your learners' experience with the new language?
24. In what ways can you use resource people in your community?

6 Developing the Communicative Abilities

INTRODUCTORY COMMENTS

The discrete linguistic-cultural items discussed in the preceding chapter are seldom—if ever—used outside of a piece of connected discourse or a communicative activity of listening, speaking, reading, or writing. As we saw in the chart on p. 30, *all* the discrete elements found within the four subsystems of the language system are utilized in what we have come to call "communicative abilities"; that is, the integrated skills of listening, speaking, reading, and writing. The term "integrated" or "integrative" is used to convey two ideas: a. Generally, the abilities are used together. We generally listen and speak or write, read and speak, or read and write. b. The discrete elements are combined in appropriate informational and meaningful sequences in speech acts or in longer units of discourse and text. Notice that in the following example a one-word utterance in response to a question brings together all the subsystems of language and is considered a complete communicative act. If, for example, someone says, "John got married yesterday," and the statement surprises the listener, the latter may say, "John?" with a rising intonation. The response, "John," contains elements from each subsystem. Phonologically, it contains a vowel and consonants, and is spoken with rising intonation; grammatically, it is the subject of the sentence (which could have been repeated in the response) and it is not inflected; it is a lexical item, being the name of a male person; socioculturally, it is obvious that the two speakers know John well or they would have used Mister, Doctor, Professor, or some other title.

In this chapter, we will discuss the four integrated abilities and suggest some general, brief activities under each which will lead to their appropriate and fluent use in any teaching approach. Other activities, specifically relevant to an F-N curriculum will be found in Chapter 7, "Strategies" (pp. 157–73). Any of the activities should be used in regular, long-term programs, some for language for specific purpose courses; others in intensive, crash courses. You, the teacher, will know best which are suitable for your class at a particular time. The activities in which you have most probably engaged in the past are still valid with an F-N content. They should be thought of as activities to be interspersed among the more specific F-N activities wherever and whenever feasible and appropriate for bringing about rapid and accurate production of linguistic forms—in other words, for developing linguistic competence, an essential component of communicative competence. The criteria for their use are, "Will this task or activity make appropriate language items available for learners, so that they can use them for their own purposes in fluency activities? Will it enable them to say what they want or need to say through language?"

LISTENING-SPEAKING ABILITIES[1]

Let us review the subsidiary or enabling skills students will need in order to listen with comprehension to connected discourse which may range from the face to face understanding of several utterances spoken by one or more other persons, to listening to a speech on the radio when noise in the room or radio static may cause interference.

In listening, the learner should be helped to hear and respond to (because they signal meaning):

1. the phonemic sounds of the language and, at upper levels, the personal or dialectal variations of the phonemes as spoken by some native speakers;
2. the sequences of sounds and the ways they group, the lengths of pauses, patterns of stress and intonation, the elisions or contractions;
3. the structure words and their required sound changes depending on their position before other words (e.g., English: a man, an animal; the /ðə/ man, the /ði/ animal, etc.—French: le garçon, l'homme—Italian: i libri, gli sbagli; etc.);
4. inflections for plurality, tense, possession, etc., many of which students should be helped to recognize as redundant elements;
5. the sound changes and functional shifts (involving positional shift) brought about by derivation (e.g., justice, (to) be just, unjust, justly; sequence, (to) sequence, sequential, sequentially);
6. the structural patterns (of verb groups, of prepositional phrases, etc.);

[1] Material on listening adapted from *The Foreign Language Learner* by Mary Finocchiaro and Michael Bonomo (1973) with permission from Regents Publishing Company, Inc., 2 Park Avenue, New York, NY 10016.

136

7. the word-order clues to grammatical function and meaning, e.g., the bus station/the station bus;
8. the meaning of words depending on the context or on the situation being discussed (e.g., the head of the statue, of the table, of lettuce);
9. the formulas, introductory words, idiomatic expressions, and hesitation words which occur in speech;
10. numbers, days, names, and dates;
11. other notions used to "complete" the function; and, of course,
12. the communicative expressions or formulas which express the speaker's *purpose*.

The learner's ability to comprehend (to decode) any utterance or longer text will depend on several factors: a. his familiarity with all the elements listed above, b. his ability to recognize redundant clues in the message, c. his ability to guess or to make hypotheses about some unfamiliar word or group of words from its position in the context, d. his "expectation" of all the enabling skills above because he has met them numerous times in a variety of listening tasks. Most important, too, is that the learner retain the essential details (those high in information) of the first part of the text as he continues to listen to the other parts.

These skills are developed over a long period of time. We start by giving learners listening tasks in brief utterances within one situation which students can retain easily; we proceed with the *same* situation and topic to longer sentences, then to combinations of sentences, first in the same and later within different situations and topics. From emphasis on short-term retention, we move ahead to give students practice in remembering or reconstructing material over a longer period of time—as, for example, in improvising a dialog several days (or weeks) after working on a similar one, or in discussing a film seen or a lecture heard one or two weeks before, or in performing a listening comprehension task in which the passage read is made increasingly longer.

To aid the students in retaining increasingly longer sentences and later in producing these longer segments, they may listen to the same material many times. As they hear the same piece of speech the fourth or fifth time, they will anticipate and "supplement" the sounds and sound sequences they are about to hear. This happens to us whenever we listen to our native language. The speaker whose speech style is familiar and the well-known situation we are part of or are hearing described (as well as the lexical combinations which we have grown to expect) all make it possible for us to hear perhaps only fifty percent of what is being said and yet to "decode" or understand the message at least globally—in other words, to get the gist of the message.

In developing listening skills, it is essential that we do not slow down or distort speech in the mistaken notion that it will help students to understand. Anything heard by the students should contain the typical rhythm, intonation, pauses, contractions, and elisions of the target language. (As we have emphasized above, when a word, structure, or phrase is to be isolated for intensive practice, it should first be heard in a normally spoken utterance. After its intensive study, it should be reinserted immediately in the same normal utterance or in a piece of connected speech at normal, conversational speed.)

Listening Activities

While the major focus is on increasing listening ability, you will notice that many of the activities require speaking, reading, writing, miming actions, or associating sound groups or utterances with pictures.

General Listening Activities

Among the many experiences and tasks which will promote our students' listening ability are the following (some are more appropriate at beginning levels; others at higher levels):

1. Listening to you as you
    - present sounds in sound sequences, intonation patterns, and utterances with contrasting stress and pauses;
    - give instructions related to classroom routines (taking attendance, giving homework, etc.);
    - present model sentences based on some communicative, grammatical, or lexical feature of language;
    - furnish cues or ask questions to stimulate appropriate responses in a variety of practice activities;
    - tell a story;
    - read a passage, poem, or playlet orally;
    - describe simple or situational pictures;
    - give instructions for tests;
    - engage in directed practice activities;
    - give instructions for simple listening games such as "Simon Says";
    - dramatize a dialog using pictures or real objects;
    - tell about an incident that happened to you or someone else;
    - clarify the situation of a dialog, a module, a film, a radio broadcast, or any other large chunk of listening;

- give a dictation (gradually increasing the number of syllables the students are to retain before they write) (see pp. 150–1);
- give a listening comprehension exercise (see p. 151);
- give a dicto-comp (see p. 151);
- give a lecture on some aspect of culture;
- prepare them orally for writing a composition through extensive discussion of the topic;
- greet visitors and engage them in conversation.

2. Listening to other pupils give directions, ask questions, give summaries, recount incidents (e.g., what they saw or what happened on their way to school).
3. Engaging in dialog dramatization and in role-playing of dialogs or modules.
4. Listening to outside speakers (resource persons from the community) or other school personnel.
5. Listening to the same recordings of language lesson segments, songs, plays, poems, speeches, etc., numerous times.
6. Listening to cassette or tape recordings of oral materials often enough so that they anticipate or "supplement" what they are about to hear.
7. Watching films several times—those especially prepared for language learners or short clips of feature films—and listening to selected radio and television programs.
8. Taking part in telephone conversations. (These can be simulated in class.)
9. Interviewing people in the community, where feasible.
10. Attending and contributing to lectures, conferences, language club meetings, discussion groups, and panel discussions.
11. Going to the movies or the theater.
12. Playing language games.
13. Working in pairs and/or groups to perform problem-solving tasks and other pertinent activities. (See p. 160)
14. Participating in spontaneous role-playing exercises (see, for example, Maley and Duff 1978).

We shall return to role-playing in the chapter on strategies, where we hope to emphasize that spontaneous, creative role-playing is perhaps tenth in an increasingly less controlled series of steps leading to real creativity and spontaneity.

Since two people are always involved in them, the mention of telephone conversations or "role-playing activities" brings us to a consideration of the speaking skill. Listening and speaking are interdependent to a great extent.

Although we are singling out "speaking" in this section, it is obvious that speaking often follows listening and that speaking may precede or follow reading and writing. Often, but not necessarily, improvement in listening comprehension will bring with it an improvement in speaking. On the other hand; a person may speak with a certain degree of fluency and speed without a corresponding facility in understanding the normal speech of a native speaker. In the give and take of conversation, listening may lag far behind speaking. As we mentioned above, while we can control what we say, we cannot control what others will say to us.

Speaking is a more complex skill than listening, for in addition to knowing the sound, structure, vocabulary, and culture subsystems of the language, the speakers must a. think of the ideas they wish to express, either initiating a conversation or responding to a previous speaker; b. change the tongue, lips, and jaw positions in order to articulate the appropriate sounds; c. be consciously aware of the appropriate functional expressions, as well as of the grammatical, lexical, and cultural features needed to express the idea; d. be sensitive to any change in the "register" or style necessitated by the person(s) to whom they are speaking and the situation in which the conversation is taking place; e. change the direction of their thoughts on the basis of the other person's responses. All of these interrelated acts—mental and physical—must take place instantaneously and simultaneously.

Spontaneous, creative use of language may develop only after years of learning, depending upon the age, motivation, and aptitude of the learner and on the quality of instruction. It happens gradually, nearly imperceptibly sometimes, but the F-N approach encourages—through its emphasis on the uses to which the language is put and through the major role given to fluency activities—the learner to operate creatively right from the early stages of learning. In order to engender interest and encourage communication, simple, authentic conversations should be engaged in from the very first day; absolute accuracy should not be demanded provided the utterance is comprehensible; questions such as, "What would you say?" should be asked to which students will respond in the target language. For example, after teaching greetings, you might say, on the very first day, in the students' native tongue where feasible, "You are walking to school and you meet a friend. What would you say"? As quickly as possible, the question, "What would you say"? should be asked in the target language. You could, of course, have dramatized the situation with two simple pictures. Or again, you might direct one student to "Ask X how he's

140

feeling today," and tell X to say how he's really feeling, whispering the direct questions and responses if necessary for the first lesson.

At the same time, however, each item of language and each grammatical operation should still be made available to students in a systematic, logical progression so that the appropriate features of sound, arrangement and word form are eventually internalized in order a. that they can be used without hesitation and b. that the stream of speech can become increasingly more fluent and thus more complex.

There are numerous other activities which will gradually develop innovative, confident speaking behavior. Some of those below are best done with beginners while others should be left for upper intermediate and advanced levels; for intensive crash courses; or for modular learning.

General Speaking Activities
Ranging from the simple to the more complex.

1. Reply to directions or questions given by you or by another pupil.
2. Give directions for other pupils. (For example, "Give me the .... Point to the .... Walk to the door and open it. Ask X how old he is. Ask X if he can do ....")
3. Engage in a Gouin series, associating speech and action.
4. Prepare "original" sentences with communicative expressions, structures or notions which have been presented.
5. Answer questions asked by other students based on any class or out-of-class experiences.
6. Frame questions to ask you, or other pupils, based on reading or on a common experience.
7. Tell what objects appear in a picture or on a chart. (When the picture is used again, elements of color, placement, size, etc., may be included.)
8. Tell a well-known story or retell an experience in their own words. If necessary, key words could be suggested by you.
9. Give a report on a prepared topic and be ready to answer questions on it.
10. Set up a class shop, a library, a post office, a bank, or other appropriate community resources and improvise realistic conversations for them.
11. Play a communicative language game.
12. Conduct a debate, a discussion, a forum, or some other oral group activity based on research (e.g., a cultural or professional topic) in which students are forced to listen attentively to the previous speaker

in order to agree, disagree, express uncertainty, or add other relevant information.

13. Make recordings of debates or news broadcasts for future discussion.
14. Engage in telephone conversations in which a. both speakers can be seen and heard or b. only one speaker can be seen and heard. (Other class members should guess what the second speaker is saying from what they can hear the first speaker say [respond].)
15. Read a newspaper article in the native language and give a report on it in the target language. Be prepared to ask and answer questions on it.
16. Engage in role-playing based on typical target language-using situations.
17. Take roles in well-known modern plays.

The crucial responsibility of the teacher, in all this work, is to allow students to use the language as freely as possible, so that the classroom becomes a genuine language-using community. Students must gradually get used to working in pairs or small groups without too much close supervision from the teacher. This means that the teacher must be able to specify clearly exactly what each task consists of (if necessary, explaining in the mother tongue) and exactly how much time is allowed for it. This will require careful planning and perhaps—for inexperienced teachers—the advice of a colleague. Successful timing of group work activities soon comes with practice, though, and classes are unlikely to be noisy or undisciplined if the exercises are well planned and well managed.

Group or pair practice will normally have three phases:

1. Preparation: the teacher will explain, or demonstrate, roughly what is to be done and will give out appropriate worksheets or other materials, refer to the relevant parts of the textbook, and generally make sure that everyone in the class understands the procedure;
2. Activity: students will perform the task(s) while the teacher perhaps sits in on the work of some groups, even taking part in the task if a group appears to need help;
3. Follow-up and evaluation: this is optional and will not always be necessary, but students prefer there to be some reporting back, demonstration of what they have achieved, or discussion for at least some of their group activities.

All the activities listed above may be prepared or carried out in small groups, and the less full-class activity there is, the more practice each student will have in fairly natural language-using conditions. Furthermore, much of this oral work can be combined with reading and writing activities to produce integrated language use, as we shall see below.

DEVELOPING THE ABILITY TO READ

While little has been said about reading in articles or texts on an F-N curriculum (except for advanced English for Specific Purpose courses), reading is an important, integral skill which should be taught in all types of courses using the F-N approach.

The development of reading activities will also help learners reinforce listening and speaking abilities. The amount of time to be spent on reading and writing has been recommended on pp. 105–6 for regular school programs. In crash programs (short-term, intensive programs for immediate use in the foreign situation), reading and writing skills may also need to be initiated as quickly as possible even when the writing systems in L_1 and L_2 are quite different. At the very least, learners will have to learn to read signs and forms; they will have to learn to fill in information on forms and to write notes with their names and addresses. Even functional illiterates (those who can read or write in their native tongue only at a level of very basic education) will need minimal essential skills and the possibility to increase these later through self-study or intensive programs in the country to which they have migrated.

In regular programs, reading and writing can well serve as a starting point for extensive listening-speaking activities. Oral attention-pointing questions *before* engaging students in reading and writing activities, answers or discussion related to preliminary motivating questions, summaries, recounting of relevant personal experiences, and word study are all integral facets of the teaching of reading and writing which may precede the activities themselves. Moreover, interesting reading experiences and those related to one's professional or vocational field will provide topics for oral discussion and for writing.

The teaching of reading to adult illiterates or to those whose writing system is different in L_1 and L_2 is unfortunately beyond the scope of this book and you are urged to turn to the literature on the subject if you find yourself in such circumstances.

The introduction of reading places a great responsibility on the teacher since reading presupposes two quite different subskills. Teachers help students a. bring meaning to a piece of connected discourse; b. get meaning from (decode) the printed or written material. Moreover, students will have to be given the motivation and the potential to continue reading out of class and later in their lives. As mentioned elsewhere in this book, the reading skill can remain throughout life whereas often the listening-speaking skills fade from forced disuse.

People read for many practical or recreational purposes. At some time or other they will need to read signs, forms, instructions for making or using things, instructions on medicines, menus with prices; to study written materials used in other curriculum areas; to engage in research; to prepare for writing outlines or summaries; and to read professional or vocational journals. Many students, we hope, will want to read for pleasure—fables, short stories, novels, plays, or essays on controversial subjects.

The teacher's principal responsibilities in developing reading skills and the enabling subskills needed may be summarized as follows: To

•   clarify the situations so that students can understand the major purpose(s) of the passage
•   extend and enrich the experiences of students so that they will understand the elements in the situation (people, place, time, topics and cultural allusions)
•   present the sounds and meanings of unfamiliar vocabulary
•   teach the sound-symbol correspondences
•   assist students to read words in logical groups
•   help learners understand the grammatical function of structures and word groups
•   help them comprehend and relate the formality and informality of the communicative expressions and notions to the situation
•   enable them to comprehend and/or guess the meaning of words and discourse connectors such as *moreover, on the other hand,* etc., in single statements and connected discourse
•   enable them to distinguish between the main theme and supporting details
•   increase their speed in reading since slow, labored reading decreases comprehension

Developing the Enabling (Sub)skills

1.   You can help learners extend their understanding by asking them questions about *their* likes and dislikes, their activities, and their outside reading. You can provide them with experiences of viewing pictures, films, newspapers, magazines; of listening to music and poetry; and discussing their emotions and feelings.

Through attention-pointing questions, you can make them aware of the elements in the situation. You can enrich their vocabularies in all the ways mentioned on pp. 128, 144 and, in addition, by helping them to use bilingual dictionaries and, with advanced, highly motivated students, monolingual dictionaries. Every classroom should aloud to them, pausing at logical points in the passage. b. You will have them read the same passage silently, *timing the reading*. c. You will decrease the reading time gradually for material of a similar level of difficulty. d. You will try to discourage lip movements. e. Most important, you will give them a specific purpose for reading, e.g., find the steps in the process; find five words which describe X; be prepared to complete the sentences I will put on the chalkboard; be prepared to discuss a title you would like for the passage.

Intensive and Extensive Reading

At beginning stages of reading (Stage I Reading), the material (expressions, notions, structures) will all be familiar to the learners because it will generally consist of the utterances they will have heard repeated and practiced in class. Depending upon the learners' age, needs, and ability levels, a slightly more difficult stage (Stage II) will expose them to familiar materials which are, however, *recombined* or *reorganized*.

In Stage III reading, they will finally see written material in which some of the communicative expressions, notions, structures, or cultural allusions will be unfamiliar to them.

When Stage III reading is introduced, the procedure for presentation is what is generally called "intensive"; that is, the students' attention should be focused on all expressions, notions, sounds, structures, and cultural allusions in the passage. After about a month (in regular programs) of intensive reading, you may wish to introduce extensive reading. When learners have developed reasonable facility in using both techniques, you can vary the procedures within the same lesson or in subsequent lessons.

Your selection (intensive or extensive) should depend on the complexity of the material, its interest to the students and the number of pages you may be required to cover in a year. After dividing the reading for a lesson into two or three segments so that you can use either an intensive or extensive technique, you may wish to proceed in the following ways for both intensive and extensive reading:

1. *Motivate* the reading by relating it to the students' experiences or, in the case of a longer story, essay, or technical chapter which you have begun, by eliciting a brief summary of what has been read.

2. *State the purpose* of the reading, e.g., (in the case of a long story) "What do you think will happen now?" (in the case of a short, self-contained passage) "Let's see what people like you (in the target country) would do/say/tell/," etc.

contain dictionaries of both types to which students may refe
necessary.

2. In regular programs, sound-symbol relationships are taught gr
and briefly at beginning levels. Reading is taught in two
streams. Stream I (the most interesting to learners) permits
read material relevant to their age and interests, primarily fc
comprehension. In Stream II, the reading material is often
around vocabulary which reinforces the sound-symbol relati
In English, the sound-symbol relationships may proceed fror
one-syllable words; to the same words ending in the lette
changing the sound to /ei/, to /I/ and /i/, etc.; to the sp
words with silent letters as in *know* or *gnat*.

3. You should discuss the formality or informality of the
Which expression or word is formal? which is informa
impolite? tentative? familiar? Which aspects of the situat
mined the formality or informality of the language?

4. You can ensure detailed comprehension of the passage or
tion in various ways *after* you have given students insigh
situation and the unfamiliar notions. Moreover, you should
the material aloud—pausing normally at logical points
sentences to indicate the relationships of linguistic item
followed you in their textbooks. (Remember, please, tl
means *looking at* written material.)

• At beginning levels or with difficult materials at upper lev
ask different kinds of questions on the same sentence: an inver
question; a question with *or*; a question word *(Wh)* question
stages, inferential questions with "*Why*", "*What* do you thin
you think (or feel)," etc.

• At beginning levels, you will ask questions in sequence, tl
which the students can find easily in their book.

• You might give sentences in a passage about a process o
of sequence and ask the learners to place them in the prop

• You will ask for a summary. A number of students can c
sentence each. (Notice that this will reinforce attentive liste

• You can ask for the principal idea of the passage and
supporting, subsidiary ideas.

• You can ask students to find the words which desc
which tell readers about his attitude or emotion or whateve
about.

• There are several ways to increase speed: a. You will re

3. *Clarify any difficulty* in the first portion. The difficulty may be related to factors in the situation or to communicative, phonological, grammatical, notional, or cultural elements. Place or have these placed on the chalkboard, repeat them, elicit or supply the meaning and use them in a context (from the reading itself where possible). Ask the learners to repeat the words.
4. *Read* the passage *aloud* as the students follow in their books. Now your procedure will vary depending on whether you will read the particular portion intensively or extensively.

Intensive

After reading each line aloud in logical, thought groups, with students' books open, ask several simple questions on each sentence as described above on p. 145. At the end of the paragraph, ask for a summary. If there are problems, ask questions to help elicit the summary. The summary should be sequential and thus informational.

Extensive

After reading the *entire* passage aloud, ask the students to read it silently. Give them the purpose for reading and the time which will be allowed. After they have read, check their comprehension by having them complete sentences on the chalkboard; stating whether an oral statement is true or false (giving the true answer if the statement was false); asking for the main idea; asking for the supporting ideas; eliciting a sequential summary. All of these tasks can be done in groups or pairs. Each group leader or secretary will later report their decision to the large reading or class group.

Some Reading Related Activities

• Distribute four or five questions to four or five students on numbered slips of paper in order to ensure informational sequence. A student will read a question aloud. Another will volunteer to go to the chalkboard with the slip containing the question and write the question and answer.

• When all the questions and answers are on the chalkboard, an able student will go to the board, ask others if there are errors, and make changes when necessary. You can then read the answers and have the class members read them in chorus after you.

• Read the passage again in thought groups and ask the students to read in chorus *after* you.

- Ask the students to formulate questions on the passage (*inverted, or,* or *Wh questions*) and call on a classmate to answer.
- Have the communicative expressions, structures, and notions that were clarified before the reading used in original sentences.
- Engage in numerous word study exercises (e.g., finding antonyms, synonyms, cognates, paraphrases, giving other parts of speech with the same root).
- Have students retell what happened in the passage from a list of key words you will place on the board.
- Have them look for the key words (those high in information) in *each* sentence.
- Have them summarize the passage. (To ensure attentive listening, ask each student to supply one statement only.)

Other Comments on Reading

- Assign supplementary readers at advanced and professional levels on students' areas of need and interest. Use these to create audience situations for the students (as they give their impression of the book to class members) and to stimulate oral discussion.
- Use bilingual texts (although to date there are very few good ones on the commercial market) in which text equivalents are given on facing pages. These will enable learners to see the similarities and differences in expressions and structures in L_1 and L_2.
- It is not desirable to have poor readers stand and read aloud for the entire class. It reinforces poor reading habits and thus wastes students' time.
- Occasionally—and again depending on your learners' needs—you may ask for the equivalent of a word or expression in the native language.
- Do not hesitate to use adapted or simplified versions of literary masterpieces or other materials. Students find them stimulating, and—who knows—reading them may motivate the students to learn enough of the target language to read the original.

DEVELOPING THE ABILITY TO WRITE

General Comments

- Except at intermediate, advanced, or professional levels, helping students "write" means primarily helping them to make carefully guided symbols on paper. We guide our learners through several progressively more complex stages over a period of time—depending as always on their needs, age, capacities, aspirations—to a point where they will be able to write a "creative" essay on a topic of interest to them in informational, logical sequence. The final stage will be long delayed or never reached at all if older students come to us with a totally different writing and rhetorical system.

• Little or no writing should be practiced in class (except with those learners who have always used a different writing system). Class time should be devoted primarily to listening and speaking tasks which most students may not have opportunities to do outside of class.

• Any copying of model sentences, communicative expressions ranging from familiar to formal language, structural paradigms (forms within a grammatical category), dialogs, notions, etc., should be done at a specific period of time toward the end of the lesson. This avoids an interruption in the smooth oral flow of your lesson and, in some circumstances, discipline problems because pencils, pens, blank pages, etc., cannot be found.

• Dictations, dicto-comps (see p. 151), cloze tests, and listening-comprehension tasks should be done in class. While results in these do not tell us about our students' ability to "communicate," they are of decided benefit in helping our learners internalize rules of use and of grammar; recall vocabulary items; learn to recognize informational sequence, redundancy, and contextual clues, and learn to recognize cohesive devices and coherence in connected texts or units of discourse.

• Writing should reinforce and help extend the listening, speaking, and reading abilities.

• Depending on their level, learners should be taught: a. the mechanics—punctuation, capitalization, abbreviations, spelling; b. the sound-spelling correspondences; c. letter writing—formal (business, legal, and related correspondence) and informal (personal, friendly correspondence); d. practical writing for taking notes from books or lectures, outlining a book or a composition they are going to write, and summarizing; e. the organization and appropriate expression of an idea, a process, a plea, or whatever so that it will convey the desired meaning to a reader; f. the differences between speaking and writing (the use of contractions, for example) in some languages.

• As in the reading skill we discussed above, learners at advanced levels should be provided with many viewing, listening, and reading experiences so that they will have ideas to write about. Looking at paintings, reading literary materials and others in their field of vocational or professional interest, or watching films and discussing their feelings will help them write more creatively.

• Important, too, is to give them practice in paraphrasing sentences and in finding synonyms for simple, overworked words like "said." In addition to a bilingual or monolingual dictionary, learners should be taught how to use a book of synonyms—if one exists in the target language.

Four Basic Procedures in Controlled and Guided Writing

For the reasons noted above, dictations, listening-writing comprehension tasks, cloze tests, and dictation-composition (dicto-comps) should be given regularly. Dictations and cloze tests are particularly valuable in reinforcing what students should have learned about the value of looking for redundancy clues in their writing. Listening comprehension and dicto-comp exercises require that attention be paid in listening to words or expressions that are high in information. Cloze tests, in which any logical word in a blank is accepted, help students retrieve learned material from their memory bank. Following are simple procedures for carrying out each activity.

Dictation at Beginning Levels
(This may be on a familiar dialog or reading passage; later, on new material.)

•   Motivate the need for writing and give a few words about the topic and situation.
•   Clarify any linguistic or cultural difficulty in a new conversation or passage.
•   Review punctuation marks by asking a student to write the symbol on the chalkboard as you say *period, comma, colon,* etc.
•   Dictate the passage at normal speed. (The students do not write during this first reading.)
•   Ask a student to go to a side board or to the front board and to write as you dictate to the entire class. Read the passage in thought groups, pausing after each group of words to give the students time to write. (With some "slower" groups, you may wish them to repeat the segment you have said after you.) *Dictate the punctuation marks.*
•   Read the passage again more slowly than at normal speed. Repeat the punctuation marks again.
•   Give the students about two minutes to look over their dictation to make sure that there is agreement between noun and pronoun, subject and verb, tense and adverbs, etc.
•   The students may keep their papers or exchange them with students next to them as the chalkboard dictation is corrected, in cooperation with class members, by an "able" student in your class.

- Ask the students if they understand the errors they made but do *not* give a grade for each dictation.
- Use the dictation to do choral reading, word study exercises, sentence paraphrases, or—if a communicative expression or structure was incorrectly written—to engage the class in brief practice. Use it as a "jumping-off point" for having students summarize, formulate questions and answers, or discuss the theme of the dictation.

Listening Comprehension
(With a writing task)

This may be on familiar or unfamiliar material—a dialog, an anecdote, a brief segment of material relevant to your students' age and interests.

- Motivate the material by giving a brief summary or by asking preliminary questions related to the theme of the passage.
- Clarify any difficulty.
- Review the procedure you will follow.
- Read the material through two times at normal speed.
- Ask a question two times. Give the students time to write the answer. (A student may write the answers at the same time on the chalkboard.)
- Continue until you have given all the questions. (Five are generally given.)
- Read the passage or conversation again at normal speed.
- Say the questions again.
- Give the students about two minutes to check their own work and to make necessary changes.
- Correct the material as in the dictation. (Peer discussion and corrections in small groups will develop interaction.)

Dicto-comp
(This is a combination of dictation and guided composition.)

- Select two or three short paragraphs around a topic of relevance to your students.
- Motivate the topic by relating it to their probable personal experiences.
- Clarify any difficulties in the paragraphs. When you first use this technique, leave the new expressions or notions on the chalkboard.
- Read the paragraphs sequentially three to five times. (Permit students to look at the words on the board.)

- Have students write what they remember of the paragraphs.
- Check the "composition" by distributing a sheet on which the paragraphs appear or—where feasible—by using an opaque or overhead projector to flash them on the screen. Another way of checking is to ask one or two of your more able students to read what they have written and to ask other students to indicate errors, gaps, or sequence problems. Still another way is to have the students break up into small groups. Each person in the group can give one sentence which can be discussed before individuals add it to their paper.

Cloze Test
(At beginning stages, this should be from a familiar reading passage; later, the passage may be unfamiliar.)

- If the passage is unfamiliar, clarify the difficulties.
- Have the students read the passage to be completed two or more times, as necessary. In the passage, every *fifth, sixth,* or *seventh* word is systematically omitted. (The first sentence and the last, however, are generally complete.)
- Students may fill in the blanks with *any appropriate* word, not necessarily, the word used in the original passage.
- Correct, by distributing or flashing the complete passage on a screen; by having several individuals read an entire sentence with the word they used; by breaking up the class into groups.
- Discuss any questions of appropriateness or correctness.
- Engage in related communicative activities.
  NOTE: At beginning levels, or at any time as a diagnostic device, you may prefer to omit all the articles or the nouns or the prepositions or whatever you have been emphasizing in class.

Some Controlled Writing Tasks
("Controlled" because the exact language being used is specified, i.e., controlled.)

Learners may be asked to:
- Copy model sentences, dialogs, or anything that has been spoken or read.
- Write out in full the model sentences they have practiced orally. Your instruction may be, "Use the words in the list to write sentences like sentence 1."

Would you mind going to the *store?*
Would you mind going to the *library?* etc.

- Change the sentences in a familiar dialog, short paragraph, or series of action sentences in any one of the following ways:
    A. Change the subject and verb to the plural.
    B. Change the gender of the subject (the name of the person or pronoun).
    C. If the subject and verb are in the plural, change them to the singular.
    D. Change by adding *yesterday, later, or tomorrow.*
    E. Change the point of view of the paragraph, e.g., "I went to the movies. I liked the film. The plot was excellent," to "I went to the movies. I didn't like the film at all. The plot was so childish that it was insulting."
- Add to a familiar dialog using newly learned communicative expressions, structures, and notions when these are appropriate.
- Answer a series of specific questions on any activity or on a reading passage.
- Complete a series of related sentences in any way they wish. The completed sentences will constitute a short "composition." For example:

    I asked X _____ the other evening.
    The music was _____.
    We heard _____.
    After the concert he said he felt like _____.
    So we _____ to a _____ and _____.

Some Guided Writing Tasks

("Guided" because the content is guided but the language is more and more the student's own.)

- Write a summary of material which has been read.
- Complete an outline form of material they have read.
- Write an outline of material which they have read.
- Write a letter (after the appropriate form has been taught and practiced) in which they expand the ideas given by you.
For example:
- Write a letter to your friend. Tell him what country you are planning to go to; why you are happy about it; how you are preparing yourself to go. Ask him about his plans.
- Write a report on an article or book read.
- Write a short paragraph for each picture in a series (three or four at the most) related to one theme.
- Write an original ending to a story they have read.

- Write an ending to a story they have *not yet* completed reading or hearing.
- Write a simple dialog using (or recombining) familiar functional expressions and structures.
- Complete a dialog when the first few lines have been given.
- Prepare a narrative paragraph from a dialog.
- Prepare a dialog from a narrative paragraph.
- Reconstruct a dialog from one or two words given in each utterance.
- Write a complete dialog when only the utterances of *one* speaker are indicated.
- Write a core module based on a specific professional or vocational activity.
- Expand the module.

In this book we shall not touch on the writing of longer essays for the advanced or professional level student, although every activity noted above will lead to that. There are many excellent books on the subject and we should like to recommend one in particular.[1]

In conclusion we should like to reaffirm that although each of the communicative abilities has been treated separately they are integrated in real life. One of our principal tasks is to help students build a repertoire of expressions, notions, and ideas that will be available to them. This availability will more easily occur if the expressions, notions, and structures are reintroduced many times in appropriate sociocultural situations (and topics), so that students will learn to *anticipate* them in listening and reading and produce them fluently in their own speech and writing.

Ideas will be recalled more easily if they result from a variety of stimulating viewing and listening experiences to which our learners can relate because they hold affective values for them. We need not say that availability and recall are favored in an accepting, warm classroom atmosphere which only you, the teacher, can create and nurture.[2]

[1] Ann Raimes, *Focus on Composition* (New York: Oxford, 1978).

[2] For examples of drills, see Appendix.

SUGGESTIONS FOR DISCUSSION

1. Why are listening, speaking, reading, and writing called "integrated (integrative)" activities?
2. What should the learners be helped to hear and to identify in a listening activity?
3. What is meant by items which are "high in information"?
4. Describe five "pure" listening activities.
5. Discuss five listening activities which would necessitate the use of the speaking skill as well.
6. Why is speaking considered a more complex skill than listening?
7. List ten activities which would require the learners to speak either after listening or reading.
8. Why are dialogs particularly suited to the development of listening and speaking?
9. Discuss some of the major purposes of reading.
10. What are the teacher's principal responsibilities in developing the reading skill?
11. What are some enabling skills in reading?
12. Explain the techniques of teaching reading in two parallel streams.
13. What steps in the reading process do intensive and extensive reading have in common?
14. What are the important elements in extensive reading?
15. Prepare five reading-related activities for elementary, intermediate, and advanced levels.
16. In the elementary, junior, and senior high schools, what types of writing activities are possible?
17. What are some enabling skills in developing the ability to write?
18. Would you demonstrate giving a dictation to your colleagues?
19. Can you give a dicto-comp? How would you go about it?
20. Select an anecdote or a brief passage and demonstrate giving a listening comprehension task.
21. What are the major steps in a cloze procedure?

22. How could you use a cloze procedure as a diagnostic device?
23. Discuss five guided writing activities.
24. How can we help students toward the writing of longer essays?

7 Strategies: Activities, Tasks, Techniques

In this chapter we have set ourselves three tasks: a.) to discuss some of the interpretative and production activities which will reinforce the knowledge of how and when to use the communicative expressions not only in the situations we have presented but also in numerous others in which they would be appropriate; b.) to review a number of time-honored activities for practicing structures which have been effective with several teaching approaches and which will be found equally effective with the F-N approach; c.) finally, to make some recommendations related to general techniques in classroom procedure which should help sustain the motivation of learners.

INTERPRETATIVE AND PRODUCTIVE ACTIVITIES

An F-N curriculum recommends that recognition and conscious awareness be combined with or precede production. Teacher activities that have been found helpful in bringing about awareness of language communicative use include the following:

Oral

1. Preparing brief statements, utterances, or mini-dialogs incorporating one or more functions within one social situation or work activity and asking the students whether the speech they hear or see is formal, polite, informal, or familiar.
2. Asking what the primary purpose of the message embedded in an utterance, statement, or mini-dialog is, that is, what function the speaker is trying to express.
3. Saying or having students listen to brief conversational exchanges within one functional category and asking them to indicate whether

the second utterance made by the same speaker is appropriate or inappropriate, whether it is of the same level of formality, whether it would be socially acceptable.

4. Describing a situation that highlights a functional category and eliciting whether the short conversational exchange that follows it is appropriate or not.

5. Reading or having students listen to a conversation and helping learners indicate where it is taking place, the social role of the speakers or their attitudes to each other, the major topics of conversation, and its communicative purpose.

6. Giving two utterances made by two different speakers and asking whether the response utterance is appropriate, i.e., of a similar degree of formality or informality possible within the particular function and situation.

7. Making a statement followed by a sequence or comment sentence by the same speaker and asking whether the sequence is appropriate.

8. Presenting a mini-dialog and asking a. whether the "register" is formal, informal, or familiar; and b. what elements in the situation make that register appropriate.

9. Preparing a brief dialog which lends itself to different interpretations depending upon the tone of voice. Saying the dialog and each time asking about the speaker's attitude, "How do you think he felt toward X? When do you think the conversation is taking place? Where?"

Written

These should generally be of the multiple-choice or matching type:

1. Give three sentences and ask which of the three makes a suggestion (or expresses gratitude or some other specific function).

2. Have learners match utterances in two columns which express the same function.

3. Give an utterance with two, three, or four choices of a place where the utterance could be said.

4. Give an utterance and tell which function it expresses.

5. Present an auditory stimulus (a sound or a sequence of sounds) and give two utterances between which the students will choose. For example, the sound is of an approaching train; the utterances may be, "Let's hurry or we'll miss it," and "That sounds frightening."

6. Give a word (or sound) stimulus, for example, *rain*. The two utterances could be, "Let's go to the beach," and "Let's take an umbrella."

158

7. Match *segments* from two columns which will form a logical utterance.

Performance (Production) Activities

Oral
(with Viewing, Reading, Actions, or Writing)

These tasks are not given in order of use. Your choice of any one of these depends on all the factors in the learning situation which have been discussed and any special ones in your circumstances.

Learners may be asked to:
1. Transpose a prepared dialog centered around one or more communicative functions to a formal or less formal style.
2. Dramatize a dialog illustrating (through different intonation patterns) varying emotions, for example, "Is that your new car?" in anger (parent-child) or as a compliment.
3. Ask for information about days, hours, prices, fees, etc., at a museum, a railroad, post office, etc., in the native or target language (where feasible) and report back to the class in the target language.
4. Give utterances which contain the same surface structure but which convey different meanings, asking where each question could have been asked and in what situation, for example, compare "Do you have a match?" and "Do you have a stove?"
5. Give a paraphrase of a single utterance, for example, "Is that your new coat?" spoken in anger and spoken in an admiring tone of voice.
6. Paraphrase utterances or short passages using appropriate alternatives a. in the same register, b. in a different register.
7. Prepare appropriate alternative utterances in a mini or long dialog maintaining the same functional and notional core (that is, the same purpose and topic).
8. Add one or more comment or sequence sentences to one's own statement or question, for example, "It's very hot. Let's go to the beach." or "Would you like a glass of lemonade? You must be very thirsty."
9. Formulate appropriate rejoinders to statements or questions and, conversely, tell what statement or question could have preceded a given response, for example, "Yes, he's gone to Paris," may have been preceded by, "I haven't seen George for a week or so. Do you know whether he's left?"

10. Perform many tasks with previously learned dialogs. Brief dialogs, as we know, are excellent vehicles for production. Two dialogs can be combined to focus on a different function; the original dialog situation can be changed (retaining the function); a familiar dialog can be expanded, with newly acquired language material added appropriately at the beginning or end; questions and answers of all kinds based on the dialogs can be formulated by one group of students and answered by others; original dialogs can be prepared by one group of students and dramatized by others; mini-dialogs can be prepared by a group or a pair of students centered around a function and based on a given situation; the dialog can be changed to reported speech or vice versa. Any of the dialogs can also be dramatized, illustrating different attitudes or emotions. For more advanced students there may be fluency activities of various types.

11. Talk about what they have heard in a speech, a film, or on television. (Their language may vary, from the very simple to the more rich and complex.)

12. Comment on information they have heard in which they can show concern, disagree politely, offer congratulations, or request further explanation.

13. Engage in prepared or spontaneous role-playing when statements are supplied on role-playing cards by the teacher or, for more able students, when only an outline of a situation is given. Ask the other students to tell what the role players tried to convey, where they were, what their attitude to each other was.

14. Cope with embarrassing statements or questions by asking other questions, by moving tactfully to another topic, or by closing the conversation. Ask other students to indicate the communicative strategies used by the speaker.

15. Ask groups of learners to solve a problem. After selecting a problem of relevance to the students (for example, they can't get into their house because no one is home and they have lost the key) have them break up into groups for discussion of the problem; have each group arrive at a decision which is then submitted to the entire class for questions and agreement, doubt, or disagreement.

16. Study many sections of a newspaper depending on their age and interests and comment on, discuss, ask questions, or summarize what has been read after saying which functions have been focused upon. (If no foreign language newspaper exists, native language newspapers or magazines can supply the content for discussion.)

17. Play games in which the students have to guess the locale of a picture

they cannot see and that someone is holding and describing. (The place should be a familiar feature of the native or target culture.)

18. Duplicate a design which has been described or is being described.

19. Compare two pictures or drawings (you can find them in many newspapers) in which the artist omitted or added some elements. Groups of students can study the sketches and report to the class, "There's (a)/There are _____ in"; "There's/There are or There isn't/aren't _____ in _____ ."

20. Study the portrait of a person and tell how old they think the person is, what his occupation probably is, and any other relevant characteristics.

21. Make appointments or reservations for planes, restaurants, concerts, or other places by phone. (A cardboard or toy phone will be useful.)

22. Cancel appointments or reservations, suggesting another time.

23. Listen to a telephone conversation and deduce from the utterances they hear what the person at the other end of the telephone line has said.

24. Study a map of a community or highway (with road signs) and give directions to someone on how to get someplace.

25. Prepare a map based on directions you will give to get to a place, indicating turning points, landmarks, etc.

26. Think of appropriate captions for cartoons.

27. Take telephone messages and report them clearly to the rest of the class.

28. Pretend their briefcase has been stolen. Describe a. what was in the briefcase and b. what the thief looked like.

29. Tell what they would take on a trip and why (nature and purpose of trip, fellow travelers, weight restrictions, etc.)

30. Pretend a crime was committed in their neighborhood and that they have to supply an alibi. (Where were they at the time? What were they doing?) The other students in the class should be asked to judge whether or not the alibi is plausible and tell why they feel that way.

31. Play the roles of some well-known person who lived in the past. (Other class members will guess who the person was.)

32. Simulate brief scenes related to food, for example:

Would you pass the salt please?	Here you are.
Won't you have a (cup of tea)?	Yes, thank you.
Won't you have another (sandwich)?	Yes, thanks very much.
	No, thank you. I can't have anything right now.

May I get you a (cup of coffee)?	Yes, thank you. I'd like one although I know I won't be able to sleep later.
I'd be very grateful if you got me (a cup of tea).	Of course. I'll be happy to.

33. Simulate utterances like those above related to shopping for food or clothing, making reservations, inviting people who will accept or refuse, asking for directions, requesting information.

34. Engage in directed practice related to any function and situation, "Ask X whether she/he knows how to swim," "X tell Y that you never learned how."

35. Say briefly what they would do or say in a certain situation. Here are some examples:
   - Making an appointment (with a doctor, professor, a friend).
   - Breaking an appointment with the same person and trying to arrange another one.
   - Discussing an art exhibit with a friend as you are viewing it and agreeing with each other.
   - Discussing an art exhibit with a friend when you are at home or on the telephone and expressing different viewpoints.
   - Suggesting an outing with a friend on a hot day.
   - Giving an acquaintance advice on courses to take at the school he wants to go to.
   - Giving a member of your family advice about courses, migrating, taking a trip.
   - Complimenting someone on his success.
   - Disagreeing with a friend's opinion.
   - Agreeing with a friend's conviction.
   - Expressing gratitude for a favor received.
   - Persuading someone who seems reluctant to do something for you.
   - Asking about some mutual friend whom you have not seen for several weeks.
   - Asking for directions to a certain place.
   - Asking someone in a foreign country what to call something you wish to buy.
   - Refusing —tactfully—food or drink at a party.

36. Expand the core activity above in one or more ways.

37. Prepare mini-dialogs with a partner on the above situations.

38. Add sequence sentences to the mini-dialogs prepared above.

39. Expand the mini-dialogs by adding other functions, other people, or an incidental (but related) topic of discussion.
40. Prepare a module in which you and a partner will simulate a series of logical, sequential language acts that have been practiced separately. For example, accepting an invitation to a party, getting lost, calling to get better directions, arriving, greeting the hosts, being introduced to other guests.
41. Expand the module above in several ways, e.g., you decide not to go at all, your host becomes angry, your host or another guest offers to come and get you. (You'll have to describe exactly where you are.)
42. Listen to tapes of longer dialogs centering about one or more functions. After a suitable motivation and explanation, they should be played *through* once or twice and general questions can be asked about the main idea. Later, they should be played again but stopped at several (three or four) logical points. Learners can be asked to repeat certain utterances or beginnings of sentences. For example, "What words did X use to invite Y to the movies?" The students' answers may be followed by a brief discussion and a similar question in greater depth. "What words did X use to invite Y to the movies for the following Saturday evening?"

    The tape is turned on again with instructions to the students to listen for something else, e.g., "How did Y apologize for not being able to go?" Then perhaps, "Was X convinced? How do you know? What did you hear him say?" Then at another point, "What did X say to convince Y to go to the movies? At still another point, "Was Y convinced? How do you know?"
43. Outline the possible utterances in the dialog above.
44. Prepare a dialog with a partner on any topic which lends itself to similar treatment, e.g., you should stop smoking; you should see a doctor; you should change your job; etc.

Written

Except when it is a culmination of group discussion, we would recommend that written activities should not be done in class. The lesson should be devoted primarily to listening-speaking activities and, at later levels, to reading-speaking or oral preparation of written essays.

Most of the tasks listed above could be written out but there are also several other brief written activities which have been found particularly useful.

Written activities for individuals, pairs, groups, or classes may include:

1. Completing a dialog when words are omitted either at random or at the end of each utterance.
2. Completing a dialog when entire utterances are omitted.
3. Preparing mini-dialogs based on a carefully outlined situation and revolving around one or more functions.
4. Preparing multifunctional dialogs based on a stimulus sentence or on a cue word alone.
5. Paraphrasing mini-dialogs, that is, using utterances which express the same communicative function but with different words and structures.

   Paraphrasing—that is, using alternative utterances—is essential if learners are to move beyond the confines of the textbook and be made to realize that the dialogs they have learned will never occur in exactly the same way in actual conversation with native speakers. The way each speaker uses the language is a result of his background of experiences, frames of reference, and personality.
6. Filling in a dialog when the speaker and listener have little or no prior knowledge of what will be heard or said.

   For example:
   A _____ change—money here?
   B _____ identity card?
   A _____ passport?
   B _____ lapsed.
   A _____ do now?

7. Expanding a basic dialog around a function (see pp. 81–83), e.g., expressing gratitude. Core dialog: making little of the favor done; expanded version: explaining that X had always wanted to do Y a favor because their parents had come from the same town (or anything the learners wish to say).
8. Rewriting groups of words from two columns to make acceptable utterances centered about a communicative expression.
9. Changing reported speech to dialog form.
10. Changing a dialog to reported speech.
11. Preparing several core modules on a delimited work activity. (Give the situation—people, place, setting, job.) This can be a group or pair activity.
12. Expanding the core modules above in any appropriate way.
13. Summarizing a dialog, a text, or a unit of discourse.

14. Writing a brief essay in which they discuss two possible points of view of a controversial subject.

TIME-HONORED TASKS AND ACTIVITIES

Oral guided production activities for practicing discrete communicative expressions, structures, and other lexical items are many and varied. Your choice should depend not only on the learning level and age of the learners but also on the structure being presented and, where feasible, on the native language of the learners. Not all drills are equally effective with all language items. With some structures—the placement of adjectives, for example—integration and expansion exercises would be appropriate. With others, conversion (or transformation) activities—changing one verb aspect to another, for example—would be more appropriate.

These tasks and activities have been and are still used in other teaching approaches. They are still valid and appropriate with the F-N approach but they are a means to a functional end, not the end itself. While some are primarily intended to make the use of certain linguistic features automatic, others demand the more active, mental involvement and total participation of the learners.

All the tasks and activities will contribute to the development of fluency and reasonable accuracy in speaking and in writing and to a firmer grasp of listening and reading skills. Today, the idea that the ability to speak fluently without necessarily achieving complete accuracy has gained increasing currency. Again, however, the amount of time and effort to be devoted to helping students attain grammatical accuracy will depend on numerous factors, not the least of which is consensus on the part of all teachers in the community and country that fluency should take precedence over accuracy. Essential also, would be to ascertain the use to which our students wish to put the language they are learning. Future teachers or broadcasters, for example, should express themselves both accurately and fluently and should be helped to achieve active control of grammatical and lexical items. In other jobs and professions, some linguistic features may remain receptive/interpretative, that is, the learners will understand them but not necessarily use them in speaking or writing.

Widely used habit-forming or skill-building exercises include *repetition*, single or multiple slot *substitution*, *replacement*, *expansion*, *reduction* and *integration* or *embedding*. In some school systems *translation* may be advocated and may be an effective means of integrating language skills, as well as a means of analysis of language in context (by translation is meant the use of semantically equivalent expressions and not word for word transfer).

Discussion and exemplification of habit-forming drills can be found in many methodology texts (e.g., Finocchiaro and Bonomo 1973; Robinett 1978; Celce-Murcia and McIntosh 1979). A teacher using the F-N curriculum should be able to use such procedures skillfully, for they have been found useful by many students, particularly as a means of becoming sensitive to correct forms of strongly ingrained errors. Short and intensive repetition exercises have a place in initial presentation of pronunciation and structural work, but it is essential that such procedures are only used briefly (just long enough to enable students to get some "feel" for the correct form). The justification of the F-N approach is that it enables students to move rapidly to appropriate language use, so it must be clear that drilling is, for the students, a means to an end, and a means which occupies only a small amount of class time.

BASIC TECHNIQUES

All teachers develop a stock of procedures which help to motivate learning. Some of these are not the particular province of second language learning, nor indeed, of any special stage in the teaching process. They are basic techniques with which good teachers improvise in response to the needs of the class, or of individual students, at a particular time.

You undoubtedly do many of the things listed below. We have selected them because we have found them particularly pertinent and fruitful in developing language use.

1. Use the probable experiences of your learners as the starting point for motivating the presentation of any functional expression, structure, or notion.
2. In presenting a new word or concept, use *yourself and* the *students* (clothing, addresses, activities) wherever possible to clarify the meaning and to associate sounds and concepts. Reinforce this initial association through pictures, objects, etc., but use yourself and the students first.
3. Assemble a picture file of individual persons and items, a series of situational pictures with people and items, and a series of situational pictures with people and items seen in an experiential setting. The pictures should be related to the categories in the spiral Sociocultural Themes (p. 36) and to any theme of interest to *your* students.

4. Spend very little time giving the meaning of an isolated word. To ensure meaning, use yourself and the students, show a picture, pantomime an action, or draw something quickly on the board. Remember always to insert the word in a normal utterance using familiar expressions or structures.

5. Devise hand signals which you have carefully explained to your students. Use these to vary the participation of learners and to ask for choral, group, or individual response; for forming groups, or pairs; for rapid practice or fluency work; or for moving from one activity to another in the classroom. Discuss with the students, particularly in areas of the world where pointing may be considered impolite, that pointing or signaling saves times for the important work of the language class—listening and speaking by the students.

6. At beginning and intermediate levels, develop a pattern of interaction with your students and among them. The following has been found effective:

   Teacher model: repetition by class, half-class, smaller groups, and individuals. (It is desirable to start with your more able students first.)

   Teacher-individual student: the teacher asks the question or makes the first statement. The student responds.

   Student-student: in chain drills, group and paired practice, or random selection of two students from any part of the room.

7. Keep the pace of the lesson brisk. a. Write all cue words on a card which you will hold in your left hand. b. Establish a definite order for individual practice or for chain practice—again in the interest of saving time. It is important, however, to ensure the active involvement of all class members even during rote drill (drill "around the room") or chain practice. Through prearranged hand signals, you may quickly indicate that a group in another section of the room is to start a new chain or to continue a drill.

8. Good questioning techniques are essential. One procedure follows:
   A. In order to ensure the participation of everyone, ask a question.
   B. Allow a few moments for *everyone* to think of the answer.
   C. Call on one student—by name or by gesture.
   D. If the student called upon cannot give the answer, you may do one of two things: 1. give him the answer and have him repeat it, or 2. call on another student to give the answer. You may then ask the first student to repeat the correct answer. This should be done only if you are sure that the student who made the error and the one making the correction have a good personal relationship. In general, it is more desirable for you merely to say, "Listen,"

followed by the question, statement, or response in which there was an error *impeding comprehension*. (If necessary, have the class or group practice briefly the item or answer which caused difficulty.)

9. With further relation to questioning, it is unwise to elicit a *choral* response to a question. Students may give varied answers to what you may consider a simple question, e.g., "What day is today?" thus causing disorder or confusion. By dividing the class into *groups*, you can practice choral questions and answers *based on your initial model*. (One group will ask the question; the other will answer.)

10. In general, you will find it desirable to call on the more able students first. This will give the others more practice in hearing and in silently rehearsing answers that will probably be correct.

11. If the same question will be asked of several students, you may wish to repeat the correct response without having to tell a student who has just answered that he has made errors in pronunciation. A good way of giving the model response yourself is by asking a student or several students individually to ask you the question.

12. Short answers, one-word answers, and "yes" and "no" answers are not merely permissible in the language class—they are desirable since they are the more normal forms of real-world speech. If you wish to practice "complete" sentences, set up situations which normally call for them, e.g., "What did you do last night?" or practice them in writing.

13. Motivate each new step in the lesson. Use transition (introductory) sentences from one activity to the other so as to relate what has just been done to what is going to be done. For example, after giving the vocabulary needed for the dialog or reading selection, you might say, "Now that we've learned some of the words people use in talking about...."

14. Discourage lengthy pauses for guessing. Supply the answer.

15. If many students have trouble with an activity, for example, a substitution drill, go back to the repetition step of your lesson. If necessary, go back and present again the aspect of the expression or structure causing the problem.

16. Focus attention on the items being taught. If students ask questions about matters that are extraneous or tangential to what you are doing, tell them you will "get to that" shortly or ask them to see you after class. Don't discourage questioning, however.

17. Although students may make pronunciation errors at several points in their response, concentrate on correcting only one or two sounds

during any one session. Moreover, if a student is expressing an idea, try to avoid interrupting. When he has completed the utterance, *say something complimentary* and then make one or two corrections. In this way, you will avoid discouraging students. Remember that high student motivation smooths the difficult task of language learning. Always praise whatever can be praised.

18. Although different intonations and word combinations may be possible—depending upon the situation, the emotional implication, or other factors—in the early stages, it is desirable to practice only one intonation and one form for each utterance. There are important exceptions to this rule, however. For example, in teaching a simple greeting formula such as, "How *are* you?" it is necessary, in order to maintain authenticity, to train your students to give the normal response form, "I'm fine, thank you. How are *you?*" In general, it is wise to help the students learn one way or one meaning thoroughly (the most frequently used with a person at a certain age level or in an important social role) before drawing attention to an alternate form or a different meaning.

19. If you require marks or grades, give short announced tests often on the items you have been practicing. Give longer tests occasionally—at the end of a unit or module or when the school requires them.

20. Clarify all directions in the textbook and in your test questions. Give several illustrations of what you expect of the students. Use the native language of the students if necessary.

21. Present related forms together. For example, we present together *I, you, we, they* in English because in simple tenses and many of the compound ones they govern identical verb forms. Choose vocabulary items carefully. For example, present and practice plurals with /z/ together and then with /əz/ or /s/. After these have been thoroughly practiced, use the principle of "conscious selection" by "mixing" the forms and encouraging the students to make the correct choice. (Use visual aids where possible to facilitate the task.)

22. When the students repeat in chorus, do not repeat *with* them after the first two or three times. This will enable you to detect problems which may require brief practice or changing a learner's seat so he will be placed with other learners who have a better pronunciation or are more fluent.

23. When you give homework, assign it (in writing on the chalkboard preferably) *at the beginning of the hour* even though the homework assignment will be an outgrowth of the lesson you are planning to teach that hour. (Let the students write it in their notebooks as soon as

they enter the room.) Have it corrected by asking several students to read out one sentence or to write it on the chalkboard at the beginning of the next hour, particularly if the new lesson presupposes an understanding of the previous lesson. Often give them the chance to revise their own work in pairs or groups before you see it.

24. Prepare visual materials which will lend interest to your teaching. *Flannel boards, pocket charts, vocabulary wheels,* and *flannel-backed pictures* which can be moved from place to place are very effective. Learn about materials in other subject areas which you may use with profit in the language class.

25. Set up a library corner with books and magazines related to the students' interests and needs in the target language.

26. Tell the students what is expected of them—on the very first day of the first semester. Teach the words *look, listen, repeat, say, ask,* and *answer* as early in the semester as possible.

27. When you think it is necessary, simplify listening and reading passages at two levels of difficulty before asking learners to hear or read the original version. Ask different types of questions for each version, for example, *Yes/No* questions for the simplest version, *Wh* questions for the second version, and these plus *inferential* questions for the original version. In the first version depending on the learning level, we would omit *subordinate clauses* and many *adjectives* and *adverbs*. In the second, we would reinsert the adjectives and adverbs.

28. Do everything within your power to help the students retain pride in their native language and culture.

29. Sustain motivation by giving students a feeling of achievement and success. Help them to say increasingly longer utterances fluently or to give one or two sequential utterances after their initial statement.

30. Motivation is fostered also when students realize that the same communicative expression can be used in numerous real-life situations and with a variety of topics.

31. Since "composition" writing is frightening to some students, allow us, please, to make some suggestions.
    • When you plan to assign an essay of several paragraphs, go over ideas with your students; discuss the appropriate informational sequence; supply some expressions, structures, and notions.
    • Allow five minutes in class for the students to begin writing their introductory paragraph.
    • Give them a few days to write their composition.
    • Do not cover the composition they give you with red ink. Merely underline the errors and write a symbol above the word, e.g., T (for

tense), Sp (spelling), N (notion), F (function). (You will have gone over the symbols beforehand.) You may prefer to ask that a one-inch margin be left at the right or left side of the paper. This will be divided into seven columns: F (function), Sp (spelling), M (mechanics), N (notion), St (structure), Seq (sequence of ideas), R (register—formality or informality). Again, you will underline the error and put a check in the appropriate column containing the error.

- Give them a few days to rewrite the composition, returning the original and the corrected one.
- Do *not* grade all compositions. *Before* you assign grades, discuss with students the points to be taken off for each type of error. (If the same error reoccurs in the composition, take points off *only one time*.)

In conclusion, each and every class activity should be designed to encourage the students to communicate and interact with you and with each other. Study pictures, practice in pairs, dramatize, or play games, but make certain that your students grow in communicative competence as they do so. Even more important, ensure—through your humane and humanistic approach—that they remain well-integrated individuals and that they grow spiritually and intellectually as they grow in communicative competence.

SUGGESTIONS FOR DISCUSSION[1]

1. Discuss five oral interpretative (recognition) activities related particularly to an F-N curriculum. Give examples.
2. List five written interpretative activities.
3. Discuss ten oral performance activities giving examples of utterances, or mini-dialogs.
4. How would you prepare learners for later spontaneous role-playing from the very beginning of the language program?
5. Demonstrate the use in class of activities 21, 22, 23, 25, and 27 above on p. 161. Use the actual words of the speakers.
6. Prepare five written mini-dialogs. Then rewrite them using alternative utterances, or changing the order of the utterances but retaining the same function, situation, and topic.
7. Paraphrase a dialog found in any one of your textbooks.
8. Write a core dialog which could stand alone. Then expand it by introducing another function in it. (See pp. 81-3 for examples.)
9. Why is it desirable to put cue words to be used in drills on small cards?
10. What guidelines should you observe in preparing tasks and activities for practicing the discrete items of language?
11. Why should one start the presentation of some language element or skill by relating it to the pupils' experiences?
12. Why are hand signals preferable to utterances in calling for repetition?
13. State the four steps in a possible teacher-student interaction pattern.
14. How can questioning be made effective?
15. What strategies should you use in correcting students' oral errors?
16. Why should related forms be presented and practiced together?
17. When and how should homework be assigned and corrected?
18. How might longer "compositions" be marked for errors? What system of grading do you generally use in grading compositions?

See further discussion of strategies in Appendix.

8 Learning Resources and Materials of Instruction

We should like to begin this chapter by reaffirming our basic credo about learning and teaching: you, the teacher, are the crucial resource in the instructional process. It is only you who can create the favorable classroom climate which will promote a mutually accepting relationship among your students and between you and your students. You are able to do this because you make your learners aware of your liking and respect for them and because you are always ready to demonstrate your obvious enthusiasm for the language you are teaching and for the native speakers of that language. You are of primary importance in engendering and sustaining your learners' motivation through your organization of materials which are effective in presenting and practicing communicative activities and your willingness to adapt your students' textbook—adding mini-dialogs and illustrations, doubling the number of utterances in a difficult task, and, most important, setting aside material which is not of high frequency for your particular students during that specific year.

Only through the attitudes and the planning noted above can you give each learner a feeling of success and achievement which is essential in learning. While you, the teacher, can accomplish this through your preparation and actions alone, we would like to urge that you consider some simple materials which are generally at your fingertips before mentioning some available commercial equipment—none of which is indispensable, however.

Let us begin this discussion by talking about those instructional aids which are generally "ready, willing, and able."

THE TEACHER, THE LEARNERS, AND THE CLASSROOM ITSELF

Teacher and Learners

Your hands, arms, face, and clothing can be used effectively in several ways. You can, for example, indicate the type of pupil participation you desire by:

• Making an encircling gesture with both arms if the entire class is to repeat after you.

• Indicating whether a row or a small group is to repeat.

• Lifting your right arm with the palm of your hand turned away from you when you would like the half of the class on the right side of the room to repeat and doing the same with your left arm for the left side of the class.

• Pointing to individual students who are expected to repeat, react, or respond—explaining in advance that pointing saves time and does not interpose a name between your model utterance and student repetition of the model.

• Encouraging learners to turn towards each other for paired practice activities.

• Using a downward movement of your right arm to indicate falling intonation and an upward movement for rising intonation.

• Demonstrating the relationship of the lips and tongue in producing sounds.

• Demonstrating rounded or stretched lips and open or closed jaw in making particular sounds.

• Placing your fingers on your vocal chords (inviting your learners to do the same) to distinguish between a voiced and a voiceless sound.

• Blowing on a piece of paper in front of your lips (encouraging your students to imitate you) in order to indicate a phoneme produced with a puff of air as the /p/ in English, for example, in pull, and /p/ with no puff of air as in spill or cup.

• Pointing to yourself, items of clothing you are wearing, things you are carrying to teach notions, structures, and communicative expressions.

When you indicate items of clothing, for example, follow this step by a. indicating similar items worn by your students (or pictures of the same items); b. sweeping your hand over the entire item. This would be true for teaching a word as simple as pencil, for example. If you show only a long, yellow pencil with an eraser (depending on how you are holding the pencil) and you do not dramatize the action of writing, learners may mistake the concept pencil for yellow, long, or eraser. It is desirable, therefore, to show several pencils: long, short, of different colors, and with or without erasers.

174

Parts of the Room

Many structures and vocabulary items can be presented and practiced by pointing to or touching various parts of the room or asking students (younger ones particularly) to walk to various parts of the room. (Questions such as, "What's he doing?" "Where did she go?" "Where was he?" "Where is he now?" etc., can be used to practice location and verb tenses or aspects.)

The seating arrangements can be utilized most effectively to teach ordinal numbers ("Who's sitting in the first row, third seat?"), as well as utterances with prepositions followed by one-word responses or by a name and an appropriate short form of the verb, for example, "Who's sitting *next to/ near/ in back of/ in front of/* you or X?" "Joe" or "Joe is."

The chalkboard (if one exists) can be a worthy supplement. Here are some of the uses you can make of it.

• Sketch (or ask a student to sketch) simple stick figures on the board or paper to indicate the speakers in a conversation. Point to each as he speaks.

(a boy) (an older man) (a girl) (an older woman) .

• Sketch simple faces to indicate young, old, sad, happy, tired, hungry, sleepy, angry.
• Sketch a number of stick figures to teach, "How many people are there?" "How many women (boys, men, girls)? Erase one or more and elicit answers to, "How many were there?" "How many (boys) are there now?"
• List hours on the board and practice greetings and leave-takings for the hours listed—pretending at times that you are greeting someone your age, someone older, someone you don't know very well.
• With younger children, teach concepts of weather daily by drawing the sun, rain, an umbrella or snow, either on a large calendar or separately in one corner of the chalkboard.
• Teach prepositions by drawing a square (representing a park, a plaza, or a public square) and with broken lines indicating *around, to the end of, through* or *across, on the other side,* etc.
• Use lines to introduce comparisons (longer, shorter, higher, longest, etc.). (It is not a good idea *ever* to ask students to come to the front of the room to represent *short, shorter, shortest.*)
• The verb chart on p. 123 should be sketched on the board so that it can be used whenever any tense or aspect is presented.
• Model sentences containing communicative expressions can be written on the board for repetition and more intensive study. The significant

175

parts and/or the relationships among them may be underlined. Drawing stick figures of children of the same age, children and older people, people having different social roles next to each utterance will clarify the use of familiar or polite language.

• Intonation lines and arrows (rising or falling at the end of the utterance) can be drawn permitting you to sweep your fingers under the lines to indicate the change of pitch, and to indicate rising or falling intonations.

• Prefixes and suffixes can be listed to be used in conjunction with the word chart on p. 103.

• Cognates in L_1 and L_2 (words having the same root and a similar meaning) should be written under each other so that the similarity becomes apparent.

• Utterances in which redundant features can be found should be placed on the board. In English, for example, *many* at the beginning of a sentence signals two important points needed for listening comprehension and writing: the nouns will be plural; the verbs will also be plural.

• In teaching reading, the board can be used to list words or cultural allusions which may present difficulties, as well as to list questions, incomplete sentences, or multiple choice items which learners will look for as they read silently (see p. 147).

• In guiding students' writing, short model utterances or paragraphs may be placed on the board to be transposed to another register, connected, placed in proper sequence, or paraphrased.

• It is *not* a good idea to place out-of-sequence words next to each other for students to put into appropriate, informational order. It is not only a waste of time but the incorrect sentence on the board may be remembered by some students. If you do want to reinforce knowledge of word order (where this is an important feature of your target language) place five or six words under each other.

• By the same token, if you wish students to reconstruct a sentence, use slash marks, e.g., John/go/beach/yesterday//play baseball. (Learners would have had prior practice in reconstructing sentences like that to read, "John went to the beach yesterday. He did not play baseball.") Notice the double slash lines before "play baseball" which signal a new (but sequential) sentence. Notice, moreover, that it would be most undesirable to give that type of sentence orally.

There are numerous other uses of the chalkboard. Allow us to mention two: a. In doing group work, write the specific assignment for each group on the board. b. At beginning levels, when giving practice in pairs, write the model pair of sentences on the board and, under the appropriate slot, indicate eight or ten words which can be used in place of the word in the model. (Later, students may use any appropriate word.)

REAL OBJECTS

A collection of everyday objects can be of great help in enabling learners to
a. associate concept and sound, b. contextualize notions in authentic
speech acts, c. prepare sustained or mini-dialogs, d. engage in role-playing
and dramatization of all kinds, and e. play language games (for example,
"Kim's Game," where they are given thirty seconds to see several objects
and then say what they saw).

Train, bus, or plane tickets; menus; small flags; buttons made of
different materials and in different sizes; cartons and containers; puppets
(made of paper bags or pieces of cloth) of different colors and weaves;
thermometers; books; magazines; newspapers; calendars; and a cardboard
clock with movable hands can all be effective. Where students are studying
the target language in their native country, artifacts of their native land are
essential to give them a feeling of pride in their culture and to enable them
to use the target language terms for the artifacts in real communicative
exchanges. This will help them realize that the new language is an
instrument of communication as is their native tongue. Similarly with
younger children they may assist simulation.

PICTURES

A file of simple pictures is invaluable. Each language teacher may have a
file—prepared by him, the students, parents, or community aides. A school
picture file may be kept in a central office. (Teachers can indicate on a
sheet of paper which category they will need during which week.) This is
not an ideal situation but we can learn to live with it if we do not have our
own classroom. Another solution would be to keep the file at home and to
bring to class the pictures which will be needed for a particular teaching
lesson.

Some criteria to be used to make the pictures effective for class use
include the following. They should be
- Large enough to be seen from all parts of the room.
- Clear and simple in design.
- Without captions (so that they can be used for diverse purposes).
- Both in black and white and in color for practice in more advanced
units.

• There should be more than one picture of each concept: person, animal, or thing in different situations for the reasons mentioned below on this page. The pictures should be kept in categories related to the cyclical topics on pp. 71–4 and their importance in your teaching situation. A box of flash cards corresponding to the name of each item (person, thing, or animal) in the pictures should be available in order that young beginners, adult illiterates, functional illiterates, or students who need to be given individualized instruction can match the picture and the associated word. For teacher use, the back of the picture may contain an indication of the subject to avoid turning the pictures when engaging in contextualized substitution, replacement, or other drills.
• Where feasible, there could be two pictures files: one with pictures related to the lives and experiences of learners in their native land; one with pictures related to the target country.

PICTURE CHARTS

There are numerous kinds which can be used to motivate learning and develop fluency. Several practical examples are suggested here:

1. A series of pictures containing *count* and *mass nouns* separately and others containing count and mass together, can be used to present and practice practically every communicative expression and structure in a number of languages. The same series can be used at all levels of learning. In harmony with the spiral approach recommended, the familiar notions can be used in increasingly longer (more complex) single utterances or—by the same speaker—in multiple utterances. Learners will not be bored with the same vocabulary because they will be using it to talk about a variety of situations and topics in more complex utterances.

2. A chart with clocks showing morning routines can also be used at various levels.
   • What time is it? What do you see?
   • What's the person doing?
   • What did he do before having breakfast? Did he have breakfast before he got dressed?
   • What time did he leave the house?
   • What time did he get the bus/the train?
   • What time did he get to work/school?

3. Two pictures of people performing some action placed side by side

178

can elicit not only the answer to, "What's she/he doing?" but "What was he doing while she was (sew)ing?" "What does he usually do while she (sew)s?" etc.

4. Three separate foldable stacks of pictures with six rings on top can be used most effectively. The first stack can contain pictures of individuals, couples, groups, people playing or walking with animals; the second stack can contain pictures of places; the third, means of transportation. These, too, can be used at all levels with groups of students flipping the pictures over in order to provide *varied utterance combinations*, for example, individual pictures showing:

Who's this? That's (Mr.) _____
What's this? A library.
What's this? A bicycle.

Two pictures (people and places)
Where is (Mr. X) going? To the library.
Where did Mr. and Mrs. X go? To the post office.
Where are Mr. and Mrs. X going later?

Three pictures (using all tenses and verb aspects)
(Ms.) K is going to the library by car.
Mr. and Mrs. X went to the park by bus.
You or a student may point to one of the three stacks to elicit questions with *who, with whom, how,* or *where.*

As you can see, the possibilities for presentation, practice, and creativity are many and varied. The students can say anything they wish about the two or three pictures they have before them.

MISCELLANEOUS CHARTS

Many useful charts can be prepared and hung on a line if necessary with clothespins. Charts which can be used to sustain motivation and enrich learning include: the verb chart (see p. 123); a list of topics for discussion relevant to the learners' ages and interests; a face indicating vocal organs; the Vowel Triangle for daily ten-second practice; clustered formats centering around one or more communicative functions.

OTHER TEACHER-MADE MATERIALS

Flash Cards

These should include expressions, groups of words, or single words and numbers. As noted above, pictures and cards may be matched; the cards can be used in brisk substitution drills as the last step in a series of cues; two action words can be used to practice making suggestions, refusing but offering an alternative, to practice structures such as, "I like _____ but Y prefers to _____ , (or) enjoys _____ more."

Flash cards can be given to group leaders to play games, create dialogs, engage in problem-solving, or prepare crossword puzzles.

The Pocket Chart

This can be made inexpensively with a piece of cardboard and three cardboard strips. It can be used for numerous purposes: to dramatize word order; to reinforce the use of a form of *do* with questions; to teach *not* with *let's*, negatives with *be*, negatives with regular verbs, etc.

It has been used most effectively in preparing language (reading) experience charts with young learners or illiterates. Simply stated, the learners in a class-wide activity—or an individual—engage in an experience (feeding fish, playing ball, jumping rope, taking the subway for the first time, shopping in a supermarket, etc.). He tells the teacher about the experience, who, in turn, prepares three short sentences from what is said and places them on individual word cards with appropriate punctuation in each pocket of the chart. The student learns to read it, copy it, take cards out, and recall what each card said, etc. These personal language experience charts are copied into the student's notebook and later transformed to the plural, the negative, the past, etc.

In order to simplify the use of the language material for the *class* pocket chart it is recommended that separate small envelopes be kept with punctuation marks, communicative expressions, subject pronouns, some base verbs, the major morphological changes in your target language, and whatever else you use frequently.

It would be a good idea in regular (extensive) courses, for each learner to make his own pocket chart so that he can perform the same manipulations as the teacher is doing in the main pocket chart. An individual chart is particularly essential for the "language experience" technique noted above.

The Flannel Board

This is the less expensive and simpler-to-carry version of the magnet board. Moreover, the flannel board has other advantages. Not only can a piece of flannel be glued or tacked to the back of the pocket chart, but it can also be thrown over the back of a chair or taped to the chalkboard.

Furthermore, the objects to be placed on it can either be made with other pieces of flannel (flannel adheres to flannel) or on thin cardboard on the back of which you have pasted a piece of flannel or a piece of sand (emery) paper.

Let us outline several ways of using the flannel board to present, practice, dramatize, or enrich innumerable language items.

• To play games, for example, a large figure of a boy is cut up, then put together, then clothed; we talk about his illnesses (stomachache or sore throat); we put on and take off his jacket, tie, shoes, etc.

• To tell folk or fairy tales in logical sequence—"Goldilocks and the Three Bears," "The Three Little Pigs," "Cinderella"—and for little ones— "The Little Engine That Could" provide enjoyment while reinforcing language. Remember that the figures can be stick figures and that settings can be represented by a single object, e.g., one tree is a garden or park, a stove is the kitchen, a bed is the bedroom, etc. Remember that any object represents what you and your students decide it is.

• To practice personal pronouns, ages, and comparative. Prepare ten name cards, five with boys' names and five with girls. Then prepare ten cards with numbers (two of the cards should have the same number). Place the boys' names in one column with an age card next to each and the girls' names in another column. Practice utterances such as:

> Joe is twelve.
> How old is Jane? She's fourteen.
> Which boys are the same age?
> Who's older, Joe or Jane?
> Is Jane younger/older than Jack?
> Who's the oldest?

• Prepositions and phrases of place can be practiced through table settings or through the use of a flannel (or cardboard) table and a small colored circle or square. Utterances such as, "Could you put the glass to the right of the plate?" "Where's the ball? Is it under the table/on the table/next to the table, etc.," can be practiced.

• Another very interesting form of communicative and structural practice involves making stick figures of people, places, and things and simple symbols, for example, a "?" to indicate a question, an "X" to indicate the negative, an "→" to indicate *going to* or *went*, an "←" to indicate *he'll be back/come back*, a "ᴧ" to indicate a place. (Under the place may be a tree, a book, a loaf of bread, or whatever, as symbols of park, library, bakery, etc.)

Questions and responses such as:

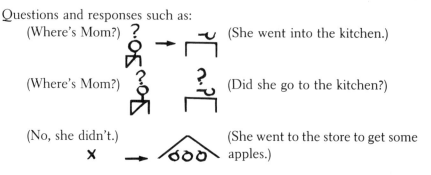

(Where's Mom?)   (She went into the kitchen.)

(Where's Mom?)   (Did she go to the kitchen?)

(No, she didn't.)   (She went to the store to get some apples.)

Songs and Games

In extensive courses and even in intensive, short-term courses, songs and games can make for an enjoyable change of pace while reinforcing language. Books of games and songs are recommended but we would like to add a personal observation. Many educators prefer that the music and the words of a song be those of the target country. We have found that students enjoy writing target language words to well-known native language songs and vice versa. And why not? We have heard "Frère Jacques" in at least ten languages. It lost nothing in adaptation. And what about "Parlez-moi d'amour"? Delightful in any number of languages.

COMMERCIALLY AVAILABLE EQUIPMENT

We move now from inexpensive teacher-made materials to more expensive electrical equipment. We shall only mention these since many excellent books have been written on the subject but we shall permit ourselves one or two comments.

Language laboratories, film strips, television programs, overhead or opaque projectors, films, and other machines our technological age will devise could, of course, vitalize teaching. Films, particularly, could illustrate aspects of the target culture which explanation could not equal. But none of them is indispensable. There are only two components in the learning-teaching process that we cannot do without—the learners and the teachers.

We should like to make a few—a very few—comments on some of the equipment mentioned above:

1. A language laboratory—except in crash, intensive courses—should be used after your initial oral presentation in class. Language laboratory work should be preceded and followed by work in the classroom which will a. prepare learners for the type of listening, speaking or listening, or writing that they will be expected to do in the laboratory; and b. permit them to demonstrate in the classroom their increased knowledge of whatever they had practiced. Playback facilities are generally not useful at very beginning levels where learners are not really capable of hearing their mistakes. Self-checking devices for upper level students should be made available in the laboratory. A good tape recorder or cassette recorder in a classroom could be used effectively for listening comprehension and for giving dictations or dicto-comps with about forty students.

2. Except at advanced levels (unless the sound is turned off) filmstrips or videotapes are more useful than films since they can be turned back instantly to focus upon a scene, a caption, or whatever.

3. Live radio broadcasts (except at advanced levels and then only with motivating questions and prior clarification of purpose, topic, setting, notions, and cultural allusions) should be taped and simplified as suggested on p. 170.

In conclusion, everything we have mentioned above (except for you, the teacher, and your learners) should be included in your teaching plans if they answer all or most of these questions affirmatively: Do they help the students maintain a positive self-image? Do they enable them to develop attitudes of appreciation toward the target language and its speakers and of other people they may meet later? Will they give the learners the potential and the motivation to continue their studies? Will they bring them closer to the attainment of communicative competence—our primary goal in language learning?

SUGGESTIONS FOR DISCUSSION

1. How can the teacher use her hands and arms to clarify difficulties or to request specific student responses?
2. What cautions should be used in presenting vocabulary items?
3. How can seating arrangements and parts of the room be used to teach prepositions or ordinals?
4. How can the chalkboard be used effectively? Give ten examples of its possible use.
5. Mention some real objects which would be easy for you or your students to gather.
6. What criteria should be used in selecting or sketching pictures?
7. Why should there be more than one picture of each concept?
8. What might the main headings of your picture file be?
9. Give ten different utterances (progressively more complex) which could be used with *each* picture of a series of count nouns starting with a communicative expression.
10. Do the same for a series of mass nouns.
11. Prepare ten sentence patterns that you could practice with the three stacks of pictures on rings, using appropriate communicative expressions.
12. Prepare a vowel chart, a verb chart, and a list of twenty topics which would be relevant to your students' interests.
13. Mention several ways in which you could use flash cards to teach pronunciation, communicative expressions, structures, and notions.
14. Talk about three ways in which you could use the pocket chart.
15. Talk about five ways of using a flannel board.
16. What advantage does a flannel board have over a magnet board?
17. Make a flannel board with name and number cards. Prepare practice activities with pronouns, comparatives, and ages using questions and statements.
18. What is your experience with a language laboratory? How have you used it effectively?
19. What electric equipment (overhead projector, opaque projector, other) is available in your school? How have you used these effectively?

184

9 Evaluation

We have chosen to use the term "evaluation" instead of testing because we consider it much broader and therefore more suited to our purpose. For we wish not only to measure the growth of our learners toward the goals set for them in the curriculum but the curriculum itself: the activities recommended in it for enabling our students to attain its objectives in the shortest possible time; the effectiveness of materials of instruction; our own presentation and practice strategies for bringing about the desired growth toward goals which are relevant to our pupils, in our school and in our community.

SOME "WH" QUESTIONS

There are several important questions that we should keep in mind as we plan our testing program for the academic "year"—whatever its duration. What kinds of tests are generally used in language testing? Why do we test? When? How? What do we test? What criteria should we consider in planning tests? What do we do with test results?

What Kinds of Tests Can Be Used?[1]
There are several types of tests.

1. Aptitude tests (also called prognostic tests)—before a person starts a program, to determine whether or not he will be successful in language study. The test measures such factors as short term memory; ability to associate sounds and pictures; and the ability to make structural generalizations (by recognizing the same part of speech, or grammatical or communicative function in different sentences). We

Material on testing reprinted from *The Foreign Language Learner* by Mary Finocchiaro and Michael Bonomo (1973) and *English as a Second Language: From Theory to Practice* by Mary Finocchiaro (1974) with permission from Regents Publishing Company, Inc., 2 Park Avenue, New York, NY 10016.

are suspicious of these. Not only do we not think that a person's "aptitude" remains stable—and we do not know enough about the human mind to make hypotheses about the role of aptitude in language learning—but, more importantly, we have often found that an enthusiastic, patient, well-prepared teacher can overcome poor "aptitude" if it does in fact exist.

2. Proficiency tests—to measure what a person already knows in the target language a) whether or not he has studied the language in a formal learning situation, and b) with whatever textbook or material he may have used. The Council of Europe plans to use proficiency tests widely in granting credits to newcomers (both youngsters and adults) to a different school system in the same or a different country, and the unit-credit system specifically assists this.

3. Achievement tests—to be used daily; weekly; after the completion of a unit, module, or text segment; or at the end of the academic year to determine the degree to which the various enabling skills or terminal goals for a particular corpus of material have been attained.

4. Diagnostic tests (which may be part of achievement tests)—to note strengths, weaknesses, or problems in some area of knowledge or skill.

Why Do We Test?

There are various reasons why we test, the most important of which is to give a learner—and parents in the case of youngsters—a report on the progress the learner has made towards the attainment of goals. We test to move the person who is having problems to another group in the same classroom, to certify that he can progress to the next level in a regular program, to award credits for units or modules completed which will be accepted by another region or country, to ensure an employer or a professional graduate school that the person can function in the work or school situation.

Other reasons for testing are a) to set realistic standards for our students and schools, b) to measure the effects of experimentation (e.g., what advantages or disadvantages are there in beginning to teach a foreign language in the first grade of elementary school when the child is not living in the target language country?), c) to retain the confidence of the community in the instructional program, d) to ensure that many persons in the community or country will be able to communicate appropriately with others at all levels of public life.

When Do We Test?

Certainly we test at the completion of a unit, at mid-term, and at the end of the academic year, but some teachers like to give a thirty-second test at the beginning of every lesson. Nothing gives learners such confidence and motivation as getting a perfect or near perfect score on the "daily quiz." Below are hints to achieve greater effectiveness and efficiency:

1. Base the quiz on what you had taught thoroughly the lesson before.
2. Announce *exactly* what students will be expected to do on the test (e.g., match communicative expressions; paraphrase them in different "registers"; convert sentences to the negative; choose or write antonyms, etc. Tell students exactly what to study—giving seven or eight items—but test them only on five for ease in grading).
3. Have the papers collected. (The papers should be all of the same size—from a small note pad, for example.)
4. Correct the test items immediately. These should still be on the chalkboard if they have been written on the chalkboard. (The correcting is done cooperatively—with an able student writing on the board as others volunteer to give each answer.) Please remember that as far as we know from the psychological sciences the knowledge that our answer is correct reinforces the answer.
5. Ask the students to indicate if they had any problem with an item.
6. Have a student (preferably one who had made an error) take the set of papers home to grade them. (On the basis of ten, any incorrect or missing answer will have two points taken off.)
7. Return the papers quickly during the next lesson. (Paper should be distributed and collected quickly by putting a pile on the first desk of each row or circle and asking the first person to take a paper and pass the others back or around. (They should be collected by asking the last person to pass his paper to the person in front or next to him who will put his paper on top—continuing the process until all papers are collected.)
8. Ask the students to keep the grades received in a notebook. These grades should be averaged by the students themselves and included—using any weight you, other teachers, and supervisors devise—in the final course grade.

How Do We Test?

Our principle objective—that of developing fluency in communicative competence—requires that we give *oral* as well as *written* tests; that we give *discrete point* tests (on individual language and cultural items) as well as *integrative* tests (those which will test communicative competence, interaction, fluency, and the appropriateness of what is said in the social situation in which the speech act is taking place by testing all the items together in realistic situations), as well as reading and writing abilities.

Another way of differentiating tests is by labeling them *objective* or *subjective*. An objective test (multiple choice, matching, fill-in, true or false) is one in which only one answer can be correct. Thus the fatigue, bias, or lack of efficiency of the rater can make no difference on the final score. On the other hand, in objective tests, it is extremely difficult and well-nigh impossible to judge sequence of ideas, richness of vocabulary, fluency, and the ability to communicate. Also, the decision about what items to test cannot be made objectively.

While subjective tests such as oral interviews or written essays can give some measure of ideas, vocabulary, culture, coherence, or creativity, they are more difficult to grade and subject to the personal inclinations of raters. Even lengthy orientation sessions with raters do not do away with a wide range of scores given by different raters for the same student in an interview or on a written paper. We would recommend, therefore, a. that both objective and subjective types of tests be given; b. that raters receive continuous training; c. that in oral interviews—especially when an admission to a higher school of learning or employment are at stake—there be three raters (where feasible), and that the three discuss and average their grades. Only in this way can we ensure that no injustice has been done to individuals.

When tape recorders in the class or in the language laboratory are used in testing it is important to make sure that students have been exposed to the machines before; that the voice on the recording is clear and comprehensible; and that the instructions are given in simple, unambiguous language. At beginning levels and where feasible, the instructions may be given in the students' native language. Test stimuli—particularly for discrete point tests—can be varied. We can use oral cues in the target or native language—for a translation exercise, for example: single pictures or groups of pictures, real objects, situational pictures, written words, multiple choice, true-false, fill-in items, etc.

What Do We Test?

We should measure the learning of everything we have considered important enough to teach. That means that we should test the students' use of communicative functions in actual conversation; their ability to use formal or informal speech when the factors in the situation require it; their skill in encoding and decoding language in integrated listening, speaking, reading, and writing tasks; their knowledge of the four subsystems of language and the subsidiary elements subsumed under each.

To illustrate, we should test their ability a. to understand the reasons for the formality or informality of communicative expressions, and the formulas and hestitation words of the target language; b. to formulate and answer questions; c. to make authentic responses; d. to add comment or sequence sentences; e. to sustain or change the direction of a conversation; f. to give reports and summaries; g. to engage in spontaneous conversation.

At more advanced levels, we may wish to test the specialized vocabulary and knowledge of their vocation or profession to ascertain if they can remember details of a lecture given some time before, to note if they can understand and use a variety of "registers," or to gauge the number of presuppositions they have internalized.

What Criteria Should We Consider in Planning Language Tests?

Keith Morrow (Brumfit and Johnson 1979, pp. 143–57), who has been working intensively in this field for several years, has written a particularly clear chapter on some aspects of testing which are concerned primarily with communicative competence. He makes some points which we find especially sound and interesting in discussing reliability and validity.

Test reliability (its objectivity) is not nearly as important as test validity, that is, does a test actually measure what examiners think they are measuring and does it test what it ought to be testing? In this regard, he lists the five types of validity which were identified by Alan Davies (1968).

1. Face—the test looks like a good one.
2. Content—the test accurately reflects the syllabus on which it is based.
3. Predictive—the test accurately predicts performance in some subsequent situation.
4. Concurrent—the test gives similar results to existing tests which have already been validated. (Morrow does not consider this aspect of validity as important as the others.)
5. Construct—the test reflects accurately the principles of a valid theory of foreign language learning.

He notes and comments on some features of language use which do not seem to be measured in conventional tests:

- They are not based on *interaction* between or among people.
- They do not take into consideration the *unpredictability* of a listener's or reader's reaction. He states, "The processing of unpredictable data in real time is a vital aspect of using language."
- Language use is not tested in *context*.
- The *purpose* of the speaker or writer is not clear to the receiver of the message. The listener especially should be able to prepare an appropriate response as he is listening in order to achieve his own purpose.
- *Authenticity* of language while important should take account of the linguistic level of the addressee.
- A test should be *behavior-based*. In other words what can the speaker (reader)-listener (writer) *achieve* through language? The performance should be measured on the basis of *quality* and not necessarily on quantity.

On this last criterion, he quotes B. J. Carroll (Morrow 1979) who distinguishes different levels of performance by comparing the student's learning behavior within the following framework:
- Size and complexity of text which can be handled.
- Range, e.g., of enabling skills, structures, and functions which can be handled.
- Speed at which language can be processed.
- Flexibility shown in dealing with changes of, e.g., topic.
- Accuracy and appropriateness with which, e.g., enabling skills, structures, functions can be handled.
- Independence from reference/sources and interlocutor (interviewer, speaker).
- Repetition and hesitation in processing text.

In addition to Morrow's and Carroll's criteria, we should also consider the factors of *fatigue* when the test is too long, the testing *environment* (comfort, light, air, space) and the *skill* of the individual rater or rating commission. (In some countries, a commission of two or three people from other cities is sent to examine candidates' performance. This often leads to failure and frustration since the examiners do not generally know the strategies the classroom teacher has used, or the language in which the teacher has generally worded his test instructions.)

Test instructions should be simple and clear. Often, unfortunately, they are more difficult than the test items themselves.

Moreoever, we would urge that until test norms are clearly established by worldwide commissions for possible transfer credit, that tests which have been normed in the United States, for example, should not generally be used in other countries with other student populations and with teachers who are not native speakers of English.

What Do We Do With Test Results?

Results of tests will help us gauge three essential components of our program.

1. The curriculum itself—is there too much or too little emphasis on listening comprehension, for example? Is there a close correlation among communicative functions, situations, notions, and exponents? Should more time, with older students especially, be spent on giving them insight into grammatical functions? How is fluency developed? Should more attention be placed on simulated and role-playing activities? Are the objectives realistic? Do our learners need more time to acquire certain categories of knowledge about the target country, etc.? Does some aspect of the curriculum at any level need revision?

2. The materials of instruction—are they effective? Is too much adaptation needed? Do they contain mini-dialogs which illustrate language in use in a variety of situations? Do modules go from the simple to the complex, that is, from "core" to "expansions"? Are there sufficient numbers of tasks and activities which provide for group, pair, or individual practice? Do our materials need to be made more suitable to the goals we have set ourselves?

3. Ourselves as teachers—do we try to motivate our students? Do we involve all of them in each lesson? Do we give them a feeling of pride in their language and culture? Do we praise them? Do we correct them gently? Do we understand their problems when they cannot do their homework, go to the library, or perform other tasks we may ask of them? Do we try to incorporate new ideas into our teaching—gleaned from journals, talks with other teachers, or attendance at conferences where possible?

Let us hasten to add, however, that many times lack of success on the part of some of our students may have nothing to do with our lesson planning or teaching. The fault may lie with problems at home, sickness, personality factors, discouragement, and all the ills that assail ordinary mortals at some time or other.

Test results serve many other purposes, as we noted above. They help us make crucial decisions about a. selecting students for admission into a school program and placing them in appropriate special classes or groups within a class; b. whether or not the student is ready to enter the mainstream of the school or foreign language track; c. whether we can certify that he has completed specific units of work and with what degree of success; d. whether we can recommend him to a higher school of learning; e. whether we feel he is ready to undertake a job in industry, for example, and what weaknesses, if any, there are still to be overcome; f. whether, after many sessions with other teachers, counselors, and supervisors, we may rechannel a student to another type of profession or job where a perfect or near perfect knowledge of language is not required.

For these and all the other humane reasons which may affect the very life of an individual, it is imperative that the preparation, giving, and recording of tests be considered a serious responsibility of teachers and administrators.

And now, let us turn to some examples of test items which will measure both interpretative and productive skills. You will note that some of these may be done with oral cues and answered with check marks; some may be done with written or other visual stimuli and answered orally or in writing. Only you, the teacher, can judge when you can use these test items with your students.

TESTING COMMUNICATIVE COMPETENCE

Items designed to test communicative competence should be related to real-life situations and should be given in authentic contexts. The ideal mode of conducting such testing would be through actual performance by older learners, for example, such as telephoning, ordering meals, making airline reservations, or applying for a job, in which knowledge of appropriate functions and notions in real use and in real time could then be judged. Many of these tasks can only be simulated in the classrooms or often be demonstrated on paper-and-pencil tests. Communicative competence, as we have noted, can be tested both on the receptive (interpretative) and on the performance level.

SOME EXAMPLES:
Interpretative

1. Tell whether the language being used is *formal* or *informal*. Circle *F* if you think it is *formal*; circle *I* if it is *informal*.
   A. He's a fool. He'll never make it.   F   I
   B. I don't believe he has any chance of success.   F   I
   C. That man I'm married to thinks a woman's place is in
      the kitchen.   F   I
   D. My husband prefers that I do not work outside the
      house.   F   I

2. Study this situation. Tell whether the language is *appropriate* or *inappropriate* by circling A or I.
   A. A man is applying for a job in a bank. He asks:
      1. How about a job?   A   I
      2. What's the pay?   A   I
      3. I'd like to know if you have an opening.   A   I

3. Study these conversations. In each case, mark whether you think the *second* utterance is appropriate or not. Circle A if it is *appropriate*; circle *I* if you think it is *not*.
   A. How do you do?
      Hya.   A   I
   B. Do you mind if I smoke?
      I prefer that you don't smoke in this room.   A   I
   C. May I have the next dance?
      No. My feet are killing me.   A   I

4. Circle the response or responses which you consider *appropriate* and *tactful*.
   A. My mother is quite ill.
      1. That's a break.
      2. That's great.
      3. I'm so sorry.
   B. I failed my exam.
      1. How could you be so stupid?
      2. It must have been a very difficult one.
      3. I told you you should have studied.

5. Match the communicative expressions which express the same function.
   1. Let's go to the movies.
   2. I prefer the other (tie).
   3. Can I get _____?
   4. Could you help me?
   5. I beg your pardon.

   a. I'd rather have the green one.
   b. Shall we go to the park?
   c. I wonder if you would tell me _____?
   d. Excuse me.
   e. Do you mind if I buy _____?

Productive Knowledge

The students' productive knowledge can be judged through oral or written activities. For example:

Written:

1. Make a statement disagreeing politely:
   A. I think X doesn't know a thing about medicine.
   B. _____

2. Give a statement showing concern:
   A. My wife was just taken to the hospital.
   B. _____

3. Give a statement expressing congratulations:
   A. My father just got that new job he wanted.
   B. _____

4. Give a paraphrase changing *familiar* to *polite* language.

   EXAMPLES:

   I'm gonna (going to) leave now.

   Would you mind if I left now?

Oral:

(Including listening, reading, and/or writing.)
1. Describe a situation and ask the student what he would say.
   A. You're at the bus station. Your bus will leave in a few minutes. You cannot miss an important appointment. What could you say to the people on the ticket line ahead of you?
   B. A stranger asks you for directions to the castle he wants to visit. What would you say?
2. Engage in role-playing.
   A. Two students will take the place of the employers; the other, that of a job seeker. After the interview, the two employers will discuss the job seeker.
   B. A friend cannot come to the baseball game that afternoon. Console him and fix another: appointment, negotiating time, date, place, circumstances, e.g., "If it rains, we'll..."
3. Two students will receive cue cards. On one is a statement which the first student will read, on the other is an instruction, such as, express joy, anger, congratulations, etc.

4. Give a brief statement in writing or orally. A student is to ask a question about it, e.g., "My best friend has moved to another city."
5. Ask the students to complete the dialog between two people in a restaurant.

   Please pass the sugar.

   (You use too much sugar—you know it's not good for you.)
6. Conduct an interview in which the student is asked to report on his studies or job experiences in his native land.
7. Ask the student to tell about his aspirations for the future.
8. Ask the student to report on an article or book he has read.

TESTING THE DISCRETE FEATURES OF LANGUAGE

Many of the items listed below include skills other than the one being tested. For example, some writing tasks may include reading or listening. (Only a few sample items will be given here since similar ones can be found in several books on testing (e.g., Vallette 1977).)

To Test Their Knowledge of the Sound System

Have students:
1. Indicate whether two sounds—given orally or in writing, isolated or in words—are the same or different.
2. Mark the syllable having the loudest stress, e.g., again/never/turn on/ apple tree.
3. Indicate (by prearranged code) rising or falling intonation, e.g., Is he at work? Why can't you help me?
4. Imitate sentences of varying lengths, e.g., I'd like a scarf. I'd like a printed scarf. I'd like that printed scarf in the window.

To Test Their Grasp of Grammatical Items

Have students:
1. Select the appropriate word from two or three words by underlining, numbering, or filling a blank on an answer sheet, e.g., Those boy/boys are very well-behaved. They/we/he always walk to the door.
2. Perform any of the conversion exercises indicated in the Appendix, e.g., make this a question: "He went to the door." "Say you want two." "May I have a box." "Ask a question with 'who'." "Mr. X is a mailman."

3. Use the words *have lunch* (for example) in these sentences, e.g., It's noon. I'm _____ now. Yesterday I _____ at noon, too. I usually _____ at noon every day.
4. Ask direct questions based on indirect questions, e.g., Ask X how old he is. Ask someone whether he knows Mr. X.
5. Give the paired sentence, e.g., "Mary is going to read later. The boys are going to study later/Mary reads every day. The boys _____ ."
6. Put *I wonder* before the question, "Who is he?"
7. Complete sentences, e.g., I ____ sleepy. ('ve/'m/have) I'd go if I ____ money. (have/get/had)
8. Answer questions of various types. Indicate whether you want a *yes* or *no* answer; whether you want a short answer or a long answer; whether you want a combination short and long answer, whether you want them to agree, disagree, express surprise, sympathy, anger, etc.
9. Combine sentences, e.g., "She's a doctor. She's considered very good."/"That man is my uncle. He's talking to the Mayor."
10. Match the stimuli and possible responses. Have one less response than the stimuli so that guessing will be minimized, e.g.,

I	II
1. Thank you.	A. Better.
2. How old is he?	B. He's twenty.
3. When are you leaving?	C. Of course.
4. How are you feeling?	D. You're welcome.
5. May I go out?	E. Tomorrow.
6. Where does he live?	

11. Select the appropriate coordinating conjunction when two are given, e.g., (and/but) I'd like to come ....I feel sick.
12. Select the appropriate connector, e.g., It was raining hard, (however/otherwise) we left for the country.

To Test Their Knowledge of Notions

Have students:
1. Indicate whether a statement is true or false, e.g., Monday comes before Wednesday.
2. Select the unrelated word from a group of words, e.g., meat/soup/eraser/peas.
3. Give a synonym or choose one from a list, e.g., commence (begin).
4. Make nouns from the following verbs, e.g., achieve/deny/permit.

5. Use the prefix meaning *not* in these words, e.g., ability/able/rational.
6. Use the suffix meaning "pertaining to" in these words, e.g., national, mental.
7. Select the appropriate word, e.g., (too/very) I can't drink the tea. It's _____ hot.
8. Choose the appropriate word, e.g., (breakfast/lunch/dinner/supper) We always have _____ at seven in the morning.
9. Translate from mother tongue into English.

TESTING THE BASIC COMMUNICATION ABILITIES

To Test Their Listening Comprehension:

Have students:
1. Carry out a request. Use one utterance with beginners and more than one with more advanced students.
2. Take an oral comprehension exercise.
3. Complete the sentence when a choice is given, e.g., It's raining. I'll have to take an _____ (examination/umbrella/envelope).
4. Answer questions according to the cue or direction, e.g., (visit friends) What did you do last evening?
5. Select an appropriate rejoinder (when several choices are given) to a statement or request, e.g., May I smoke? (Not at all./Of course.)
6. Identify the central theme or the nature of a talk when listening to a news broadcast, e.g., social/political/artistic/educational.
7. Tell which statement (given orally or in writing) embodies the main idea of a passage they hear. Give one supporting statement in the passage.
8. Give a simple summary of a talk they have listened to.
9. Take the role of listener or speaker in a dialog.
10. Engage in role-playing exercises.

To Test Their Speaking Ability

Have students:
1. Say (or read) a passage, poem, or dialog they have learned.
2. Take one of the roles in a dialog.
3. Make a rejoinder to a statement or request.
4. Read a passage containing new material which they have not seen before.

5. Ask direct questions when an indirect statement is given, e.g., Ask me how I came to school yesterday.
6. Convert sentences according to the direction given.
7. Give the equivalent of a short native language utterance (if feasible).
8. Formulate questions on a passage.
9. Tell what they would say (or do) in a certain situation.
10. Tell about something they did at some particular time (before coming to school perhaps: something that happened, or something that they hope is going to happen.)
11. Elaborate on or add comments to something they have said.
12. Comment on something another speaker has said.

To Test Their Reading Ability

Have students:
1. Complete sentences based on a passage read when a choice is given.
2. Complete sentences when a choice is not given.
3. Complete a logical inference, e.g., He had worked for many years without ever taking a vacation but he was not (rich/lazy/stupid).
4. Read an unfamiliar passage aloud and answer questions on it.
5. Formulate questions on a passage.
6. Answer several questions on a passage read silently.
7. Give definitions or paraphrases of selected words in a passage.
8. Indicate a possible rejoinder or sequence to a statement or a series of statements.
9. Outline a paragraph.
10. Summarize a passage.
11. Indicate the characters in a story who had expressed a point of view or performed some actions.
12. Read a passage crossing out irrelevant words.
13. Read a passage silently within a limited time and answer questions on it.
14. Discuss the cultural allusions in a poem or passage.
15. Give synonyms, antonyms, or paraphrases of certain words or expressions.

To Test Their Writing Ability

Have students:
1. Insert punctuation marks and capital letters in a paragraph.

2. Write out in full the words for symbols or abbreviations, e.g., +, %, Mr., Inc.
3. Reconstruct a sentence from several words, e.g., girls/theater/last week.
4. Answer questions substituting pronouns for all nouns.
5. Complete a sentence using the same verb in both spaces, e.g., (run) He _____ as he had never _____ before.
6. Expand several sentences into a letter, a dialog, or a paragraph.
7. Add logical details to a topic sentence.
8. Answer questions about themselves or some material they have studied.
9. Take a dictation or a dicto-comp.[2]
10. Take an aural comprehension exercise to be answered in writing.
11. Rewrite a passage or story from their point of view, or in the past or future.
12. Write what they would say or do in a situation.
13. Write what they see in a scene.
14 Summarize a passage.
15. Formulate questions on a passage.
16. Rewrite a paragraph using a more familiar (or more formal) style.
17. Write an essay on one of three topics you indicate (based on their professional or vocational reading, a cultural topic, a news item, etc.).
18. Take a cloze test.
19. Give the foreign language equivalent of a passage in the native language or vice versa.
20. Write an expanded module for a specific situation.

Testing Cultural Understanding

Objective tests and essay tests may be used to test knowledge of facts and insight into cultural behavior.

Following are some examples. Students may be asked to:

1. Complete a sentence, e.g., The _____ is the center of social life in (country).
2. State which is true or false, e.g., Most Xs have lunch at noon. Southern cities are industrialized in (country).
3. Choose (by circling, underlining, or writing on a separate sheet) the correct answer, e.g., People in X belong to unions. (Some/All/None).
4. Define or identify by completing a sentence, e.g., New Year's in the United States falls on _____ .

[2] You may have noticed that many tasks include listening or reading.

5. Indicate which behavior may be considered typical, a or b, e.g.,
   A. In _____ people go to the theater at 2 p.m.
   B. People go to the theater at 9:30 p.m.
6. Write a brief paragraph when a topic sentence is given, e.g., Migration to a new country should be considered carefully.

Testing Literary Appreciation and Professional Knowledge

Again, both objective tests and essays will be useful. The objective tests can be of the types indicated above under Cultural Understanding, p. 199. Students may be asked to *complete* sentences when a choice is given or when no choice is given, to *identify*, to *match*, to *define*, or to *give an explanation*.

The knowledge tested will depend on the material taught. It may be related, for example, to:

1. authors and the names of their works,
2. story line or plot,
3. cultural allusions in a poem, play, or novel,
4. the use and meaning of certain words or expressions in a literary work.

Vocational and professional knowledge can be tested through specialized vocabulary tests and through completions, multiple choice, or true-false items. These should be based on job analyses and students' immediate needs. Experts in the fields (future employers, hospital superintendants, and others familiar with the subject matter) should be asked to collaborate in the test preparation. Examples:

> T or F: A drill press bores holes in metals.
> Therapeutics is concerned with anatomy.
> Pei is a famous American architect.

> Complete: Registered nurses must have _____ years of specialized training.

Essay tests should be required in certain situations. If we feel that the student has the necessary ability to read a technical manual, a professional journal or literary work in the original, we must also assume that his writing ability has kept pace. Only through an essay can we judge the student's ability to express himself in informational sequence and in the appropriate register.

In the majority of secondary schools, however, such abilities cannot be assumed even if the foreign language was started in the elementary school. Again, each school will have to decide whether such steps are possible with its particular student population and resources.

PROFICIENCY TEST SCALES

We are including two scales which have been used widely to measure basic and professional communicative abilities. It is very likely that the Council of Europe will adopt or adapt one of these. Their content and the terminal behavior noted should still be of use to you in any case.

While it is true that teaching and learning are more important than testing, it is nonetheless true that success, on tests of performance especially, is perhaps the most motivating component in the learning process. Well-planned tests, graded fairly, can do more for a student's ego enhancement than the best planned lesson.

The Foreign Service Institute in the United States, which prepares persons for assignments in government posts, uses the following scale:

FSI Absolute Language Proficiency Ratings[3]

Elementary Proficiency (Level 1)

Able to satisfy routine travel needs and minimum courtesy requirements.

Can ask and answer questions on topics very familiar to him; within the scope of his very limited language experience can understand simple questions and statements, allowing for slowed speech, repetition or paraphrase; speaking vocabulary inadequate to express anything but the most elementary needs; errors in pronunciation and grammar are frequent, but can be understood by a native speaker used to dealing with foreigners attempting to speak his language; while topics which are "very familiar" and elementary needs vary considerably from individual to individual, any person at the S-1 level should be able to order a simple meal, ask for shelter or lodging, ask and give simple directions, make purchases, and tell time.

Limited Working Proficiency (Level 2)

Able to satisfy routine social demands and limited work requirements.

[3]Extracted from circular, *Absolute Language Proficiency Ratings*. Washington, D.C. Foreign Service Institute, November 1968.

Can handle with confidence but not with facility most social situations including introductions and casual conversations about current events, as well as work, family, and autobiographical information; can handle limited work requirements, needing help in handling any complications or difficulties; can get the gist of most conversations on nontechnical subjects (i.e., topics which require no specialized knowledge) and has a speaking vocabulary sufficient to express himself simply with some circumlocutions; accent, though often quite faulty, is intelligible; can usually handle elementary constructions quite accurately but does not have thorough or confident control of the grammar.

Minimum Professional Proficiency (Level 3)

Able to speak the language with sufficient structural accuracy and vocabulary to participate effectively in most formal and informal conversations on practical, social, and professional topics.

Can discuss particular interests and special fields of competence with reasonable ease; comprehension is quite complete for a normal rate of speech; vocabulary is broad enough that he rarely has to grope for a word; accent may be obviously foreign; control of grammar good; errors never interfere with understanding and rarely disturb the native speaker.

Full Professional Proficiency (Level 4)

Able to use the language fluently and accurately on all levels normally pertinent to professional needs.

Can understand and participate in any conversation within the range of his experience with a high degree of fluency and precision of vocabulary; would rarely be taken for a native speaker, but can respond appropriately even in unfamiliar situations; errors of pronunciation and grammar quite rare; can handle informal interpreting from and into the language.

Native or Bilingual Proficiency (Level 5)

Speaking proficiency equivalent to that of an educated native speaker.

Has complete fluency in the language such that his speech on all levels is fully accepted by educated native speakers in all of its features, including breadth of vocabulary and idiom, colloquialisms, and pertinent cultural references.

Rating Language Proficiency in Speaking and Understanding English[4]

Name of applicant _____ Date _____

Name of interviewer _____ Place _____

I. Comprehension

— 5. Understands everything; no adjustments in speed or vocabulary are needed.

— 4. Understands nearly everything at normal speed, though occasional repetition may be necessary.

— 3. Understands fairly well at slower-than-normal speed with some repetition.

— 2. Obviously has trouble understanding; frequent adjustments in speed and vocabulary are necessary.

— 1. Understands only very general conversational subjects at slow speed with frequent repetitions.

— 0. Cannot be said to understand even simple conversational English.

II. Pronunciation (including word accent and sentence pitch)

— 5. Speaks with few (if any) traces of "foreign accent."

— 4. Pronunciation understandable, but one is always conscious of a definite "accent."

— 3. "Foreign accent" necessitates concentrated listening and leads to occasional misunderstanding. Words and sentences must sometimes be repeated.

— 2. Many serious errors in pronunciation (e.g., *still* sounds like *steel*, *laws* sounds like *loss*), word accent (words are frequently accented on the wrong syllable), and sentence pitch (statements have the "melody" of questions, etc.). Frequent repetitions are required.

— 1. Definitely hard to understand because of sound, accent, pitch difficulties.

— 0. Pronunciation would be virtually unintelligible to "the man in the street."

[4] Reproduced by permission of the American Language Institute of Georgetown University.

III. Grammar and Word Order

— 5. Uses English with few (if any) noticeable errors of grammar or word order.
— 4. In general uses "good English," but with occasional grammatical or word-order errors which do not, however, obscure meaning (e.g., "I am needing more English," "He gave to me the letter").
— 3. Meaning occasionally obscured by grammatical and/or word-order errors.
— 2. Grammatical usage and word order definitely unsatisfactory; frequently needs to rephrase constructions and/or restricts himself to basic structural patterns (e.g., uses the simple present tense where he should use past or future).
— 1. Errors of grammar and word order make comprehension quite difficult.
— 0. Speech so full of grammatical and word-order errors as to be virtually unintelligible to "the man in the street."

IV. Vocabulary

— 5. Use of vocabulary and "idioms" is virtually that of a native speaker of English.
— 4. Rarely has trouble expressing himself with appropriate vocabulary and "idioms."
— 3. Sometimes uses inappropriate terms and/or round-about language because of inadequate vocabulary.
— 2. Frequently uses the wrong words; speech limited to simple vocabulary.
— 1. Misuse of words and very limited vocabulary make comprehension quite difficult.
— 0. Vocabulary is inadequate for even the simplest conversation.

V. General Speed of Speech and Sentence Length

— 5. Speech speed and sentence length are those of a native speaker.
— 4. Speed of speech seems to be slightly affected by language problems.
— 3. Both speed of speech and length of utterance are apparently affected by language difficulties and limitations.
— 2. Speed of speech and length of utterance seem *strongly* affected by language difficulties and limitations.

— 1. Speed of speech and length of utterance are so far below normal as to make conversation quite difficult.
— 0. Speech is so halting and fragmentary as to make conversation with "the man in the street" almost impossible.

Comments:

Total Rating _____ (25 possible points)

x 4_____(multiply by 4 to convert score to percents)

SUGGESTIONS FOR DISCUSSION

1. What kinds of tests do you use in your school system?
2. What is the attitude of educators in your country about aptitude and aptitude testing?
3. How often are you required to give tests?
4. For what purposes are test grades used?
5. Why is a brief daily quiz important?
6. What is meant by a discrete-point test?
7. What do we mean by an integrative test?
8. What are the advantages of an objective test? What disadvantages are there at advanced levels?
9. In using tapes or cassettes for testing, what cautions should we observe?
10. Which three basic elements of the learning-teaching process should we evaluate? Why?
11. What does Davies include in the term validity?
12. Prepare five items for an interpretative test of communicative competence.
13. Prepare five items for a performance test of communicative competence.
14. Discuss Carroll's criteria for judging performance.
15. How could you test the learners' knowledge of features of pronunciation.
16. Indicate five ways of testing students' grammatical knowledge.
17. Prepare a vocabulary test asking for antonyms.
18. Prepare a vocabulary test in which students add prefixes or suffixes to basic words.
19. How could you test listening-speaking ability?
20. How could you test reading-speaking ability?
21. Give five ways of testing reading ability.
22. Indicate five ways of judging students' writing ability.
23. How could you test literary, cultural, or professional facts or insight?
24. Could you use the two proficiency tests scales included as they are printed now? If not, how could you adapt them?

Conclusion

We have tried in this book to show how the theoretical discussion, originating in the work of the Council of Europe, on functional-notional syllabus design can be integrated with the traditional concerns and practices of second and foreign language teachers. The movement towards communicative syllabuses is not a total revolution but a reorientation of our work towards the needs of the students and the demands of authentic communication. Many teachers have been doing this for years, though they would describe their activities in rather different terms from those used by theorists. It is certainly possible, however, for the experience of teachers and the insights of applied linguists to come together fruitfully to build on and improve existing classroom expertise. If such an improvement is to take place on a large scale, it can only result from detailed discussion of implications for the classroom within the framework of existing practice.

We hope that this book will provide teachers with a basis for the development and improvement of their own work and that of their colleagues. Meanwhile discussion will continue. This can only be an interim statement, for our ideas continually develop as our societies and students change in their demands and needs. In a sense a book like this offers a challenge: to those who feel it is too cautious and conservative there is the challenge to show how more radical ideas can be adapted to the realities of most classrooms and most teachers' schedules; to those who feel that they do not need yet more innovation there is the challenge to show how traditional procedures have been as sensitive as the F-N approach to the demands of communication. The next decade is going to be an exciting one in language teaching as teachers, materials writers, and administrators respond to the many new ideas which are emerging. We hope that we have been able to show the implications, for typical classrooms, of some of them.

Appendix *

Before listing a number of drills briefly which can be used profitably in practicing a large number of language items, it may be desirable to review some criteria which should be considered in drill preparation and to make two recommendations: a. After having taught a unit, make a simple chart with separate columns of all the structures, notions, and miscellaneous items you presented in it. For example, your headings may be: date, unit, functional expressions, situations, structures, verbs, nouns, adjectives, adverbs, structure words, idioms, and miscellaneous words (days, dates, numbers). These should be noted briefly so that you can keep all the units together on long sheets of paper for easy reference in order to ensure that you will reenter familiar items with new items in drills and other activities. b. When you present a lesson, write all the *cue* words for drills on a card or slip of paper which you may keep in your left hand. This will make for the smooth flow of the lesson (since the words are immediately available to you) and permit you to walk to different parts of the room and use your hands to signal the type of repetition or interaction you would like.

Guidelines for Teacher-Controlled Tasks
(Beginning level)

Among these:
- Separate drills should be prepared for each structure as well as for specific functions and notions centered around a theme (e.g., going on a picnic, choosing a vocation).
- The changes required when beginning the practice of a new structure (or aspect of a structural category) should be minimal; that is, only one major change should be required at one time. When the students are ready for more advanced practice the drills may be so contextualized that learners will be forced to make more than one change. For example, a beginning drill of the pattern, *Where is she?* may involve the substitution of *he, it, the boy,* etc. Later, *the men, they, Mr. and Mrs. X* will require a change from *is* to *are.* (This is one facet of the teaching stage of "conscious choice.")

*Adapted from *The Foreign Language Learner* by Mary Finocchiaro and Michael Bonomo (1973) with permission from Regents Publishing Company, Inc., 2 Park Avenue, New York, New York 10016.

- The change required should be consistent. For example, in practicing frequency words, you might start with *always* with the verb *be* and say, "Use *always* in each of these sentences." You may in another lesson use frequency words with other verbs. Still later you may give a drill using *be* and regular verbs encouraging learners to make a "conscious" choice.
- Initially the vocabulary around which an exercise is built should center around one topic (food, recreation, daily routines) and, where logical, one function (e.g., requesting something).
- It is desirable that even rote drills be contextualized. In this way the drills practiced can lead immediately to real conversation.
- At beginning and intermediate levels, the drill sentences should be short so that students can concentrate on the change to be made without having to worry about keeping a long sentence in their minds. This is particularly important in drills on complex structures or communicative expressions (e.g., "I wonder if you would mind if . . . ").
- The utterance elicited should be a complete one, not a sentence segment or an isolated word. However, as we have noted elsewhere, in many responses a phrase or even a word would be considered a complete utterance. For example, a normal response to, "Who did you see last night?" could be, "Laurie." The normal response to, "What did you do last night?" would have to be, "I went to Laurie's house." On the other hand, an *oral* cue such as, "I went—the store," eliciting the response *to* alone, would not be desirable even if you indicate the dash by clapping or using some other gesture or pausing. Both the stimulus sentence and the response would be confusing and un-natural.
- Several (six to eight utterances) should be given for each type of accuracy activity, since the first one or two are often said hesitantly.
- The drills should be varied. In the initial presentation of a structure or communicative expression, repetition and substitution drills and two or three additional drills of different types should be given—the type depending on the expression or structure being practiced.
- The directions to the students, emphasizing the changes to be made should be brief and explicit. For example, in a substitution drill you could say, "Use the new word I will give you (or show you) in place of the word swimming. Do you enjoy swimming?" (Sustained pause.) "Hiking?" If it is feasible and you judge it essential, you may give the instructions for new drills in the native language of your learners. (Phase out the native language after two or three days, however.)
- After giving clear instructions, do several examples with the students. Give the model for repetition, the cue, the newly derived sentence and engage in repetition. Give help for as long as required, but move as quickly as possible to group and paired practice with student leaders.

- All cues and responses should be in the target language except for the Translation Drill below.
- All drill responses should be oral. (The drills done orally in class or in the language laboratory may later be assigned as written homework but they should be done orally first—using normal rhythm and speed.)
- In order to avoid confusion, drill responses should be given by individuals. If you wish to confirm a student's response by repeating it, make sure that there is a long enough pause between your confirmation and your next cue so that you will avoid your students hearing confusing sentences like, "I'd like to go swimming/hiking."
- Drills should be graded. For example, an expansion drill may start with cues requiring no change in word order, e.g., (new) "Should we buy a (new) fridge?" to (I wonder if) "Should we buy a new fridge?"/"I wonder if *we should* buy a new fridge?"
- Questions and answers could be practiced at first with the class divided into two groups. Based on your model, half the class will ask the question; the other half will give the answer (preceded at beginning levels by your model). Then the roles can be reversed.
- Pupil participation should be varied often enough to prevent boredom or "selective" listening. Most students enjoy group and paired practice, for example.
- All drills should be clearly related to the aims of the program—increasing communicative competence, while using formal, informal, and familiar language appropriately and fluently.

Basic Tasks

(Controlled)

Following are some commonly agreed upon names and examples of oral structure practice activities which will help students grow in their control of grammatical inflections, word order patterns, and notions, while promoting fluency and appropriate social interaction.

Substitution: In this drill, students use another word of the same class in place of a word in a sentence position (slot). A noun is replaced by another noun, a verb by another verb, an adjective by another adjective, a determiner (an article, possessive, etc.) by another determiner, etc.

At beginning levels particularly, and wherever needed, in substitution exercises you can use four different types of cues.
- Show the object or picture of an object or action while saying the word to be substituted.
- Give the cue word alone.
- Show the written word on a flashcard or on the chalkboard. (This cue can only be used if the learners can read.)
- Show the object or picture alone.

You will have noticed how the cues above adhered to the principle of "diminishing" help. First, students heard the word *and* saw a picture or object: Concept and sounds were reinforced, then they heard the sounds alone, then they saw the referent but had to supply their own word.

Substitution drills can be used with any communicative expression or structure and at all levels to help develop rhythm and fluency, e.g., "I wonder if (he'd) have (bought) a (car) if he'd really won the money."

Replacement: Students will be expected to replace one *class* of word or expression by another, e.g., nouns or names by pronouns: "Does (John) or (the boy) have any money today?" to, "Does (he) have any money today?"

It is pedagogically sound to cluster the items: Give only masculine singular nouns first, then feminine only, then both in random order. Giving items in random order becomes the essential step of "conscious" selection.

In replacement of noun to pronoun, sentences like, "I'd like to see that man," require a change of stress and intonation in English, "I'd like to see him." In other languages, French for example, *J'aime cet homme* (I love that man) becomes *Je l'aime*, while *Est-ce que tu vois cet homme?* becomes *Est-ce que tu le vois*.

Transformation (sometimes called *Conversion* to differentiate it from transformational analysis): Learners may be asked to change utterances from singular to plural; from affirmative to negative or interrogative; from present to present progressive, past, or future; and from active to passive, for example. (It is not necessary to use grammatical terminology unless your students have learned such terminology in their native language or unless they plan to become teachers.)

You may say, "Make a question," or "Let's use *not* in these senten-ces," or "Let's use *yesterday*," etc. Question word transformations make for effective practice. Starting with a sentence like, "Mrs. Galant got some money last week," you might ask questions like, "Who, What, When, or What happened to...?" Later, students can be encouraged to ask ques-tions of each other.

Expansion: Depending on the target language, the insertion or addi-tion may require a change in word order, in agreement or in verb aspect. Notice these examples, in increasing order of difficulty. Say:

> Let's add the word *too* to these sentences. Listen: The soup is cold. I can't drink it.
> Let's add *always*: I get up at seven. What about you?
> Let's add *efficient*: Mrs. X is a secretary.
> Let's put *I think* in front of this sentence (or Let's begin these sentences with *I think*): They're world famous.
> Let's put *He said that* in front of this sentence: I prefer to go to the beach.
> Let's use *yesterday* in this sentence: They're going to the museum.
> Let's put *The woman asked me* in front of this sentence: Where do you live?

In some languages the new expression in the main clause will require the subjunctive in the subordinate clause. In many of your classes, an extensive amount of repetition and substitution practice will have to precede an expansion activity because of the possible multiple changes required.

In *Integration* or *Embedding* tasks, learners combine two sentences. For example: "Look at my briefcase (a school bag). It's new." ("Look at my new briefcase.") "You saw that woman yesterday? Well, she's my math professor." ("That woman (whom) you saw yesterday is my math professor," or an appropriate variation.)

In *Nominalizaton* tasks, a subordinate clause is changed to an *-ing* form. (This activity should be reserved for upper levels.) For example, "As he walked across the road, he was hit by a car." "Walking across..."

In *Restatement* tasks, students practice expressing an utterance in different ways. For example, "Is this a new stove?" "Is this stove new?" "Is this message urgent?" "Is this an urgent message?"

Paired Sentences are popular tasks and help reinforce verb forms, personal pronouns and adjectives. Say:

> Joe likes to drink coke. What about Harry and Jim? (They like to drink coke too.)
> Rosemary is very pretty. What about Tina and Fay? (They're very pretty also.)
> Sal doesn't like pizza. What about Martha? (She doesn't like pizza either, or Neither does Martha.)

Association: Give the students a communicative expression or a structure to start their response (e.g., I'd rather have) and a cue word (e.g., milk) which they would use with its common concurrent element: "I'd rather have *a glass of* milk," or, "What would you rather have?" "A glass of milk."

Progressive Replacement (sometimes called *Moving Slot Substitution Drill*): This is a challenging multiple substitution drill which requires that learners listen attentively, since each new sentence to be created is based on the immediately preceding one.

Teacher (or Student)	Student
How about going to the beach?	How about going to the beach?
What	What about....................?
coming	What about coming.............?
swimming pool?	What about coming to the swimming pool?
How	How about ....?
How would you feel ....?	How would you feel about........?

Directed Practice: This is an effective task for going from guided manipulation to freer communication. One student is directed to ask another student a question. The other student is told what to answer (at very beginning levels only) or told that he may answer in any way.

X ask Y what he had for breakfast.
Y tell X that you only had a cup of tea.

(When you first start doing this drill, you may whisper the direct question to the first student and the direct answer to the second one.)

Translation (giving the equivalent): We have deliberately left this task to the end of the series. Translation drills have been the subject of controversy until recently. Now, the majority of educators appreciate their value. Only teachers who know the native language of the students (or who have a bilingual informant or some other aide in the classroom) can engage in this drill and only in classes where all learners speak the same native language.

At the beginning levels the translation should be on a clearly specified communicative expression or on a *limited* structural point, on one point only and contextualized (given in a clear utterance or preceded or followed by one). Ideally, the student should not say the native language but this is unrealistic in some circumstances, and you might wish to do a translation exercise in two steps *within the same lesson:*

I. **Teacher** (target language)	**Student** (native language)
What have you been doing all day?	L_1
What have you been doing for the last hour?	L_1
What have you been doing for the last month?	L_1
What have they been doing all day?	L_1
What has she been doing all day?	L_1

II **Teacher** (native language)	**Student** (target language)

(Use the same examples as above in the initial stage.)

Question-Answer Practice: (This should be interspersed with activities of the type listed above.) There are several basic types of question-answer drills. Moreover, each drill can be done in several ways, for example:
1. You will ask the students a question; one student will answer.
2. A student will ask you a question; you will answer.
3. A student will ask another student a question.
4. Pairs of students will face each other and practice questions and answers.
5. Pairs of students or groups of four students will question each other in chain fashion. This, too, has several variations. A. Student

1 will ask Student 2 a question. Student 2 will answer. Student 3 will ask the same question of Student 4 who will answer. B. Student 1 will ask Student 2 a question. Student 2 will answer and ask the same question of Student 3, who will answer and ask the question of Student 4. C. Student 1 will ask Student 2 a question, e.g., "Have you got a pencil to lend me?" Student 2 answers, "Yes, I do" or "Yes, I have" or "Yes, here you are." Student 3 will ask Student 4, "Does he (or she) have a pencil?" or "Has he got a pencil?" referring to Student 2. Student 4 will answer. Student 5 will start a new chain with the same or similar question.

Let us examine briefly several basic question-answer drills which can be used effectively in teaching communicative expressions, grammar, and notions.

Notice the progression in the students' responses (at early levels particularly) with affirmatives and then with negatives.

Answer Yes: "Would you like a coke?" "Yes." (Here listening comprehension alone is stressed.)

Answer Yes. Give a short answer: "Would you like a coke?" "Yes, thanks" or "Yes, I would."

Answer Yes with any appropriate sequence: "Would you like a coke?" "That'd be great."

Answer No: "Do you want a coke?" "No, thank you."

Answer No. Give a short answer: "Do you have a coke?" "No, I'm sorry, I don't."

Answer No. Tell what you have, want, etc. (or tell what it is): "Would you like a coke?" "No, I wouldn't. I'd like/I'd rather have a beer."

When an item is first introduced, you or an able student may give the cue which tells the students what to answer. Later, students may give any appropriate answer.

- Choose one or the other. "Do you need a red crayon or a blue one for this picture?" "A blue one." At the beginning level, make your second alternative the "correct" one so that the sounds the students are to produce are fresh in their minds.
- Patterned Response. You will ask a question such as, "May I borrow your X?" The student will answer with the utterance being practiced, for example, "Yes, here it is." "Do you like salad (ice cream, swimming, etc.)?" "Yes, very much."

At intermediate levels, the patterned response drill can be used to practice changes in word order or substitute expressions. Notice:

"I'm hungry." "So am I."
"I'm thirsty." "So is he."

"Do you think she's pretty?" "Yes, I think so" or "Yes, very."

"Do you think it's going to rain?" "Yes, I'm afraid so" or "It looks like it" or "I think so. Don't you?"

"Would you like a sandwich" "Yes, thank you" or "Yes, I would" or "No, thank you, not right now."

The drill can be made more interesting by adding an appropriate patterned clause to a reply (e.g., "Will you play soccer this afternoon?" "Yes, I will if you'll play too," or "Will you study for the test?" "Yes, I will if you'll study too.") In another lesson *if* can be expanded to *but only if*.

- Question-word (*Wh*) Questions.

  Who's in the first seat? (*Joe*)

  Who's at the door? (Frank *and* Bill)

  What do you need?

  Where's the railway station?

  When will you see your friends?

  How long have you studied English?

  How many times have you been there?

  How far is the capital from here?

  Why do you look so tired?

- Question-word questions and inverted questions can be combined in realistic conversational exchanges. Notice:

  Have you seen X recently?

  Yes, I have.

  When did you see him?

  I saw him two days ago.

- Echo Response. You or a student will ask a question and the student called upon will echo a segment of it before responding, e.g., "Where's your coat?" "My coat? It's in the closet."/"Where did you go last night?" "Last night? I went to the movies."

- Free Response. Depending on the learning level and the items with which students are familiar, you might ask anything from, "What do I have on my desk?" to "What new pictures do you see on the bulletin board?" to "What do you like to do on weekends?" or anything on which the students may wish to focus.

To help students with ideas, you or a student could again use cues—spoken words, pictures, objects, or written words—to elicit responses. Gradually, however, no cue should be used at all and you will find that none will be needed.

Glossary

This includes brief, simple definitions of terms which have been used in this book and which may be unfamiliar.

ACCURACY WORK In this book, work in class where the intention is to produce correct or appropriate language, rather than to perform a genuine communicative act.

ACOUSTIC Information about sounds, gathered by technical instruments.

ACTION SERIES (or Gouin Series after its originator) A series of utterances which reflect a series of actions being performed at the same time, e.g., "I'm standing up," etc.

ACTIVE VOCABULARY The words which learners can use effectively themselves.

ALLOPHONE One of the varied sounds, acoustically detectable, which are perceived by native speakers of a language to be the same sound phonemically, e.g., the *p* sound in *pout, spout,* and *lip* is a different allophone in each example.

ATOMISTIC Use of learning or testing in which items are presented or tested in isolation, out of context.

AUDIO-LINGUAL An approach to language teaching where imitation and drilling preceded spontaneous production, relying heavily on habit-forming drills.

AUDIO-VISUAL A development of the above using visual materials in addition.

AUTHENTIC MATERIALS Materials used in the classroom, but not specifically designed for teaching, e.g., newspaper articles.

AVAILABILITY Used about language items which can be easily recalled by the learner. In this book, accuracy work leads to availability, but fluency work enables learners to use the item appropriately in genuine social interaction.

BEHAVIORISM A psychological theory which maintained that we should be concerned only with phenomena which can be observed and measured. In language learning, associated with stimulus-response learning theory.

CASE A term for the semantic relations which link nouns to other items in the sentence. These may be deep semantic relationships which are not revealed in the morphology, or they may be shown through inflections.

CLOZE A test in which students replace words which have been deleted from a text on a random basis (e.g., every seventh word).

COGNATE A word in one language which looks like one in another and has a similar meaning. (This may confuse learners when the meanings are not exactly the same.)

COGNITIVE CODE A theory which believes that language learning is best achieved by conscious understanding of the rules underlying language behavior.

COMMUNICATIVE COMPETENCE The ability to use the language system appropriately in any circumstances.

COMMUNICATIVE EXPRESSION An utterance which conveys a functional meaning and is particularly appropriate to the circumstances for which it is produced.

COMMUNICATIVE GRAMMAR A grammar which relates the structures specifically to the meanings and uses for which they might be used.

CORE Basic parts of teaching units which may, but do not have to be, expanded further.

CUE A stimulus provided (in class) to produce a response (from students).

CURRICULUM The knowledge, skills, materials, learning activities, and terminal behavior required in the teaching of any subject.

DECODING The process by which a listener or reader works out the whole meaning of a message.

DEIXIS A feature of words like *he, this*, etc., whose meaning results from referring to other parts of the text (e.g., *he* refers to a person already mentioned).

DIAGNOSTIC TEST One which enables the tester to diagnose the strengths and weaknesses of the candidate.

DIALECT A variety of a language, usually, but not necessarily, associated with a geographical area.

DIPHTHONG A sound which consists of two vowel sounds which run into each other, e.g., /au/.

DIRECT METHOD Language teaching through intensive spoken work entirely in the target language.

DISCOURSE A coherent stretch of speech or writing which communicates a message.

ENABLING SKILLS The skills which assist the learner to achieve success in a complex process such as reading, which consists of a range of different skills all operating together.

ENCODING The process by which a language user turns a message into the forms of the language.

ERROR ANALYSIS The study of mistakes made by language learners in order to assess their significance for learning theory and pedagogy.

EVALUATION The whole process of determining the effectiveness of teaching—which may be by means of formal tests and examinations, or by informal or subjective feedback from students and teachers.

EXPONENT The utterance containing the language items used to express the communicative purpose of the language. These stem from the integration of function, situation, structure, topic, and notions.

FEEDBACK Monitoring and adapting one's actions on the basis of the perceived effect on the environment. In language work, response to the reactions of listeners and readers.

FLUENCY In this book, language work in which the learner is acting naturally, in the same way as when using the mother tongue (contrasted with accuracy work).

FORMAL 1. Relating to the patterns, or "forms," of the language;
2. A style of speaking appropriate to situations which are strongly socially structured.

FORMULA A fixed expression which is used habitually, e.g., *Thank you*, in predictable circumstances.

FUNCTION The communicative purpose of a piece of language.

GRAMMAR-TRANSLATION A method of language teaching which concentrates on the memorization of grammatical rules and translation of (usually literary) texts.

GROUP WORK Work in which the class is broken into small groups of from three to eight people. They may work simultaneously on the same task, or be given different tasks of varied types or levels.

HOLISTIC An approach to learning in which language is considered in its totality for each act of communication, and not broken into separate parts.

IDIOLECT The system of language used by a particular individual.

INCREMENTAL LEARNING Learning in small steps, each step adding a little to the previous one.

INFLECTION A change in the form of a word to indicate that it is plural, or to show possession, or a tense, etc.

INFORMANT A native speaker, or someone with extensive knowledge, who can provide information about linguistic or cultural behavior of the taget language.

INFORMATION GAP The missing or incomplete part of a message which makes communication necessary. Communicative exercises in class make use of this to establish a need for genuine communication.

INPUT Oral, written, or visual stimuli from the formal or informal learning setting.

INSTRUMENTAL MOTIVATION Learner's desire to learn a language for the rewards which may result from knowing it.

INTEGRATIVE MOTIVATION Learner's desire to develop a close relationship with members of the target language community.

INTERFERENCE The influence of one type of behavior (e.g., mother-tongue linguistic behavior) on one that is learned later (e.g., foreign-language linguistic behavior). This may be either beneficial or harmful.

KINESICS The study of body movement, facial expression, etc., in relation to the messages they convey and in relation to language use.

LEVEL OF FORMALITY The extent to which language is formal or informal (see FORMAL).

METHODOLOGY The study of the whole process of language teaching with the aim of improving its efficiency.

MINIMAL PAIR Two words which differ only in one phoneme, e.g., box, fox. Often used, especially in audio-lingual procedures, as a device for teaching the sounds of the language.

MODE The form which language takes, e.g., spoken or written.

MODULE A self-contained, minimal special purpose unit.

MORPHEME The smallest meaningful unit analyzable in a language, e.g., cows consists of two morphemes: cow + s, a morpheme meaning "cow" and a morpheme meaning "plural."

MORPHOLOGY The study of changes in the forms of words.

MULTIPLE CHOICE QUESTIONS Questions in which several possible answers are given and the student has to select one or more appropriate answers.

NEEDS ANALYSIS The analysis of the purposes for which students may require the language. These may be objective and predictable, or subjective and difficult to predict.

NOTION A unit of analysis of meaning in a language. General notions refer to the ways in which a language expresses categories like space, time, result, causality, etc. Specific notions may be simpler meaning elements and are often interpreted to be simply the lexical items, or vocabulary, in a language.

PAIR WORK Work in which students operate simultaneously in pairs on a task, or on different tasks.

PATTERN A regular organization, e.g., the grammar in a language, in which the same basic arrangements recur.

PEDAGOGIC GRAMMAR A description of a language modified so as to be useful for teaching purposes.

PHONEME The smallest sound unit which contrasts meaningfully with other sounds in a language, e.g., /b/ and /p/ in bit and pit—those sounds create a difference in meaning.

PITCH The position of a sound in language on a high-low scale.

PRAGMATICS The study of how language and situations interact to produce meaningful messages.

PROFICIENCY TEST A test which measures the knowledge of a language in relation to external criteria of competence (without relation to formal classroom learning or specific textbooks used).

PROGRAMMED LEARNING A procedure for teaching in which the material to be learned is broken into the smallest possible pieces and presented as a sequence of simple steps.

PROXEMICS The study of the physical distances maintained by language users in relation to each other.

PSYCHOLINGUISTICS The study of language in relation to psychological processes and personality.

RECEPTIVE ACTIVITIES Those which are concerned with the process of understanding language rather than producing it.

REDUNDANCY The way in which the same piece of information may be provided in several different ways in the same utterance, e.g., in the sentence "The students *are* reading *their* books," there are three separate indicators of the presence of more than one student.

REFERENT The object or situation to which a word refers in the real world.

REGISTER The varied styles of language which are used for different purposes, varying according to such dimensions as setting, role of speakers, topic, mode (speaking or writing), and so on.

RELIABILITY The extent to which a test measures its results consistently.

RHYTHM The variability and regularity of 1. stress and pause in speech; 2. the individual's pace of learning.

ROLE-PLAY A teaching activity in which students act the parts of language users in specified situations.

SEMANTICS The scientific study of meaning in language.

SEMIOTICS The study of sign systems in the world; not simply language, but clothes, architecture, eating habits, and all ritual events.

SITUATIONAL APPROACH An approach to syllabus organization which bases work on predicted situations in which students are likely to need to use the language.

SPEECH ACT What a speaker does with a piece of language, e.g., apologize, threaten, persuade.

SPIRAL APPROACH A method of presentation in which the same item recurs in progressively greater depth as the syllabus develops.

STRESS The prominence of sounds in speech.

STYLISTICS The linguistic analysis of different styles of language, often with particular reference to literary texts.

SYNTAX How words are arranged systematically to form sentences.

TARGET LANGUAGE The language being learned.

TEXT A piece of spoken or written language.

THRESHOLD LEVEL The specification, made for the Council of Europe (for English, see van Ek 1975), of the minimum level of attainment in a language for adequate communication.

TRANSFORMATIONAL-GENERATIVE GRAMMAR An influential model of language structure, originating in the work of Chomsky, which attempts to derive all sentences of a language from a series of transformational rules operating on a series of base structures.

UNIT-CREDIT SYSTEM A scheme devised by the Council of Europe to enable language learners to acquire credits through completing a series of units which are standardized across languages.

UTTERANCE A stretch of language, in speech usually marked off by silence at the beginning and end.

VALIDITY The extent to which a test measures exactly what it is supposed to measure.

Bibliography

Alatis, James E., Altman, Howard B., and Alatis, Penelope M., eds. 1981. *The Second Language Classroom, Directions for the 1980's.* New York: Oxford University Press.

Alexander, L.G. 1975. Grammatical inventory of T-L English. In van Ek, *The Threshold Level.* Strasbourg: Council of Europe. Reprinted 1980. Oxford: Pergamon Press.

_____. 1976. Where do we go from here? *ELT Journal* 30:89-103.

American Language Institute. Rating language proficiency in speaking and understanding English. Washington, D.C.: Georgetown University.

Anthony, E. 1963. "Approach, method and technique." ELT Journal 17:63-7.

Brumfit, C.J. 1979. Accuracy and fluency as polarities in foreign language teaching materials and methodology. *Bulletin CILA* 29:89–99.

_____. 1980. *Problems and Principles in English Teaching.* Oxford: Pergamon Press.

_____. 1980a. Linguistic specifications for fluency work: How meaningful a question? In Richterich and Widdowson, eds. *Description, Presentation et Enseignement des Langues.* Paris: Hatier.

Brumfit, C.J. and Johnson, K., eds. 1979. *The Communicative Approach to Language Teaching.* Oxford: Oxford University Press.

Bung, K. 1973. The input-output relation in language behavior. *CCC/EES* 12.

_____. 1973. The specifications of objectives in a language learning system for adults. *CCC/EES* 34.

Celce-Murcia, Marianne and McIntosh, Lois, eds. 1979. *Teaching English As a Second or Foreign Language.* Rowley, Mass.: Newbury House.

Davies, Alan, ed. 1968. *Language Testing Symposium: A Psycholinguistic Approach.* Oxford: Oxford University Press.

Finocchiaro, Mary. 1969. *Teaching English as a Second Language.* 2d ed. New York: Harper and Row.

_____. 1974. *English as a Second Language: From Theory to Practice.* rev. ed. New York: Regents Publishing.

_____. 1979. The functional-notional syllabus: Problems, practices, problems. *English Teaching Forum* 17:11-20.

Finocchiaro, Mary and Bonomo, Michael. 1973. *The Foreign Language Learner: A Guide for Teachers.* New York: Regents Publishing.

Foreign Service Institute. 1968. Absolute language proficiency ratings. Circular. Washington, D.C.

Gardner, R. and Lambert, W. 1972. *Attitudes and Motivation in Second Language Learning*. Rowley, Mass.: Newbury House.

Halliday, M.A.K. 1973. *Explorations in the Function of Language*. London: Edward Arnold.

————. 1975. *Learning How to Mean*. London: Edward Arnold.

————. 1979. *Language as Social Semiotic: Social Interpretation of Language and Meaning*. London: Edward Arnold.

Hymes, Dell. 1970. *On Communicative Competence*. Reprinted in *Directions in Sociolinguistics*. Gumperz, J. and Hys, N., eds. Toronto: Holt, Rinehart and Winston.

————, ed. 1964. *Language in Culture and Society: A Reader in Linguistics and Anthropology*. New York: Harper & Row.

Johnson, K. and Morrow, K. 1975. Meeting some social language needs of overseas students. Mimeographed. University of Reading.

————. 1976. The production of functional materials and their integration within existing language programmes. Mimeographed. University of Reading.

————. 1978. Communicate: the function of social interaction. Mimeographed. University of Reading.

Joos, Martin. 1967. *The Five Clocks*. New York: Harcourt Brace Jovanovich.

Kelly, Louis G. 1969. *Twenty Five Centuries of Language Teaching*. Rowley, Mass.: Newbury House.

Krashen, S. 1981. *Second Language Acquisition and Second Language Learning*. Oxford: Pergamon Press.

Lee, W.R. 1979. *Pergamon Dictionary of Social English*. Oxford: Pergamon Press.

Leech, G.N. and Svartvik, Jan. 1975. *Communicative Grammar of English*. London: Longman.

Littlewood, William. 1981. *Communicative Language Learning: An Introduction*. Cambridge: Cambridge University Press.

Maley, Alan and Duff, Alan. 1978. *Drama Techniques in Language Learning*. Cambridge: Cambridge University Press.

Maslow, Abraham H., ed. 1970. *Motivation and Personality*. 2d ed. New York: Harper and Row.

Morrow, Keith. 1979. Communicative language testing: Revolution or evolution? In Brumfit and Johnson, *The Communicative Approach to Language Teaching*. Oxford: Oxford University Press.

Prabhu, H.S. and Carroll, D.J. 1980. *Introduction to Teaching English as Communication*. Newsletter Special Series 1, no. 4. Bangalore, South India: Regional Institute of English.

Raimes, Ann. 1978. *Focus on Composition*. New York: Oxford University Press.

Richterich, R. 1971. Analytic classification of the categories of adults needing to learn foreign languages. CCC/EES 71-5. Reprinted. 1973, 1980 in *Systems Development in Adult Language Learning*. Oxford: Pergamon Press.

_____. 1973. A model for the definition of adult language needs of adults learning a modern language. CCC/EES. Reprinted in *Systems Development in Adult Language Learning*. Oxford: Pergamon Press.

_____. 1980. *Identifying the Needs of Adults Learning a Foreign Language*. Oxford: Pergamon Press.

Richterich, R. and Widdowson, H.G., eds. 1981. *Description, Présentation et Enseignement des Langues, Actes du Colloque de Berne 1980*. Paris: Hatier.

Rivers, Wilga. 1972. *Speaking in Many Tongues*. Rowley, Mass.: Newbury House.

Robinett, Betty W. 1978. *Teaching English to Speakers of Other Languages: Substance and Technique*. Minneapolis: University of Minnesota Press. Reprinted 1979. New York: McGraw-Hill.

Schools Council. 1973. Modern Language Project. York: University of York.

Trim, John L.M. 1973. Draft outline of a European units-credits system for modern languages learning by adults. CCC/EES. Reprinted 1980. Oxford: Pergamon Press.

_____. 1973a. Modern languages in adult education with special reference to a projected European unit-credit system. *Consolidated Report, EEE Symposium* 57.

_____. 1973b. Research and development project for European unit-credit system for modern language learning by adults. *Progress Report, CCC/EES* 26.

_____. 1977. Total English. Mimeographed. Cambridge: University of Cambridge.

_____. 1980. *Developing a Unit Credit Scheme of Adult Language Learning*. Oxford: Pergamon Press.

_____, et al. 1980. *Systems Development in Adult Language Learning*. Oxford: Pergamon Press.

Vallette, Rebecca M. 1977. *Modern Language Testing: A Handbook*. 2d ed. New York: Harcourt Brace Jovanovich.

van Ek, Jan A. 1975. *The Threshold Level*. Strasbourg: Council of Europe. Reprinted 1980. Oxford: Pergamon Press.

_____. 1978. *The Threshold Level for Modern Language Learning in Schools*. London: Longman.

_____. 1980. *Threshold Level English*. Oxford: Pergamon Press.

_____, et al. 1980. *Waystage English*. Oxford: Pergamon Press.

Widdowson, Henry G. 1971. The teaching of rhetoric to students of science and technology. *CILT Reports and Papers* 7:31-40.

————. 1978. *Teaching Language as Communication*. Oxford: Oxford University Press.

Widdowson, Henry G. and Brumfit, C.J. 1981. Issues in second language syllabus design. In Alatis, Altman, and Alatis, eds. *The Second Language Classroom, Directions for the 1980's*. New York: Oxford University Press.

Wilkins, D.A. 1973. An investigation into linguistic and situational content of the common core in a unit-credit system. Strabourg: Council of Europe.

————. 1973a. The linguistic and situational content of the common core in a unit-credit system. Strasbourg: Council of Europe. Reprinted 1980. Oxford: Pergamon Press.

————. 1977. *Notional Syllabuses: A Taxonomy and Its Relevance to Foreign Language Curriculum Development* London: Oxford University Press.

Index

Communicative competence, definition, 13ff; interpretative (recognition) 157, 158ff; production (performance), 159ff; purposes, 13, 14, 137; tasks leading to, 157, 158ff; testing of, 192, 193

Communicative grammar, communicative expressions, 15

Communicative views of language learning, 94-98, 125; from accuracy to fluency or vice versa, 97, 98

Community, factors within, affecting learning and teaching, 57; involvement of, 57; utilization of resources, 57

Compositions, preparation and correction, 170-71

Comprehension, development of, 136ff, 144ff; listening, 136ff; reading, 144ff

Consonants, chart of, 115; producing, 117; teaching, 118

Content words, 30, 127ff

Context, definition of, 66

Conversation, techniques for stimulating, 85ff, 100, 145-48, 157ff

Conversion drills, 211

Copying as guided writing, 148ff

Core module, and expansions of, 41, 164

Correcting techniques, choral responses, 168; homework, 169; pronunciation, 167, 168

Cost effectiveness, 21

Council of Europe, objectives, 10-12

Courses, planning for, extensive (long-term), 58; intensive, 59

Credits awarded on unit or module completion, 11, 12; current thinking on, 19ff

Cue cards, use of, 167, 210

Cued responses, 214

Culminating activities, dialogs as, 159-60

Cultural immersion, 26, 27

Cultural island, creating a, 130

Cultural pluralism, 132

Cultural subsystem, 30

Cultural understanding, development of, 26, 27, 128ff; incidental, 129; native and target country, 74, 129; interdisciplinary approach, in native and target country, 131; use of literary masterpieces, in native and target country, 131; pupil projects in, 130; spiral approach, sociocultural themes, 36; systematic, 129; testing of, 199; teaching of, 128ff; variety of techniques in, 129

Curriculum, aims, 48-50; considerations, general, 47; content, 47ff; criteria, long and short-term courses, 58; evaluation, 59, 60; examples of secondary school units, 77-80; factors in curriculum planning, 56-57; levels, 58, 59, 76

Curriculum, mini-, chart, 38-39; criteria for selecting functions and items when writing the curriculum, 76; division of units into teaching lessons when writing the curriculum, 76ff; modules (and chart), 80-83; planning a curriculum, 50-54; premises and priorities in, 42ff; spiral approach in, 37; variables in a second language situation, 55

Daily schedule, suggested, 106-7

Davies, Alan, 189

Decoding, definition and steps in, 31, 137

Definition of terms, F-N approach, 13ff

Deixis (a general function), definition and examples, 32

Derivation, 30, 136

eral categories, 23; of Finocchiaro, 23; of van Ek, 23; of Wilkins, 23; specific categories, 61–66; of Finocchiaro, 65–66; of van Ek, 63–64; of Wilkins, 61–63

Function words, categories, 23, 24, 61–65; teaching of, 127ff

Games, use of, 139, 160

Gardner, R., 33

Generalizability, importance of, in item selecton, 29, 40, 43, 124

Generalization, 114; essential features in giving, 114, 122; student discovery of, 122–26

Global comprehension, in listening, 136ff; in reading, 143ff

Glossary, 216–20

Gouin series, 5–6

Gradation, in practice and presentation, 40, 43, 124

Grammar presentation and practice, 122–25; role of, 124; testing, 196

Grammar translation method, 4–5

Grammatical categories, 68–70; of Alexander, 68; of Finocchiaro, 68ff; of van Ek, behavioral specifications, 71

Grouping students, 34, 109ff; criteria in, 109–10; need for, 109; organization in, 109

Group practice, 106ff, 139, 142

Groups, teaching, 109ff; teacher's division of time, 109–10

Guided writing, activities, 148–53

Habit formation, operant conditioning, need for, 9, 165–66

Halliday, M.A.K., 32–33

Homework, assigning, 169; correction of, 169

Humanistic base of F-N curriculum, 57–58, 132

Hymes, Dell, 108

Idiolect, 25

Individualizing instruction, 50–55

Inductive process (cognitive code), 100–125

Input, 21, 26

Integration drill, 212

Intensive courses, 59

Interaction, importance of, 21; patterns of, 167

Interdisciplinary approach, 43, 132

Interpretative activities, oral, 157, 158; written, 158ff

Intonation, cautions in, 119, 169; examples of, 120; pitch levels in, 119; rising, 119–20; rising-falling, 120, teaching of, 121; in questions, 120; in statements, 120; in tag questions, 120

Johnson, K., 90

Juncture, internal (pause), 120

Kinesics, 102

Lado, R., 8

Language, interrelationship of subsystems, 30; redundancy in, 102

Laboratory, language, cautions, 183; uses of, 183

Lambert, W., 33

Language learning, factors affecting, 56ff; in the community, 56–58; in

Opaque projector, 182

Operant conditioning theory, 9

Organization for grouping of students, 109ff; possible schedule in, 109, 110; problems in, 109ff; written assignments in, 109, 110

Overhead projector, 182

Overview, language learning and testing, 3ff

Paired sentence task, description and examples of, 212

Pair practice, 106, 139, 143. *See also* Role-playing

Pantomime, use of, 158ff

Paraphrasing, necessity of, 102, 159–64

Pattern practice activities, criteria for preparation, 208; need for variety in, 209; use of association, 212; use of directed practice, 212–13; use of expansion task, 211–12; use of paired sentences, 212; use of progressive replacement, 212; use of question-answer, 213–14; use of replacement, 211; use of restatement, 212; use of substitution, 210–11; use of transformation (conversion), 211; use of translation, 213

Performance activities, oral, 159–63; written, 163–65

Phonemes, charts of, 115; teaching of, 115ff; use of transcription, 118

Phonology, definition of, 30, 117; testing of, 195

Picture file, utilization, 128, 167, 177ff

Picture series, types of, 178; uses of, 178

Pictures, individual types of, 177ff; situational types of, 177ff

Placement of items for presentation, 29, 40, 43, 124

Planning, a balanced program, 104ff; lessons, 105ff; time allotments to integrative skills, 105–6; time schedules, 105–6; writing the plan, 107

Pocket chart, 180

Practice activities, types of, communicative, 157ff; question-answer, 213–14; affirmative, short and long answer, 214; free response, 215; negative, 214; patterned response, 214. *See also* Appendix

Presuppositions, cultural, definition, 22; problems, 22, 26; teaching, 26, 27

Productivity, importance of, in item selection, 40, 43, 124

Proficiency tests, 187, 202ff; American Language Institute rating scale, 204–6; Foreign Service Institute rating scale, 202–4

Program, ensuring balance in teaching, 104ff; varied daily schedule, 106; weekly schedule, 105

Progressive replacement task, 212

Projects, student, 130; cross-cultural comparisons, 130

Pronunciation, teaching features of, 117ff, 121

Psycholinguistics, 27ff, 50–54

Psychology, contributions of, to F-N approach, 33ff, 50, 54

Punctuation, teaching of, 149

Questions, basic, asked by educators, 3

Questions in teaching, 167–68

Quizzes, advantages of frequent, 169; content of, 169; criteria in preparing, 169; grades in, 169

Radio, use of, 183

Reading, activities, 145–48; bilingual

dictionaries, 144, 148; bilingual texts, 148; development of, 143–48; extensive, development of, 147; initial, 143; intensive, development of, 146; materials, teacher-prepared, 86; motivation, 144, 146; supplementary, 148; teacher's responsibilities, in clarifying difficulties, 147; in enriching experiences, 144; in ensuring initial global comprehension, 144; in increasing speed, 145, 146; in preparing prereading questions, 143; in summarizing, 148; in teaching sound-symbol relationships, 145; in teaching subskills, 143, 144; testing of, 198

Reading method, 6

Real objects, 128, 130, 178

Receptive learning, 40, 42. *See also* Interpretative

Recombination, in dialogs, 75, 84

Record player, use of, 130, 182

Redundancy in natural languages, examples of, 102

Registers, definition, 24; formality, 24; mode-oral, written, 25; profession or vocation, 25

Relationships of linguistic and cultural subsystems of language, 30

Repetition, sequence of, 114; class, group, individual, 114

Replacement drill, definition and use of, 211

Resources (people and places), use of, 53, 75, 98, 132, 173–74

Responsibilities of teachers, 98ff; encouraging discussion of native culture, 101; guiding controlled and free activities, 100; permitting student creativity, 100; relating teaching to learner's world, 100; using cognitive-code and habit-formation theories, 100; utilizing native language when necessary and feasible,

101. *See also* Teachers

Rhythm, teaching of, 120–21

Richterich, R., 65, 67

Rivers, Wilga, 96

Role-playing, in testing, 194; steps in, 86, 87, 139, 160

Rules, descriptive, 114, 122; discovery by students, 122, 126; learning of, 114, 122

Schedules, daily, 106; weekly, 105–06

School, factors in, 50; organizational practices, 55; physical plant, 50, 51; resources, 51; supervisory staff, 52; teachers, 51; testing program, 54

Second language learning, 56; factors in, 55; psycholinguistic theories of, 27ff

Selection and gradation of language items, criteria in, 40, 43, 124

Setting (place where communication is taking place), 17, 26, 166ff

Simplifying listening and reading materials, 170

Simulation activities, 161, 162, 163

Situational method, 8–9; differences from F-N teaching, 8–9

Situational topics (cyclical), 71–74

Situations, categories of, 15, 66–68; factors: agents (people), 15, 67, 68; place (setting), 15, 67, 68; time, 16, 67, 68; topic, 16, 67, 68

Skills, development of integrated skills, 135ff; emphases, at different levels, 105; listening-speaking, activities in, 136–39; importance of dialogs in, 75, 84; proportions of time allotted, 105; reading, activities, 143–48; writing, activities and tasks, 148–52

Skinner, B. F., 6, 9

Sociocultural, insights, 128–32; themes, 35–37

Sociolinguistics, contributions of, 22ff
Songs, using, 130, 182
Sound-symbol relationships, 145
Sound system, allophones and phonemes, 117; consonant chart, features of, 115; intonation, 119–20; liaison, 120; pause, rhythm, 120–21; stress system, 198; teaching of, 117ff, 121; testing of, 195; use of phonetic symbols, 118, 119; vowel charts, 116, 117
Speaking skill, complexity of, 140ff; teaching, 141, 142; testing, 197–98
Speech acts, 13, 19, 20, 22
Spiral approach, desirability of, 35, 37, 58, 59, 99, 113, 124, 127, 129, 170; sociocultural themes, 36; in structural topics, 36; in vocabulary, 127
Strategies, types of, teaching, in communicative competence, 157ff; interpretative (receptive) activities, 157, 158; pattern practices, 210–15; performance, oral, 157, 159; performance, written, 157, 159; translation tasks, 213
Streams approach, in developing cultural understanding, 128ff; in developing reading, 145
Stress (word, phrase, sentence), 119; teaching of, 119
Structural approach, 6–7
Structural topics, 36
Structures, categories of, 68ff
Structure teaching, 122–25; testing, 196. See also Grammar
Students, aims, 50–55, 98; grouping, 34, 109; motivations, 34, 50–55, 109; needs, 56–57, 98, 101; participation, 11, 109–10
Substitution task, description of, 210–11
Subsystems of language, 30
Suggestions for teacher-class discussion (group work and research), Ch. 2, 45–46; Ch. 3, 88–89; Ch. 4, 111–12; Ch. 5, 133–34; Ch. 6, 155–56; Ch. 7, 173; Ch. 8, 185; Ch. 9, 207
Summaries, of dialogs, 164; of lesson, unit, 84, 106, 111; of reading, 148
Supplementation in language learning, 137
Svartvik, Jan, 135
Symbols, for sounds, 118
Synonyms, use of. See Paraphrasing
Syntax, definition of, 121; teaching of, 121
System and subsystem, 30

Tape recorder, uses of, 163
Teachers, attitude of, 98ff; crucial role of, 98–101; tasks of, giving learners awareness of cognates, redundancy, 102–3; tasks of, reintroducing same linguistic items in different situation, 102–3; use of students' native language, 22, 40, 43, 93
Techniques of instruction, 166ff; choral repetition procedures, 169; conducting pattern practice activities, 165–67; correcting errors tactfully, 168–69; creating a cultural island, 130; dialog teaching, 75–84; engaging in role-playing, 139, 160, 194; ensuring understanding, formulation of rules, repetition, fluency, 113–14; enlisting community participation, 132; essays, preparing longer, 170–71; grouping students, 166; homework assignment and correction, 169–70; individualizing instruction, 166; motivating every lesson step, 169; picture file, preparing and using, 166; playing games, 139, 160;

234